TRUE NORTH

A Prophetic Call to Faithfulness

TRUE NORTH
A Prophetic Call to Faithfulness

Editorial Team: Mark Finley, Clinton Wahlen, Ken and Phyllis McFarland
Cover Design: Mark Bond / Red Canoe Creative
Interior Design: Page One Sentence Doctors

ISBN-13: 978-1-954730-13-7

Hart Books
PO Box 2377
Fallbrook CA 92088

Review & Herald Publishing Association
12501 Old Columbia Pike
Silver Spring MD 20904

CONTENTS

Before You Turn This Page v

CHAPTER 1 | *Who Are We As a Church—and Where Are We Going?* 1

CHAPTER 2 | *The Authority of Scripture* 13

CHAPTER 3 | *Why Creation Matters* 27

CHAPTER 4 | *Jesus and Doctrine* 41

CHAPTER 5 | *Prophetic Interpretation* 59

CHAPTER 6 | *Hope From Above: The Good News of the Sanctuary* . . . 71

CHAPTER 7 | *"What Hath God Wrought!"* 85

CHAPTER 8 | *Fanaticism and Extremes* 105

CHAPTER 9 | *Behind the Scenes: The Great Controversy* 123

CHAPTER 10 | *Faithfulness in Mission* 139

CHAPTER 11 | *Spiritualism* 159

CHAPTER 12 | *Biblical Standards* 179

CHAPTER 13 | *Focus on Financial Faithfulness* 193

CHAPTER 14 | *A Messenger Sent from God* 211

CHAPTER 15 | *A Prophetic Call to Faithfulness* 229

BEFORE YOU TURN THIS PAGE

THE BOOK YOU HOLD IN YOUR HANDS, *TRUE NORTH: A PROPHETIC CALL TO FAITHFULNESS,* is an unashamedly straightforward, no-nonsense presentation of biblical truth. Each of the thirteen authors is committed to the authority of Scripture. We believe the Bible is the infallible, inspired Word of God.

Each chapter here is based on the fundamental truths of the Word. We discuss topics that are absolutely essential for God's end-time people. Each page will speak to your heart as well as to your mind. Eternal truths will leap off the pages and move you deeply. The goal of each author is to present the truths of the Word in a clear, powerful way, to prepare each of us for the coming of our Lord.

You may wonder about the phrase *Truth North.* It is actually based on Ellen White's classic statement:

> "The greatest want of the world is the want of men—men who will not be bought or sold, men who in their inmost souls are true and honest, men who do not fear to call sin by its right name, men

> whose conscience is as ***true to duty as the needle to the pole,*** men who will stand for the right though the heavens fall" *Education,* 57, emphasis added.

When the "needle points to the pole," it is pointing true north. It provides a clear sense of direction and orients weary, lost travelers to their destination. This book is a clarion call to faithfulness, pointing us heavenward on our journey to eternity.

The critical need of this crisis hour of earth's history is not more technology, institutions, administrative units, plans, or programs—as important as each of these are. The critical need of this hour is for men and women totally committed to Christ, filled with His Holy Spirit, anchored in the truth of His Word, focused on the advancement of His kingdom, and proclaiming His last-day message to the ends of the earth. Men and women of courage are needed who are unafraid to "call sin by its right name." Men and women of faith are needed who will "stand for the right though the heavens fall." Men and women of commitment are needed who "in their inmost souls are true and honest."

We are convinced that no half-hearted, superficial religious experience is sufficient for this time of earth's history. We are living on the edge of eternity. Seventh-day Adventists are a divine movement raised up by God with a special message of three angels to be preached to every "nation, kindred, tongue and people." To this end—to produce a people ready for the coming of Jesus—this book is written. As you prayerfully read these pages, open your heart to the ministry of the Holy Spirit and let Him radically transform your life.

Mark Finley, *Executive Editor*
Dan Houghton, *Publisher*

AS YOU BEGIN THIS FIRST CHAPTER...

Those who count such things say that the world has about 4,200 different religions. The largest, Christianity, is estimated to have some 45,000 denominations around the world – of which 200 or so can be found in the United States.

Is it even possible to settle on just one Christian denomination that most closely represents Christ and His teachings in the world today? Does the Bible help identify such a Church?

Yes, the Bible does indeed reveal just such a group – a last-day Remnant of the Church Jesus founded as He lived here on Earth. This Remnant carefully follows Jesus and His truth. Coming up in the first chapter of this book are the marks of that Church as God's Word brings it to view.

That Church is marked both by its three-part Message and by the Mission it follows in sharing it with the world. The marks of this Church are clearly set forth in the Bible's last book, Revelation – marks that describe the only "True North" Church in the entire New Testament.

In the chapters just ahead, listen as God issues to His people a "prophetic call to faithfulness" – a call to honor His truth, to follow Him wherever He leads, and to love as He loves.

Robert Costa has served as a pastor, departmental director, and administrator since 1980 in South America and North America. A native of Uruguay, he received his higher education in Argentina and in the United States. He is the volunteer Speaker-Director of the telecast *It Is Written* in Spanish, which is broadcast via satellite, cable, and local channels on more than 11,000 stations, reaching 138 countries. Pastor Costa's passion is to share the Good News of God's Word, and he's had the privilege of conducting more than 420 evangelistic series in the last twenty-one years on every continent. He and his wife, Nancy, reside in Maryland, USA, where they both serve God— she as an assistant to Adventist World Radio, and he as Ministerial Associate of the General Conference, in charge of Evangelism and Church Growth for the Seventh-day Adventist Church.

CHAPTER 1

WHO ARE WE AS A CHURCH, AND WHERE ARE WE GOING?

IS OUR CHURCH JUST ONE MORE CHURCH? WHAT SETS US APART FROM THE rest of Christianity? Where are we now, and where are we headed? What justifies our existence?

God answers all of these questions. He sees us in the context of the Great Controversy that is raging on Planet Earth:

> "But you are a chosen generation, a royal priesthood, a holy nation, His own special people, that you may proclaim the praises of Him who called you out of darkness into His marvelous light" (1 Peter 2:9).

This statement defines our identity and purpose. But can't the rest of the Christian world claim the same thing? Yes, in part, but not in its entirety—and that distinction makes all the difference.

PRESENTING THE WHOLE TRUTH

Many churches do an excellent job of leading people to Jesus. But if the great truths for this hour are excluded, it's an incomplete, watered-down gospel. The Bible should always be presented as a whole—and only by studying the Old Testament can we understand the New. But deceiving is not merely lying—it is also mixing the truth with error and, more subtly, not telling the whole truth. We can guard against this by refreshing our origins, identity, message, commitment, and mission from our homes, pulpits, and classrooms.

NOT JUST ONE MORE CHURCH

We are more than a Church—we are the final movement that God has raised up in a prophetic time, with a prophetic message, centered on Jesus and His grace, to restore the whole truth and to prepare the world for His return.

God's messenger reminds us:

> "Seventh-day Adventists have been chosen by God as a peculiar people, separate from the world. By the great cleaver of truth He has cut them out from the quarry of the world and brought them into connection with Himself. He has made them His representatives and has called them to be ambassadors for Him in the last work of salvation. The greatest wealth of truth ever entrusted to mortals, the most solemn and fearful warnings ever sent by God to man, have been committed to them to be given to the world" (*Testimonies for the Church,* vol. 7, 138.)

Or, as Paul said, the Church is "the pillar and ground of the truth" (1 Timothy 3:15). For that purpose, God called Israel (Deuteronomy 7:6-9; 14:2; Isaiah 60:1-3) to be not just one more people group but His special people. He placed them at the crossroads of civilizations with a sacred purpose. He revealed to them, through the earthly sanctuary, how He acts in this rescue plan, and He did not leave it up to them to choose how to live, how to worship, or how to evangelize but gave specific instructions.

Unfortunately, they didn't fulfill God's purpose, but God's plan didn't end. At the precise prophetic moment, when somewhere beyond the stars and out of the reach of human vision, something big was about to happen in heaven that would affect every human being—something "as essential to the plan of salvation as was His death upon the cross" (*The Great Controversy*, 489), God opened the heavenly books. The world had to know!

A PROPHETIC BIRTH CERTIFICATE

For that, God raised up a people from a disappointment—prophesied by Jesus in His vision to John centuries earlier (Revelation 10:5-11)—to a sacred appointment, to restore all the light of His truth "to those who dwell on the earth—to every nation, tribe, tongue, and people," presenting "with a loud voice" the last three most solemn messages of love ever given to mortals (Revelation 14:6-12).

That divinely foreseen disappointment was actually the birth certificate of the true people of God. Moreover, if the last Church hadn't arisen from a disappointment at the prophesied moment by studying Daniel's prophecies, it could not be the true Church and would still be part of Babylon. When our pioneers understood—after the disappointment—by diligently studying the Scriptures to discern what had happened on October 22, 1844, they situated themselves by faith where Jesus was ministering. From there, they began to preach all the truths of the plan of salvation revealed in the earthly sanctuary services.

Shortly thereafter, God Himself granted the gift of prophecy to this people, thereby defining the two outstanding characteristics of the remnant at the end: they keep the commandments of God and have the testimony of Jesus, which is the Spirit of Prophecy (Revelation 12:17; 19:10). These two components appear together in the Scriptures, and they define the true people of God (Isaiah 8:19, 20).

In Ellen White's first vision, God clearly established the rise, course, and destiny of this movement that would later be called the Seventh-day Adventist Church. She described a "narrow path, cast up high above the world." The evangelical world does not have this light that we have received. And if the truth of the heavenly sanctuary is not understood, then the plan of salvation is not fully understood. It leads to the Cross and, through Christ as our High Priest, to heaven. There is a present truth for this hour, and it comes to us from the Most Holy Place of the heavenly sanctuary.

BEWARE OF DISTRACTIONS

There are certain distractions and dangers that can undermine our identity, purpose, and mission as a remnant.

Distraction No. 1: To stop presenting the present truth. The everlasting gospel was the plan of salvation presented to Adam and Eve from the very beginning. But there is also the present truth—a specific message that each generation has been commissioned to present, all within the context of the everlasting Gospel. Ellen White emphasizes that what we need to preach in the Adventist Church today is the present truth. And what is the present truth for this hour? The truths centered on the Most Holy Place, where Jesus ministers. If you want to preach the present truth today, simply find out where Jesus is now—what He is doing today—and then preach it. Sadly, there are winds of change in this approach that have distracted us from our unique message and our distinctive mission.

Some argue that, as the apostle Paul said, we must preach only Christ—the crucified Christ (1 Corinthians 1:23). That was the present truth for that hour, and they proclaimed it. The prophetic time had not yet been fulfilled for the risen Christ to enter His final work concerning the plan of salvation.

Today, the sublime truth of what Jesus did on the Cross almost 2,000 years ago is still as foundational as it was in the first century, but the element of a Christ who intercedes in the Most Holy Place of the heavenly sanctuary since 1844 is now present truth, showing us more fully the purpose of His death and perfect life. When He finishes this work of intercession and judgment, the case of each human being will have been decided.

There is an entire book in the Bible (Hebrews) about what Jesus is currently doing as High Priest. We cannot ignore this great truth for this hour, much less since we are called to proclaim it (Revelation 14:6, 7).

Distraction No. 2: To focus only on social justice and humanitarian aid, without leading people to Jesus and the full Gospel message. Many secular entities do excellent social work in helping communities. But social aid and social justice are not our main mission as a Church. Passages in Micah 6, Isaiah 58, and James 1 emphasize helping others, but this is more about personal Christian living. Jesus Himself did good works, but His mission was not just to relieve suffering but to save the human race. Yet He lived His religion—showing love and compassion within the context of His mission. We highlight "Christ's method alone" (*Ministry of Healing,* 143), and this is good. To help people with their temporal needs is important, but we cannot stop there. We need to move even farther, through the guidance of the Holy Spirit, to lead people to the foot of the Cross and to the full Advent message, focusing especially on the Three Angels' Messages. We must urge people to take steps to follow and obey Him.

Distraction No. 3: To imitate other denominations in their liturgy, music, and growth methods. For Israel, this led to catastrophic results (Numbers 22:24). Some are seeking ideas from contaminated sources, which deny great biblical truths, and then they apply these methods in our churches. Although not everything that others do is wrong, the question still remains: have any of these Protestant churches accepted the Three Angels' Messages and the truth about the heavenly sanctuary that is the foundation of our faith? Does this sound like a place where we should acquire our lifestyle, musical style, worship patterns, and evangelism methods? I think the answer is obvious!

More perplexing is that with the abundance of light we have, what motivates us as Adventists to adopt the style of worship and growth methods of churches that the Bible describes as "Babylon," when these churches despise the message of present truth? Why would we want to go back from the Most Holy Place to the Holy Place, or to the outer court in our approach of presenting the message to the world? God never suggested that Israel adopt the methods or worship styles of the surrounding nations in order to reach them. To the contrary, they were raised up to be His special and distinct people, as a light to the world (Exodus 19:5, 6; 1 Peter 2:9).

Distraction No. 4: To emphasize an existentialist Adventism where discipleship is separate from doctrine. If we speak only about the Master and His virtues and do not teach what the Master asks us to teach, how good a disciple can we actually be? How can new believers teach others the truth that they themselves did not learn?

We sometimes hear some confusing half-truths: "We must be inclusive," "We must appeal to what people like," "We must give people what they feel they need," "We must realize that different generations require different methods," "We must be pluralistic," "We must not judge anyone," "We must love and accept people unconditionally," and "What matters is love."

This change in approach has caused some to become human-centered rather than Christ-centered. It seems that the primary concern in some churches is that secular people feel comfortable in worship, and "Thus says the Lord" has been replaced by messages of motivation, convenience, and cultural contextualization. As a result, the revelations from God for this time through Ellen White are replaced by quotes from specialists.

When preaching ceases to be prophecy-based, doctrinally sound, and Christ-centered, and becomes focused only on grace, it leads to personal comfort and ill-advised spiritual satisfaction, where genuine revival is impossible. A gospel of grace by itself produces liberalism, and a gospel of warning apart from grace produces fanaticism. We are neither fanatical nor liberal. We are disciples who receive and accept the grace to live in commitment to Christ and His Word.

In some pulpits and institutions, we have gone from one extreme to another, from doctrinal formalism to a subjective existentialism. Some people have begun to assume an anti-doctrinal stance, in which the fundamental pillars of the Adventist faith are seen as mere requirements of an obsolete legalistic religion—as belonging to an old covenant. The outcome? A slide into Loadicea. This could well be classified as ministerial and educational malpractice. Millions are in the secularism of Babylon, waiting to be invited to leave and join God's remnant Church, but we cannot help them if we repeat the mistake of the historical Christian Church that lost its identity when flooded by the unconverted world and adopting their pagan customs.

Distraction No. 5: To stop looking for a genuine revival, or to look for it while neglecting any of the elements that produce it. It is clear to us that the greatest of our needs is that of a revival of primitive godliness. For that to happen, we must neither overlook any of the three basic elements of true revival nor the purpose for which the Holy Spirit revives and reforms us. The opposite is also true. All genuine revival has disappeared when one or more of these three elements or components is set aside.

GENUINE REVIVAL

1) Renewed emphasis on the Word of God.

Every genuine revival throughout history has begun with a deep searching of God's Word. His creative Word is life for our lives—that same Word that called the worlds into existence. It realigns us with the will of God, while the Holy Spirit does the dual work of cleansing (Psalm 119:9; John 15:3) and empowering for service. By opening its pages—which are comparable to the leaves of the Tree of Life—we are directly inviting the Holy Spirit to begin His transforming work in our lives, which will lead to internal and external change and genuine reform. In the Word is the formula for eternal life (John 17:3)—that of knowing God. The emphasis on His Word automatically leads us to the next element.

2) Renewed emphasis on intercessory prayer.

There can be no revival without constant and earnest prayer. But it is the Word of God, which shapes our prayers, that will now be offered more and more on behalf of others and for the establishment of Christ's kingdom—rather than for ourselves and our personal needs. Intercessory prayer is intended to bring us into harmony with God in His great rescue plan so that we pray for those we want to see in the kingdom of heaven. Disconnected from this purpose, such prayer can become an end in itself, paralyzing the machinery God has revived and reformed to accomplish His saving mission. I would venture to say that it is dangerous to pray for the descent of the Holy Spirit if we are not ready for change and for the Spirit of God to lead us to witness and be channels to carry the message to others.

> "The Holy Spirit will come to all who are begging for the bread of life to give to their neighbors" (*Testimonies for the Church*, vol. 6, 90).

3) Renewed emphasis on witnessing.

> "Every true disciple is born into the kingdom of God as a missionary" (*The Desire of Ages*, 192).

Witnessing leads us to a life of constant prayer and dependence on the promises of God. It places us at the very heart of what Jesus is doing in the heavenly sanctuary—the greatest rescue operation in the universe. How many internal problems at the local church level (as well as other levels) would be resolved if we left these matters in the hands of God—if as individuals and as a Church, we were focused on what God is focused on: the salvation of others?

The Great Commission (Matthew 28:18-20) is clear, as is the Great Promise (Acts 1:8) that supports it. But "how shall they believe in Him of whom they have not heard? And how shall they hear without a preacher? And how shall they preach unless they are sent? As it is written: 'How beautiful are the feet of those who preach the gospel of peace, who bring glad tidings of good things!'" (Romans 10:14, 15).

The apostle Paul understood his responsibility and privilege well when he exclaimed, "Woe is me if I do not preach the gospel!" (1 Corinthians 9:16.) As individuals and as a church, we are called to live in a continuous state of revival. This is not a utopia but a reality that the last generation will live. We are revived and reformed to fulfill our end-time mission, and as we fulfill that mission, we are revived. The three angels fly quickly, crying out with a loud voice. They are in constant motion until the earth is finally illuminated with the glory of God. God is counting on our faithfulness in this.

OUR GOD-GIVEN RESPONSIBILITY

Do we grasp the responsibility that God has placed on you and me in these last days of the Great Controversy between Christ and Satan?

Revelation presents us with the solemn picture of three angels flying through the sky, crying out with a loud voice the last messages of God's love to humanity, calling the world to meet on Mount Zion, symbolizing His Church. This is a message of reunion.

On the other hand, we have "three unclean spirits like frogs coming out of the mouth of the dragon, out of the mouth of the beast, and out of the mouth of the false prophet" calling for another worldwide gathering for "the battle of that great day of God Almighty." Jesus was clear in addressing the Church leaders of His day and telling them there is no neutral ground in this task: "He who is not with Me is against Me, and he who does not gather with Me scatters abroad" (Matthew 12:30; Luke 11:23). The question for us as individuals and as a Church is: Are we joining with the Lord in His gathering work—or scattering with the enemy?

> "In a special sense Seventh-day Adventists have been set in the world as watchmen and light bearers. To them has been entrusted the last warning for a perishing world. On them is shining wonderful

> light from the word of God. They have been given a work of the most solemn import—the proclamation of the first, second, and third angels' messages. There is no other work of so great importance. They are to allow nothing else to absorb their attention. The most solemn truths ever entrusted to mortals have been given us to proclaim to the world. The proclamation of these truths is to be our work. The world is to be warned, and God's people are to be true to the trust committed to them" (*Testimonies for the Church,* vol. 9, 19).

And if we don't do it, who will? What a privilege, what a responsibility, and what a call to faithfulness! We know how things will end. There will be a last generation that will stand firm and love the Lord so much that they will obey Him fully. They will be sealed for eternity, established in all biblical truth so that they cannot be moved. That generation will participate in wonderful things—the latter rain and the completion of God's work—and the earth will be illuminated with the glorious character of God (Revelation 18:1). My prayer is that we will be that last generation. *Maranatha*. Who Are We As a Church, and Where Are We Going?

AS YOU BEGIN THE NEXT CHAPTER . . .

Seventh-day Adventists see themselves as the Remnant Church of the last days, and they describe themselves as "people of the Book"—people who read and study their Bibles. Yes, they do this to learn what to believe but also, how to live. And even more, they want to know Jesus.

Strange, though, how any one man—or woman or young person—hears the Bible saying to them something far different than someone else finds in that very same Word.

Why?

Most always, these differences have to do with the rules, the principles, one uses to understand "the Book." Those principles are called hermeneutics: the principles of interpreting what the Bible says.

What the Bible says—and with what authority it speaks—depends on the set of principles one uses in approaching the study of God's Word. Such hermeneutical principles include preterism, futurism, idealism, and historicism.

Dr. Hasel presents clear hermeneutical principles that will guide you in your study of God's Word.

Michael G. Hasel, PhD (University of Arizona) is Professor of Near Eastern Studies and Archaeology at the School of Religion, Southern Adventist University and director of the Institute of Archaeology and Lynn H. Wood Archaeological Museum. He has published ten books and over 150 articles in peer-reviewed journals, dictionaries, and encyclopedias. He has appeared on documentaries for Anchor-Point Films, the Hope Channel, 3ABN, and National Geographic. His work in the Middle East as an archaeologist spans thirty years at eleven sites and currently as co-director of The Fourth Expedition to Lachish. He is the co-author of two Sabbath School studies, including How to Interpret Scripture (2020) and The Promise: God's Everlasting Covenant (2021). His wife Giselle is a professor of Art History at Southern, and their two daughters, Daniella and Sarah, are both university students.

MICHAEL G. HASEL

CHAPTER 2

THE AUTHORITY OF SCRIPTURE

THE YEAR WAS 1521, AND MARTIN LUTHER WAS FACING DEATH AS HE appeared before the Diet of Worms. Before him sat Charles V, the Holy Roman emperor, the most powerful political authority in Europe. The previous year Pope Leo X, the leading religious authority of Christendom, had issued his papal bull, *Exsurge Domine,* outlining forty-one errors found in Luther's writings. Now, as Luther faced his emperor and his church, he was confronted with the question: "What authority will you submit to?" His answer: "Unless I am convinced by the testimony of the Scriptures or by clear reason (for I do not trust in the pope or the councils alone, since it is known that they have often erred and contradicted themselves), I am bound by the Scriptures I have quoted, and my conscience is captive to the Word of God . . . Here I stand, I can do no other. May God help me, Amen."[1]

Those present in the room were stunned. Then the room erupted, and the words were repeated, published, and echoed through the corridors of history until today. The early Protestant reformers would stand with *sola Scripture*—"the Bible only"—as their final authority, as they faced life's biggest questions.

The question of authority has been at the center of human civilization from the beginning of history.[2] The temptation in the Garden of Eden revolved around the core issue of authority. When Satan, in the guise of a serpent, asked, "Has God indeed said, 'You shall not eat of every tree of the garden'?" (Genesis 3:1), the question for our first parents was this: Would they trust in the Word of God as authoritative, or would they trust their senses—reason and experience—to determine truth? This question was not merely philosophical or theoretical. Their determination of what was authoritative had a direct impact on their actions and behavior. "So when the woman *saw* that the tree was good for food, *that it was pleasant to the eyes*, and a tree *desirable to make one wise*, she took of its fruit and ate. She also gave to her husband with her, and he ate" (Genesis 3:6, emphasis supplied). Eve put her trust in what she saw as above God's Word, and she acted on her desire to be all knowing, while Adam gave in to his feelings because of His love for Eve. Trust placed in human reason and experience against God's explicit word plunged humanity into sin and darkness which continues to the present.

A multiplicity of factors must be taken into consideration when we deal with the issue of authority. For one, authority in our modern and postmodern world is not a popular idea at all. Often, individuals rebel against authority and seek complete freedom from it. However, despite our inherent search for freedom, we are ultimately bound by some form of authority—even if we make that authority ourselves. When condensed through human history, the list of sources for authority is fairly small: God, tradition, human reason, experience, and culture. Each of these sources of authority, or a combination of them, have influenced thinking throughout the ages. In the Garden of Eden, human reason and experience impacted the crucial decision Adam and Eve faced. This was before the development of traditions or culture, as defined by a people group, and how that group defines values and ethics. Subsequently, tradition and culture have played an increasingly significant role, so that today each of these sources of authority is widely influential in society. Everyone will allocate, consciously or unconsciously, a place and role to each of these sources in their pattern of authoritative criteria. Differences arise as a result of the priority assigned to each source. In modern society, we live in a humanistic world, where man has been placed in the center. This raises the question: Is there an authority higher than humanity itself?

BIBLICAL AUTHORITY

The Bible teaches that ultimate authority rests in God, who created humanity and who lovingly desires from us a response of worship and obedience (cf. Romans 13:1; Daniel 4:34; John 19:11; Revelation 14:7). The canonical Scriptures derive their authority from God because they are divinely inspired, for "All scripture is given by inspiration of God" (2 Timothy 3:16) and as such, they are "the oracles of God" (Romans 3:2). Therefore, Paul called them the "holy scriptures" (Romans 1:2). The cry of the Reformation was *ad Fontes*—"back to the sources." The reformers studied Scripture to learn how Jesus and the apostles understood authority. They discovered that Jesus affirmed the authority of Scripture and submitted Himself to it. When Jesus, in His weakest human condition, was tempted by Satan, in all three temptations, Jesus responded with the words "It is written." Notice, Jesus did not say, "It was written," or, "It will be written." Instead, He uses the present perfect tense—"It is written"—because the Word of God was not relegated to a distant culture in the past. It was not meant only for future generations. The writings of Scripture were present truth for Moses, for Christ, and for us today. The Bible and the Bible only was Jesus' method of defense against the attacks of the adversary. Jesus was God, but when attacked, He submitted Himself solely to the Word of God. His defense was not by personal opinion; it was not by an elaborate, convoluted argument; it was by the simple and properly applied words of Scripture. For Christ, Scripture had the greatest authority—the greatest power. For Jesus to quote as He did from Deuteronomy, means that He had studied, memorized, and understood their meaning. Jesus prepared for His ministry from childhood and then commenced it within the foundation of the Bible. This can be demonstrated in many examples throughout His ministry. Jesus affirmed, "Do not think that I come to destroy the Law or the Prophets, I did not come to destroy but to fulfill . . . not one jot or tittle will by no means pass from the law till all is fulfilled" (Matthew 5:17, 18). For Jesus Scripture cannot be broken (John 10:35).

On the road to Emmaus, Jesus expounded to the two disciples "beginning with Moses and all the prophets, he interpreted to them in all the scriptures the things concerning himself" (Luke 24:27, RSV). Again in Luke 24:44, 45, He says, "These are my words . . . . that everything written about me in the law of Moses and the prophets and the psalms must be fulfilled." Jesus then "opened their minds to understand the scriptures." We see that Jesus, the Word made flesh (John 1:1-3), relied on all Scripture. By referring to the totality of Scripture, Jesus was teaching the disciples by example. As they went forth to spread the Gospel message, they too were to expound all Scripture to bring understanding and power to the new converts throughout the world.

Jesus says to His disciples then and to us today, "All authority in heaven and on earth has been given to me." That authority remains rooted in the Father and the entire Godhead, for He continues, "Go therefore and make disciples of all nations, baptizing them in the name of the Father and of the Son and of the Holy Spirit, teaching them to observe all that I have commanded you" (Matthew 28:18-20). What did Jesus teach and command that He wants us to observe? His teachings are found only in Scripture. As His disciples we are called by Jesus to remain faithful to Scripture as He was. That means all of Scripture, from historical details to the great scope of divinely appointed prophecy.

THE BIBLE AND HISTORY

Jesus became flesh and dwelt among us (John 1:14) becoming the ultimate act of intervention in human history. The Bible is unique compared to all the other sacred texts of the world's major religions, because it is historically constituted. The Bible depicts a God who acts on our behalf. From the first verse of Scripture—"In the beginning God created the heavens and the earth" (Genesis 1:1)—God is separate from but intimately involved in fashioning our cosmos in time and space, and then He continues His involvement in our affairs. This unique feature allows history to be the "place," if you will, where God gives humanity an opportunity to test and confirm the truthfulness of His Word. That is why history and historical details are where the trustworthiness of the Bible and of God's Word are challenged the most and where criticism often begins first.

Since the Enlightenment, the subject of biblical history has been increasingly challenged. This is largely due to the presuppositions of the historical-critical method, which essentially denies the possibility of divine intervention in human history—the very element that sets the Bible apart.[3] As Walter Dietrich has written, "In the modern age, history must be understood and described *esti deus non deratur* ('as though God did not exist')." But he admits that this makes it difficult when assessing biblical history. In the Bible "God plays an active role . . . God gets personally involved . . . he sends prophets . . . he moves events." Dietrich concludes, "What enlightened person can accept all these things as historical accounts?"[4]

Historical criticism, by denying this element of divine interaction, rejects a special Creation, the miracles of the Bible and of Jesus, predictive prophecy, the bodily resurrection of Christ, and the possibility of a Second Coming. The Bible is reduced to a humanly written book conditioned by a primitive culture that naively believed such things. The historical-critical method is shared today both by Catholics and mainstream Protestant denominations.

One reason these two branches of Christianity—once so radically and fundamentally based on different presuppositions—can now sign new doctrinal agreements is that they have removed Scripture as the authoritative norm, interpreting the Bible on the basis of recent, modern trends.[5] This allows tradition, human reason, experience, and culture again to be placed above the Bible, just as was done in the Middle Ages. Because the Bible has become a mere human production, it can be reinterpreted and rewritten to support present norms and objectives that are derived outside of Scripture. In rewriting history it is possible to create a new future—one that is defined by ecclesiastical counsels and no longer by the Bible.

But God's acts are intrinsic to His spoken word. The two cannot be separated. If Scripture is not trustworthy in historical statements, how can we trust it on theological and spiritual questions? The repeated phrase, "I am the LORD God who brought you out of the land of Egypt" (cf. Exodus 6:7; 20:2; Leviticus 11:25; 22:33; 25:55; 26:13) would have little meaning if the Exodus never took place. His sovereignty over His people is again and again tied specifically to the historical event of their deliverance from Egypt.[6] As James K. Hoffmeier states,

> "The Old Testament Scriptures do not treat the sojourn-exodus-wilderness events as trivial matters. Rather these events stand at the heart of Israel's religious life, as evidenced by the fact that these themes are ubiquitous throughout the Old Testament itself."[7]

Otto Piper pointed out years ago: "Of the 2688 references of the OT in the NT... Exodus occupies the third place with c. 220 quotations."[8] What would occur to biblical theology if the Exodus events never took place, or took place without God's divine intervention? These events of the Bible would cease to have meaning in reality, and the rest of the Bible, which is founded on those events, would come into serious question.[9]

History is essential to the trustworthiness of the Bible. Here, archaeological investigation over the past 200 years has been invaluable to answer some of the critics who have largely argued from the basis of the absence of evidence. Today, we can say that more than 100 people of the Bible have been rediscovered on seals, seal impressions, monumental texts, and cuneiform tablets. They include well-known kings such as Nebuchadnezzar, Sennacherib, and David. They also include lesser-known officials who are only mentioned in passing, such as the Babylonian official Nebu-sarsakim in Jeremiah 39:3,[10] or the head of Hezekiah's palace, Eliakim, the scribe Shebna, King Hezekiah himself, and now possibly Isaiah the prophet, all mentioned in Isaiah 37:1, 2.[11]

Even in the details there are unexpected developments, such as the Hebrew word *pîm,* which is used only once in the Bible in reference to the Israelites getting their iron tools sharpened by the Philistines: "The price for sharpening proved to be a *pîm* for the plowshares" (1 Samuel 13:21). We know today that this was the name of a specific weight unit measuring 7.82 grams, or two-thirds of a shekel, thanks to the discovery of these weights during excavations.[12] Responding to minimalists who claim that the biblical text was written late only in the Hellenistic period, William G. Dever writes:

> "[The biblical text] cannot possibly have been 'invented' by writers living in the Hellenistic-Roman period several centuries after these weights had disappeared and had been forgotten. In fact, this bit of biblical text . . . would not be understood until the early 20th century A.D., when the first actual archaeological examples turned up, reading *pîm* in Hebrew. . . . If the biblical stories are all 'literary inventions' of the Hellenistic-Roman era, how did this particular story come to be in the Hebrew Bible? One may object, of course, that the *pîm* incident is 'only a detail.' To be sure; but as is well known, 'history is in the details.'"[13]

Today hundreds of biblical sites have been identified and even excavated, producing new evidence that illuminates the world of the Bible. New surveys and excavations at Khirbet Qeiyafa, Socoh, Khirbet el-Rai, Tel Burna, Khirbet Summeily, and Lachish (2007–2020) have now shown increasing evidence for major settlement and growth during the early Kingdom of Judah.[14] Texts demonstrating literacy in Judah have now been found at Tel Zayit, Jerusalem, Khirbet Qeiyafa, and Gezer, suggesting that Hebrew was well developed at the time of David, so that he could indeed have written the psalms attributed to him.[15] These discoveries and so many more teach us that the "absence of evidence is not evidence of absence."[16] As we await further discoveries, our faith is strengthened in our trust of the Bible's history.

THE BIBLICAL TEXT AND TRANSMISSION

Often the question is asked: How do I know whether the biblical text and translation I read today is accurate and reliable? Thousands of New Testament manuscripts from the first four centuries after Christ are preserved.[17] For Plato there are seven, Herodotus only eight, and Homer's Iliad has merely 263 surviving copies. No other ancient literature comes even close in terms of the number of copies and the shortness of time between the originals and the copies. The Dead Sea Scrolls, discovered in 1947, testify to the Old Testament's accuracy over millennia. Copyists carefully worked in the desert to meticulously reproduce manuscripts that predate the medieval Bibles our translations were based on by over 1,000 years.[18] We can compare the entire book of Isaiah and see the remarkable way in which God preserved its accuracy, owing to the work of these scribes through centuries.[19]

In 1979 one of the oldest Hebrew texts was uncovered on two silver amulets in Ketef Hinnom. The second amulet reads, "May the LORD bless you, keep you. May the LORD make his face to shine upon you and grant you p[ea]ce." This bears a striking similarity to one of the Bible's most famous prayers, found in Numbers 6:24-26. Dated paleographically and by archaeological context to the seventh century BC, it is the oldest quote from Scripture.[20] This has raised serious doubts about the date placed on the book of Numbers by historical critics, because the text predates the so-called "priestly writer" by at least 200 years.[21] In this way history, through archaeology, has provided new data that makes many of the nineteenth-century hypotheses of historical-criticism untenable.

THE BIBLE, PROPHECY, AND ADVENTIST IDENTITY

In contrast to most major world religions that have a cyclical concept of history, the Bible presents a view of time that is forward moving, with a destination firmly in mind. The unique features that contribute to that movement are both an ongoing view of history in which God is actively engaged with the nations and people and a transcendent God who is able to see forward into future events and provides predictive prophecy to keep that destination in mind for all people. The Bible is unique in that nearly 30 percent of its contents contain prophecy.[22] No other religious text of any other world religion contains prophecy, because in their worldview God is not transcendent and separate from Creation. Rather, their gods are one with nature and, therefore, have always been part of Creation.[23]

Predictive prophecy, like history, provides the Bible with an internal mechanism to test whether it is accurate and true. Prophecy assumes that: 1) God is able to communicate future events that cannot be known to or predicted by human beings; 2) that His knowledge is perfect concerning the events that will take place in the future, seeing beforehand the outcomes of decisions made; and 3) that God ultimately has a plan and purpose in mind for His people. Amos 3:7 states, "Surely the Lord God does nothing, unless He reveals His secret to His servants the prophets." That modern and postmodern approaches to the Bible have attempted to remove the authenticating nature of prophecy from the Bible should not be surprising. In denying the possibility of divine interaction in history and its communication to the prophets, critical scholarship assumes that such foreknowledge is impossible.

The apocalyptic prophecies of Daniel and Revelation largely gave birth to the Protestant Reformation. Scholars rediscovered *historicism*, a method of prophetic interpretation deriving from the text of Scripture and the biblical writers. Historicism is defined as "the continuous historical method of prophetic interpretation because it understands prophecy to be continuous and consecutive as regards predicted sequences of empires and events in the books of Daniel and Revelation."[24]

Prophecy moves forward from the time of the biblical writer until the time of the end without breaks or gaps in the process. Apocalyptic prophecy, unlike classical prophecy, is not dependent on the actions of humanity but presents God's cosmic timetable for His specific purposes in human history. These fulfillments *will* take place exactly when and where God has outlined. As such, apocalyptic prophecies have only a single fulfillment in history and not multiple fulfillments.

Through historicism Protestants were able to identify the long-range time prophecies of the 1260 years, the sea-beast of Revelation 13:1-3, and the man of sin of 2 Thessalonians 2:3, 4 as the papacy. This provided tremendous reaffirmation of their stand on *sola scriptura* and helped them understand the time in which they were living. It should not surprise us that, just as the historical reliability of Scripture has come under increasing attack, so has historicist prophetic interpretation. Today the methods of preterism, futurism (dispensationalism), and idealism severely undermine the prophetic message of Scripture.[25] These interpretations introduced during the counter-reformation take their focus away from the papacy and the Three Angels' Messages. Preterism relegates prophecy into the past so that all was fulfilled in the first through fourth centuries AD. Futurism projects the prophecies into the future, introducing a huge gap during the time from Christ's ascension to the present. Idealism spiritualizes the prophecies into multiple interpretations that diminish the specificity of the prophetic clarity of Scripture.

Today, Seventh-day Adventists alone maintain the historicist interpretation of Scripture that gave rise to the protest against Rome. As God's remnant, this should not surprise us, but it also calls us to renewed faithfulness in proclaiming the distinctive message God has given His end-time Church. It was careful Bible study that resulted in the rediscovery of the five distinct pillars of the Seventh-day Adventist Church: the Sabbath, the Second Coming, the sanctuary, the state of the dead, and the Spirit of Prophecy. The combination of our fundamental beliefs that begins with the authority of Scripture, together with the Three Angels' Messages, is understood today to give the Seventh-day Adventist Church its message and mission. We have been called to stand for Scripture as Martin Luther and the reformers stood. May we remain faithful to Scripture as we live for the mission of sharing God's Message until He comes.

ENDNOTES

1. Roland H. Bainton, *Here I Stand: A Life of Martin Luther* (New York: New American library, 1950), 144-145.
2. For further discussion on topics discussed herein, see Frank M. Hasel and Michael G. Hasel, *How to Interpret Scripture* (Nampa, ID: Pacific Press, 2019), 29-37, 93-111.
3. For a full discussion of the presuppositions of the historical-critical method, see Michael G. Hasel, "History, the Bible and Hermeneutics," in *Biblical Hermeneutics: An Adventist Approach,* ed. Frank M. Hasel (Silver Spring, MD: Biblical Research Institute, 2020), in press.
4. Walter Dietrich, *The Early Monarchy of Israel: The Tenth Century B.C.E.* (Atlanta: Society of Biblical Literature, 2007), 102, 103.
5. The following quote at the beginning of the Joint Declaration on the Doctrine of Justification states, "By appropriating insights of *recent biblical studies* and *drawing on modern investigations of the history of theology and dogma,* the post-Vatican II ecumenical dialogue has led to a notable convergence concerning justification, with the result that this Joint Declaration is able to formulate a consensus on basic truths concerning the doctrine of justification. In light of this consensus, the corresponding doctrinal condemnations of the sixteenth century do not apply to today's partner" (JD 2.13, emphasis supplied). Note that this is only possible under the presuppositions of modern, recent investigations of the history of theology and dogma, i.e., the historical-critical method—which both Catholics and Lutherans now share.
6. Walter C. Kaiser, Jr., *Toward Rediscovering the Old Testament* (Grand Rapids: Zondervan, 1990), 67.
7. James K. Hoffmeier, "Why a Historical Exodus is Essential for Theology," in *Do Historical Matters Matter to Faith? A Critical Appraisal of Modern and Postmodern Approaches to Scripture,* ed. James K. Hoffmeier and Denis R. Magary (Wheaton, IL: Crossway, 2012), 111.
8. Otto Piper, "Unchanging Promises: Exodus in the New Testament," *Interpretation* 11 (1957), 3.
9. Michael G. Hasel, "The Book of Exodus," *Andrews Bible Commentary,* ed. Angel M. Rodriquez (Berrien Springs, MI: Andrews University Press, 2020), 196-236.
10. The tablet confirming his existence is in the British Museum, BM 114789; Michael Jursa, "Nabu-šaprrūssu-ukīn, *rab ša-rēši,* und 'Nebusarsekim' (Jer. 39:3)," *Nouvelles Assyriologiques Breves et Utilitaires* 1 (2008): 9, 10.

11. On Eliakim, see Martin G. Klingbeil, Michael G. Hasel, Yosef Garfinkel, and Nestor Petruk, "Four Judean Bullae from the 2014 Season at Tel Lachish," *Bulletin of the American Schools of Oriental Research* 381 (2019): 41–56; on Shebna, see Robert Deutsch, "Tracking Down Shebnayahu, Servant of the King," Biblical *Archaeology Review* 35, no. 3 (2009): 45–49, 67; on Hezekiah and Isaiah, see Eilat Mazar, *"The Ophel Excavations to the South of the Temple Mount 2009-2013," Final Reports Volume II* (Jerusalem: Shoham Academic Research, 2018), 253–256.

12. Raz Kletter, *"Economic Keystones: The Weight System of the Kingdom of Judah,"* Journal of the Study of the Old Testament: Supplement Series, vol. 276 (Sheffield: Sheffield Academic, 1998), 85.

13. William G. Dever, *What Did the Biblical Writers Know and When Did They Know It?* (Grand Rapids, MI: Eerdmans, 2001), 227.

14. Yosef Garfinkel, Saar Ganor, and Michael G. Hasel, *In the Footsteps of David: Revelations from an Ancient Biblical City* (New York: Thames and Hudson, 2018); and most recently, Michael G. Hasel, "The Geographical Extent of the Kingdom of Judah (Shephelah and Negev) in the Tenth Century BC," in *Lexham Geographic Commentary on the Old Testament Historical Books,* ed. Barry J. Beitzel (Bellingham, WA: Lexham, 2021, forthcoming).

15. Michael G. Hasel, "Geographical Extent of the Kingdom of Judah," for references.

16. For a further discussion on the "absence of evidence" argument, see Michael G. Hasel, "New Excavations at Khirbet Qeiyafa and the Early History of Judah," in *Do Historical Matters Matter to Faith?: A Critical Analysis to Modern and Postmodern Approaches to Scripture,* ed. James K. Hoffmeier and Dennis R. Magary (Wheaton, IL: Crossway, 2012), 483–487.

17. On New Testament manuscript history, see Metzger, Bruce M., *The Text of the New Testament: Its Transmission, Corruption and Restoration,* 3rd edition (New York: Oxford University Press, 1992), 33-35.

18. On the transmission of the biblical text and modern translations, see Clinton Wahlen, "Variants, Versions, and the Trustworthiness of Scripture," *Biblical Hermeneutics: An Adventist Approach,* ed. Frank M. Hasel (Silver Spring, MD: Biblical Research Institute, 2020), in press.

19. Gleason L. Archer, *Survey of Old Testament Introduction,* Revised and expanded edition (Chicago: Moody, 1994), 29.

20. Gabriel Barkay, Marilyn J. Lundberg, Andrew G. Vaughn, and Bruce Zuckerman, "The Amulets from Ketef Hinnom: A New Edition and Evaluation," *Bulletin of the American Schools of Oriental Research* 334 (2004) 41–71.

21. Erik Waaler, "A Revised Date for Pentateuchal Texts? Evidence from Ketef Hinnom," *Tyndale Bulletin* 53 (2002) 29–55.

22. J. Barton Payne, *Encyclopedia of Biblical Prophecy* (Grand Rapids, MI: Baker, 1973), 674, 675 lists 1,279 prophecies in the Old Testament and 578 prophecies in the New Testament, for a total of 1,817. These encompass 8,352 verses or 26.83 percent of the Bible.

23. John N. Oswalt, *The Bible Among the Myths* (Grand Rapids, MI: Zondervan, 2009), 47-110.

24. Gerhard F. Hasel, "Israel in Bible Prophecy," *Journal of the Adventist Theological Society* 3/1 (1992), 124.

25. On these additional methods of interpretation, including preterism and futurism, introduced in the counter-reformation, see Gerhard F. Hasel, "Israel in Prophecy," 121-130.

AS YOU BEGIN THE NEXT CHAPTER...

You may be familiar with a table game in which a stack of narrow wooden blocks is created; then players take turns pulling out blocks one at a time—carefully, so as not to collapse the edifice. At some point, of course, the whole "Tower-of-Babel"–like pillar comes crashing down. Game over.

Something similar threatens, when the Genesis story of the Earth's seven-day Creation is pulled out from the sum total of the Bible's important teachings—its fundamental truths, or doctrines.

Without Creation, what does the Sabbath mean? It's the weekly memorial of—what? And of all the world's believers who champion biblical Creation, none do so with more fervor than do Seventh-day Adventists. It's right there, after all, in their very name!

Or, what might the First Angel's Message of Revelation 14 be about? "Worship Him who *made* Heaven, the Earth, the Sea..."? Worship the One who did—*what?*

And especially, without Creation, how do we even begin to know where we human beings came from.

Many in this world scoff at the idea of Creation. They replace it with a theory of their own: evolution—a more supposedly intellectually honest and acceptable alternative to Creation. More acceptable, because evolution requires no belief in the primary foundation of Creation: belief in a Creator.

Upcoming in the next chapter: a careful comparison of godless evolution and the Creator's Creation. After the previous chapter on the authority of God's Word, what could be more logical than its first words: "In the beginning, God *created*..."?

Clifford Goldstein is editor of the *Adult Sabbath School Bible Study Guide.* Goldstein's latest book is *Risen: Finding Hope in the Empty Tomb.*

CLIFFORD GOLDSTEIN

CHAPTER 3

WHY CREATION MATTERS

"IN MY BEGINNING," WROTE POET T.S. ELIOT, "IS MY END."[1] ELIOT HAS A point actually. Particularly when it comes to human beginnings—human origins. After all, if our beginning, our origins, were the chance products of blind cosmic forces that never saw us coming, that never intended to create us, and that don't care about us at all—which means that we are nothing but "blobs of organized mud"[2]–then we can logically assume that the same cold forces that blindly brought us into existence will one day blindly lead us blobs out as well. Hence, the entire Christian message of hope; of salvation; of eternal life in Jesus; and of "a new heavens and a new earth" (2 Peter 3:13), is all a lie, a myth, some kind of Freudian wish-fulfillment subconsciously scrounged up from the depths of damaged human psyches.

So yes, Creation matters. Origins matter—they matter greatly. In fact, one could argue, based on the seventh-day Sabbath, that origins matter more than anything else, perhaps. Think about it. What biblical doctrine, what teaching, is so foundational, so crucial, that God *demands* one-seventh of our lives, every week and without exception, to remind us of it fifty-two times a year? (It comes to us, we don't go to it.)

We don't keep the Sabbath, as a memorial of the incarnation, the cross, the resurrection, the state of the dead, the sanctuary— no, we have been commanded (right up there with *Thou shalt not murder; thou shalt not steal)* to keep the Sabbath as a memorial of the six days of Creation.

This makes perfect sense, because none of these other teachings, i.e., the incarnation, the cross, the sanctuary, mean anything apart from the biblical account of Creation. If God hadn't created us, as we have been told in Scripture, then these beliefs become nothing but myths made by blobs of mud.

However, as Seventh-day Adventists, we have run into a problem, and the problem is science. Or, more accurately, scientism, the idea that, basically, the best way, or (as some would argue) the only way to have solid and secure knowledge is through science and the scientific method, and that any view which contradicts science needs to be rejected. And so much science, at least as it is practiced today, presents a model of origins that—in every conceivable way, at the most foundational levels, the level of first principles even—contradicts the biblical Creation account. And, despite the best efforts of many well-meaning people to harmonize them, they can't be harmonized, at least not without making a mockery of the Word of God.

How, then, can we as Seventh-day Adventists, a people whose very name includes our belief in the biblical six-day Creation, remain faithful to our prophetic mission to proclaim the Three Angels' Messages—which includes the call to worship the one "who made heaven and earth, the sea and springs of water" (Revelation 14:7)—in the face of a non-stop onslaught from the media, the academy, and even many other

Christians, against biblical Creation? And, too, how do we respond to those among us who assert that evolution and biblical Creation can be harmonized?

ONE MODEL OF CREATION

Though variations to this model exist, the present scientific consensus about the origins of the universe goes, basically, as follows. About thirteen billion years ago or so (give or take a billion one way or the other), an infinitely hot, infinitely dense, *something* (speculations about the size vary, from that of an atom to a human fist), called a "singularity," was the starting point of Creation. The logical question, of course, is: *Where did this infinitely hot, infinitely dense singularity come from?* Cosmologists waffle a bit here, arguing merely from math equations that it arose from nothing or stating flatly it was a "brute fact," that is—it just was.

Putting aside the minor detail about the origins of the singularity, the model states that this singularity exploded into what is known as "The Big Bang" (originally a pejorative term), out of which time, matter, space, and energy arose. The matter and energy, because of gravity (then, too, there's the slight question of where gravity came from and why it acts as it does and not in some other way), congealed into hot globs of molten mass, some turning into stars; some into planets, such as our earth. Then, about three billion years ago, based only on the known laws of chemistry and physics, "life arose in the ancient scorched Earth from the simplest of basic raw materials: air, water, and rock."[3] Next, over time, the forces of evolution, as first proposed by Darwin, were responsible for the variety of life on earth.

A few crucial points. First, nothing in this Creation model was, in any way, the result of intention or directed purpose. More conscious thought went into someone spray painting graffiti on the side of subway car than went into the creation of the universe and all life in it. From the Big Bang to human consciousness, everything resulted from cold, blind natural laws. Even staunch atheists, such as Richard Dawkins, admit how improbable it all was but, their argument goes, given enough time, anything, even something as improbable as life on earth, could happen. Second, foundational to this model is the claim that all life, from seashells, to butterflies, to the human brain—all arose from one common ancestor billions of years ago. Whether starting in a shallow pool, in molten rock, on shale, wherever and however it went from non-life to life, this primeval entity is, ultimately, the single ancestor of all life that followed.

ANOTHER MODEL OF CREATION

In contrast, the biblical model starts out with the words, "In the beginning God created the heavens and the earth" (Genesis 1:1). From the start, Creation is seen as the result of a supernatural entity, God Himself—exclusively. Though debate exists, even among conservative creationists, as to whether this verse was referring specifically to the Creation of the entire cosmos, and then the earth in particular, or whether Genesis 1:1 was referring only to the creation of our immediate heavens and earth, no debate exists about God as the origin of all that was created (see John 1:1) and that He was not dependent upon preexisting matter in this work of Creation.

Next, Genesis 1 and 2 depict God's supernatural work of fashioning the sky, the earth, the seas, and all life in it in six, literal, twenty-four-hour days, as we understand days today. In fact, each day is depicted not only by the Hebrew word for "day," *yom*, as in a twenty-four-hour day, but also with the refrain, repeated six times (one for each day) "and there was evening and morning, day . . ." *one, two, three, four, five, six,* (Genesis 1:5, 8, 13, 19, 23, 31). It's as if the author wanted to make it clear that he's talking about each different day, an evening and morning, as we have them today. "The phrase 'evening and morning,'" wrote Richard Davidson, "appearing at the conclusion of each of the six days of creation, is used by the author to clearly define the nature of the days of creation as literal twenty-four-hour days."[4] In fact, even many scholars who don't believe in a literal six-day Creation will, nevertheless, admit that the author of Genesis intended the story to be read as literal.

A few crucial points. In contrast to the secular model, where nothing in the Creation account was the result of any purposes or conscious intentions, in the biblical Creation account—*everything* resulted from the direct actions of God. And God said let x happen, "and it was so" (Genesis 1: 7, 9, 11, 15, 24, 30)—x happened. Each time it was deliberate, intentional, and purposeful. Second, in contrast to the secular model, where all life had a common ancestor, the biblical Creation account teaches that God made the birds, the animals, the fish, and humans separately and distinctly from each other.

> "And God created great whales, and every living creature that moves, which the waters brought forth abundantly, *after their kind,* and every winged fowl *after his kind* . . . And God said, Let the earth bring forth the living creature *after his kind,* cattle, and creeping thing, and beast of the earth *after his kind*: and it was so. And God made the beast of the earth after his kind, and cattle after their kind, and everything that creeps upon the earth *after his kind*" (Genesis 1: 21, 24, 25).

Each kind, each major species, were made separately and distinctly from each other.

In short, even based on the broadest reading of either Creation or evolution models, it's hard to imagine two more contrary and opposite viewpoints on origins.

THEISTIC EVOLUTION

Nevertheless, this radical difference between Creation and evolution has not stopped many well-meaning Christians from trying to harmonize them. These Christians feel that they have no choice because, as we have been told again and again, the scientific evidence for evolution is overwhelming, as obvious as a round earth or, to use an image from Richard Dawkins, as certain "as it is a fact that Paris is in the Northern Hemisphere."[5] Thus, theistic evolution, the idea that God created our world but did so through the forces of evolution, has infected much of modern Christendom—unfortunately, too.

Why unfortunately? Because they cannot be harmonized, as so many Christians claim to do. First, all one has to do is read the various attempts to do just that, to harmonize Creation with evolution, in order to see these Christians twist, distort, or even ignore Scripture in order to try and make it fit an evolutionary model. As one theistic evolutionist states with refreshing honesty (if nothing else):

> "Of necessity, this evolutionary effort will also mean that some of the [Bible] teachings will be translated almost beyond recognition, just as our skin is so unlike that of our scaly reptilian ancestors. Then, too, some passages will have so little utility that they will disappear, just as the primate tail was lost within our lineage of apes."[6]

Take, for instance, death. No matter how often Scripture presents death as an enemy, as something bad (1 Corinthians 15:26; Isaiah 25:8; 1 Corinthians 15:55; Hebrews 2:14; Revelation 21:4; 1 Corinthians 15:22), in every theistic evolutionary model, death becomes the very means of creating life. Billions of years of violence, extinction, suffering, and death were, then, God's chosen means for the creation of the rich diversity of life on earth. That's a nice theory, but because it contradicts what the Bible says about death, then those biblical texts about how bad death is must be among those passages that "will have so little utility that they will disappear, just as the primate tail was lost within our lineage of apes."

Then, too, the cross itself—at least as taught by the Bible, especially Paul—becomes null and void. About half a dozen times in Romans 5, the apostle makes a distinct link between Adam and Jesus. Adam brought death, and Jesus brought life. "For if by the one man's offense many died, much more the grace of God and the gift by the grace of the one Man, Jesus Christ, abounded to many" (Romans 5:15; see also Romans 5:12, 16-19). Christ's death, then, was predicated on an at-first-sinless Adam in paradise, whose fall Christ came to redeem. Yet evolution is predicated on an environment of death, violence, and predation in which no Adam in paradise could have possibly existed. Thus, whatever Paul was saying in Roman 5 about Jesus coming to undo the death that Adam caused—it was wrong. After all, science says so.

Also, how in any evolutionary model would the Gospel work? The Lord incarnates into an evolved ape that was created through the vicious and painfully murderous cycle of natural selection, all in order to abolish death, "the last enemy" (1 Corinthians 15:26)? But how can death be the "enemy," if it was one of God's chosen methods for creating humans?

The Lord must have expended plenty of dead *homo erectus, homo heidelbergensis*, and *homo neanderthalensis* in order to finally get one into His own image (*homo sapiens*). So then, Jesus comes to save mankind from the very process God used to create it in the first place?

And then there's the "fall." How did that work? Christians who believe in evolution say that God uses processes of violence, selfishness, and dominance of the strong against the weak in order to create a morally flawless and selfless being who "falls" into a state of violence, selfishness, and dominance of the strong over the weak—a state from which he has to be redeemed, or else face final punishment? So, in short, we need to be saved from the very process God used to create us to begin with?

Seeing this problem, the late Desmond Ford—having accepted something called "progressive creationism," i.e., billions of years of suffering and death interspersed with God directing the process every now and then—came up with his own "solution." Ford argued that the Adam of Genesis 1–3:24, the Adam whom God created, who fell, and who was kicked out of Eden, was a completely different man—separated by 100,000 years—from the Adam in the next verses, Genesis 4:1.

Wrote Ford:

> "Adam and Eve in Genesis 1 were not the parents of Cain and Abel .... The idea that there are two Adams, separated by vast ages, may confound those who think literally .... [T]he Adam of Genesis 1-3 is different from the Adam of chapter 4. . . . The Adam of chapters 1-3 is prehistory whereas the Adam of chapter 4 onwards lives in a world of about ten thousand years ago. The Adam of chapter 4 is a different man."[7]

All this, even though, coincidentally enough, the Adam in the next verse, Genesis 4:1, this "different man," also happened to have a wife named Eve as well!

These incredible distortions of Scripture, or flat-out denials of the most basic reading of Scripture, helps reveal the incompatibility between evolution and Scripture. Numerous atheist evolutionists mock, and justifiably so, theistic evolutionists as much as they do biblical creationists, because they can see the futility of trying to meld two theories that, at the most basic levels possible, contradict each other.

A TALE OF TWO PRINCIPLES

However, a fair question could be: Why does science, which gets so much "right," at least in the sense of making accurate predictions and creating amazing technology, get origins so wrong? The answer stems from two principles that science uses, both of which, when it comes to origins, happen to be false.

The first is that science, which studies the natural world, must look only to the natural world for answers. This notion, hundreds, maybe even thousands of years old, asserts that we should not resort to supernatural causes to explain natural effects. Biologists must not explain, for instance, the extremely complicated process of blood clot formation by attributing the enzyme cascade to divine intervention. Science would not, could not, progress if everything, or anything, not understood were explained away as supernatural meddling.

This makes great sense, too. If you have a backache and go to the doctor, sure, it would be fine if he/she prays with you, but you want more. You want pills, massages, exercises, surgery; that is, you want something natural to deal with a natural issue. Science works the same way as well.

The second principle is that the laws of nature must remain constant. All things being equal, then, what a law does today it did yesterday and will do tomorrow, and any variations result from another law-like pattern that itself resulted from another law-like pattern, etc. Otherwise, science and the technology we derive from it would be impossible. We assume that the laws of aerodynamics for jet flight and those of torque and force behind bridge construction remain constant when we drive across the bridge or ascend in a Boeing 747.

The only problem? When it comes to origins, both these principles are flat-out wrong.

Take the first one, which requires supernatural causes for natural events. That's fine for hurricane tracking or for analysis of whooping crane embryology. But it is worse than worthless for origins that start out with "In the beginning God created the heavens and the earth" (Genesis 1:1) and from there go on with one supernatural event after another. God speaks the grass, the birds, the animals into existence. He *speaks* them into existence!

Everything about this process, from beginning to end, was only supernatural. But, if you automatically rule out *anything* supernatural, then whatever explanation you have for Creation will have to be wrong. It's like a detective in a murder case who, from the start, rules out as a suspect the guilty party. Whoever the detective charges with the murder will, of necessity, be innocent.

It's the same with the second—the constancy of nature. That principle makes sense, except that Romans 5:12 reads, "Therefore, just as sin entered the world through one man, and death through sin, and in this way death came to all people, because all sinned." This verse presupposes a natural environment discontinuous, and qualitatively different, from anything that science now confronts. "As they witnessed in drooping flower and falling leaf the first signs of decay," wrote Ellen White, "Adam and his companion mourned more deeply than men now mourn over their dead. The death of the frail, delicate flowers was indeed a cause of sorrow; but when the goodly trees cast off their leaves, the scene brought vividly to mind the stern fact that death is the portion of every living thing" (*Patriarchs and Prophets*, 62). What can science, which studies only an environment where everything dies, teach us about one where nothing did? And, even worse, when it rejects the very idea of an environment where nothing died?

THE EXPERTS

Of course, to reject evolution in favor of biblical Creation, means that you have to believe that thousands upon thousands of experts—the feted, the wined and dined in biology, chemistry, genetics, physics, zoology, etc., some of the world's greatest minds—are wrong about origins, and in a big way, too. Though the fact that a majority of experts believe something hardly proves it true (the experts have been wrong before), the psychological pressure on others to believe as they do can be quite compelling.

An analogy, a parallel, might help. We are Seventh-day Adventists, and if there's one doctrine, almost uniquely ours, that's so clear, so biblical, so certain, even to the point that one can all but be dogmatic about it, it is the validity of the seventh-day Sabbath. Yet how many of the world's greatest biblical scholars, experts in Hebrew, Greek, Aramaic, systematic theology, biblical history—yes, the feted, the wined and the dined, some of the world's smartest people—how many of them get the Sabbath right? Most don't.

The fact that so many biblical scholars get the Sabbath wrong doesn't prove, of course, that so many experts also get origins wrong. It proves only that the world's experts can, indeed, get it wrong.

WHY CREATION MATTERS

The doctrine of Creation forms the foundation of biblical truth. From the nature of humanity to the fall, to the work of the Godhead, to the sovereignty of God, to the story of redemption, to the origins of evil and of death—so many basic teachings derive directly from the six-day Creation account. If that's wrong, our most basic theology, right up to the Three Angels' Messages, is built on lies.

Then, too, there's the integrity of the biblical text itself. Why would God use billions of years of violence, predation, disease, and death to create human life on earth, and then give us our only "official" account of Creation, a story that in every way, from the broad principles to the most specific details was wrong? If evolution were true, then for thousands of years—from the whole Israelite period up, through the New Testament era, through the Middle Ages, the Protestant Reformation, and beyond—the Lord's Church was kept in darkness regarding human origins until God, in His infinite wisdom, raised up His divinely appointed one, Charles Darwin, ultimately an atheist, to finally reveal the truth about the proper interpretation of Genesis? If Scripture were so wrong about origins, why trust what it says about anything else?

If evolution were true, the "everlasting gospel" (Revelation 14:6), the foundation of the Three Angels' Messages, as we have seen, would become fatally compromised. And without the gospel, the judgment that follows (Revelation 14:7) would leave us hopelessly condemned. Who wants to face God in the judgment without the hope offered by the cross? And in any evolutionary scenario, whatever happened at the cross was not Jesus suffering there in our stead, in order to redeem us from death (Hosea 13:14), if death was the very process God used to create us to begin with.

Finally, in the evolutionary paradigm, eschatology becomes interesting too, especially God's promise to make a new earth. Will that creation be by divine fiat, or will life, again, endure the rigor and "joy" of natural selection and survival-of-the-fittest for billions of years until a new world, one "wherein dwelleth righteousness" (2 Peter 3:13), finally appears?

Scripture, too, teaches that "We shall not all sleep, but we shall all be changed—in a moment, in the twinkling of an eye, at the last trumpet. For the trumpet will sound, and the dead will be raised incorruptible, and we shall be changed" (1 Corinthians 15: 51, 52). God will raise the dead, some having been nothing for millennia but scattered molecules; and if He can do that, in a moment, in the "twinkling of an eye," the second time He creates life, why did He use billions of years the first go around—and then, again, give us some silly story that teaches nothing accurately about what really happened?

In our beginning, yes, the six-day Creation of heaven and earth as depicted in Genesis (1 and 2), is our end the "new heaven and new earth" depicted in Revelation 21:1?

Creation, the biblical account of a six-day Creation, matters. It matters greatly, because if that's false, all that follows, including the cross, salvation, the Second Coming, is false, which means our faith is empty, our hopes vain, the Three Angels' Messages meaningless, and, yes, we "blobs of organized mud" are still in our sins.

We know better, though. We are Seventh-day Adventists. Our very name declares to men and to angels, our belief in the biblical Creation account and not some impossible hybrid with a story that denies the Genesis account in every particular. The Creator, the Creator of the cosmos, loved us so much that not only did He create us, He redeemed us as well, and now He calls us to faithfulness to Him and to His written Word. How can we neglect so great a creation, so great a salvation (Hebrews 2:3)? We shouldn't, and by faithfulness to the truths God has given us—we won't.

ENDNOTES

1. *The Collected Poems of T. S. Eliot* (New York: Harcourt,1963).
2. Carroll, Sean. *The Big Picture: On the Origins of Life, Meaning, and the Universe Itself.* Penguin Publishing Group. Kindle Edition.
3. Hazen, Robert. *Origins of Life: Part One* (Chantilly, VA: The Teaching Company, 2005), 14.

4. Klingbeil, Gerald, *The Genesis Creation Account* (Berrien Springs, MI; Andrews University Press, 2015); Richard Davidson, "The Genesis Account of Origins," 78.

5. Dawkins, Richard (2009-09-18). *The Greatest Show on Earth: The Evidence for Evolution.* Free Press. Kindle Edition, 10.

6. Dowd, Michael (2008-06-19), *Thank God for Evolution: How the Marriage of Science and Religion Will Transform Your Life and Our World.* Penguin Group. Kindle Edition.

7. Ford, Desmond, *Genesis Versus Darwinism: The Demise of Darwin's Theory of Evolution* (Desmond Ford, 2015), 156, 157.

AS YOU BEGIN THE NEXT CHAPTER...

In the chapter just finished, the author focused on one of the most important doctrines in all of God's Word: Creation.

Many sincere Christians, though, express reservations about placing too much emphasis on the preaching and teaching of doctrines in the mission of the Church. Rather, they say, our message should be about Jesus and the importance of a personal relationship with Him.

- True, the risk is real that we can fall into presenting law and doctrine, largely devoid of any significant focus on Jesus, till we are—as the Remnant Messenger wrote, "dry as the hills of Gilboa."
- But we can also veer off the other side of the road and present a sentimental, overly emotional view of Jesus that somehow sees His teachings—His doctrines—as somehow suspect and even dangerous to the Christian life.

In the chapter just ahead, the author demonstrates that to divide between Jesus and doctrine is a false separation. All genuine doctrines, or teachings of the Word, have Jesus right at their center. And it's not possible to build a relationship with Jesus that doesn't include His teachings. To accept Jesus the Truth is to accept the Bible truths that are in Him!

Clinton Wahlen (Ph.D. in New Testament, University of Cambridge) has served as an associate director at the Biblical Research Institute in Silver Spring, Maryland, since 2008, and is the author/editor of scholarly books and many articles. Previously, he taught New Testament and Greek at the university and doctoral levels for eleven years and served as a pastor in Northern California, where he was ordained to the gospel ministry. He and his wife, Gina, have two grown children and twin grandchildren.

CLINTON WAHLEN

CHAPTER 4

JESUS AND DOCTRINE

LET'S FACE IT—DOCTRINE IS NOT A VERY POPULAR WORD TODAY. THERE ARE movements that want to minimize doctrine and emphasize Jesus only. For some, the word doctrine conjures up the idea of cold church creeds, stale traditions, boring discourses, and "proof-texting." One Seventh-day Adventist pastor sadly observes: "To some, it sounds like a swear word: 'Oh yeah! Well, you're full of *Doctrine!*'" From their skewed perspective, doctrine "might sound like a place where good ideas go to die."[1]

So uncomfortable has this word become that it even seems to be vanishing from more recent versions of the Bible. It occurs fourteen times less in the King James (fifty-six times), nine times less often in the New Revised Standard Version (eight times) compared with the original Revised Standard (seventeen times), and one less time in the 2011 New International Version (six times) compared to the 1984 edition (seven times).[2]

But the word cannot be erased completely from Scripture, because it is a biblical idea. Solomon said, "I give you good doctrine" (Proverbs 4:2).[3] Jesus said, "My doctrine is not Mine, but His who sent Me" (John 7:16). Jesus' affirmation of doctrine should not be surprising. He is, after all, *the Word*:

> "In the beginning was the Word, and the Word was with God, and the Word was God. . . . And the Word became flesh and dwelt among us, and we beheld His glory, the glory as of the only begotten of the Father, full of grace and truth" John 1:1, 14.

While some contend that Jesus and doctrine should not, cannot, be spoken of in the same breath, Scripture makes plain that Jesus and doctrine—meaning Jesus and His teachings—are inseparable. They are two sides of the same coin. To take one away is to take away both. To really know Jesus is impossible without an understanding and acceptance of His teachings, which includes what He says about Himself.

Almost everything we know about Jesus comes from the Bible, especially the Gospels and the rest of the New Testament. And a lot of that content consists of His teachings. The Gospel of Matthew, for example, is organized around five major blocks of Jesus' teaching, beginning with the Sermon on the Mount, which covers three entire chapters (Matthew 5-7), as does the final block, Jesus' Sermon on Last Things (Matthew 23-25).[4] The other three deal with discipleship and mission (Matthew 10), mysteries of the kingdom (Matthew 13), and the Church (Matthew 18). Altogether, these five teaching blocks comprise about forty percent of Matthew's Gospel. Other sayings and teachings of Jesus are found elsewhere, in addition to Matthew's own descriptions of who Jesus is.

In Luke and John the teachings (or "doctrines") of Jesus likewise predominate. Only Mark focuses attention more directly on Jesus' life, especially His miracles, sufferings, and death. Even then, in all four Gospels, the miracles illustrate Jesus' power to save from sin and His sufferings and death are shown to fulfill the prophecies/teachings of the Old

Testament about the Messiah. In other words, *the careful reader of the Gospels recognizes that they are saturated with the teachings of Jesus and that it is impossible to separate what Jesus did from what He taught, because His whole life is a lesson book for us. Knowing Jesus includes knowing His teachings and accepting them. If we don't know and accept His teachings, how can we really claim to know Jesus?*

What are some of these teachings, and why are they important? What does all this have to do with my salvation? Isn't it enough simply to believe in and love Jesus? What danger is there in focusing on just Jesus? Wouldn't this be safer, since there is so much disagreement among Christians, and even among Adventists, on certain doctrines? What is important and what is not—and how can we tell the difference? These important questions deserve clear answers. Fortunately, we can find answers to these questions in the Bible. Let's begin by looking at those who were closest to Jesus—the apostles—and discover what their attitude was toward doctrine. How important was it to them?

THE APOSTLES' ATTITUDE TOWARD DOCTRINE

It may come as a surprise to some that the early Church, from the very beginning, emphasized doctrine. The thousands who were baptized on the Day of Pentecost "continued steadfastly in the apostles' doctrine and fellowship, in the breaking of bread, and in prayers" (Acts 2:42). Doctrine is mentioned first, and their fidelity to it is emphasized—they "continued *steadfastly*" in it, using a word that means "hold fast to."[5] Furthermore, it was the *teachings* of the apostles that got them in trouble with the Jewish authorities (Acts 4:2, 18; 5:25, 28). But despite opposition, the apostles "did not cease teaching and preaching Jesus as the Christ," the Messiah (Acts 5:42).

This emphasis on doctrine, they learned from Jesus Himself. To the two disciples on the road to Emmaus, "beginning at Moses [the Pentateuch] and all the Prophets, He expounded to them in all the Scriptures the things concerning Himself" (Luke 24:27). What a Bible study that must have been! The disciples "said to one another, 'Did not our hearts burn within us while He talked with us on the road, and while He opened the Scriptures to us?" (v. 32). So moved were they that they "rose up that very hour and returned to Jerusalem" to tell the apostles all about it (v. 33). But Jesus was not done. While they were all gathered together, Jesus appeared and said, "These are the words which I spoke to you while I was still with you, that all things must be fulfilled which were written in the Law of Moses and the Prophets and the Psalms concerning Me" (v. 44). So important were these things that Jesus repeated what He had already explained to the Twelve during His ministry. Jesus cannot be separated from His teachings. They are two sides of the same coin.

THE DARK SIDE OF DOCTRINE

So why did Jesus' sufferings and death on the Cross come as such a shock to the disciples? Because they didn't believe what He was trying to teach them—they did not want to accept His doctrine. Jesus indicated the same to the two disciples on the road to Emmaus, lamenting that they were "slow of heart to believe in all that the prophets have spoken!" (Luke 24:25). Rather than accept the teachings of Jesus, they preferred to believe the widespread popular Jewish notion that the Messiah was to deliver them from the Romans and rule as an earthly monarch (v. 21; cf. John 6:15). In other words, they experienced doctrinal dissonance—what Jesus was trying to teach them didn't agree with their previously held beliefs.

Doctrine can be a bad thing if it's not in harmony with Scripture. Jesus said to the scribes and Pharisees who criticized Him for not keeping their traditions that their "doctrines" had "made the commandment of God of no effect" (Matthew 15:6, 9). As with "doctrine," the word "tradition" in the New Testament can be good or bad. Jesus told them that the Word of God had been made "of no effect through your tradition which you have handed down" (Mark 7:13). Often, that is the problem with tradition. It has simply been handed down from one generation to the next as a theory of truth rather than the living, vibrant reality that God's truth really is.

The typical design of the sanctuary in Adventist churches illustrates this phenomenon. From our earliest days, sanctuaries in Adventist churches have had a raised pulpit in the center to emphasize the importance of the preaching of the Word, and the Bible would be placed prominently in front of it to show our Bible-based message. In other denominations, the liturgy and Lord's Supper are more important, so the pulpit may be off to the side. How many Adventists are aware of the reason for the design of our churches? In most cases, the tradition has been preserved, but the reason for it forgotten. Unfortunately, the same happens with doctrine. It gets handed down as a theory of truth, but sometimes the biblical support for it gets lost. When this happens, we lose the basis upon which to decide whether or not a teaching, or doctrine, is true and important, because the Bible evidence has been forgotten or even ignored altogether.

WHY IS DOCTRINE IMPORTANT?

When doctrines come, not from Scripture, but from other sources, they can be downright dangerous. They may come from unbiblical traditions, from human reasonings, or from what some may consider a "Spirit-led" experience.

We have already seen how traditions not based on the Bible were a problem in the time of Jesus. It may seem obvious that doctrines based primarily on human reasonings could be dangerous, but that doesn't keep people from going down that false path.

But what about spiritual experiences? Surely, the Spirit wouldn't lead us astray, right? That is true. The Holy Spirit who inspired the Bible will never lead us contrary to its teachings—"the spirits of the prophets are subject to the prophets" (1 Corinthians 14:32). But not every spiritual encounter is from God. That is why John tells us: "do not believe every spirit, but test the spirits, whether they are of God; because many false prophets have gone out into the world" (1 John 4:1). Bible-based doctrine is important because it is possible for us to imagine a voice is the Holy Spirit speaking when it is really a different spirit.

Some years ago, following an evangelistic meeting held in my church, a young woman was convinced that the seventh-day Sabbath was biblical and needed to be kept holy. The very next Sabbath she was in church. However, the following Sabbath she was not there. I went to visit her to see if everything was alright. She explained the reason for her not returning the next Sabbath—"I see the Bible teaches that the Sabbath is Saturday, but the Spirit told me I don't have to keep it."

Even our own heart can deceive us sometimes. Paul warns that the time would come when people "will not endure sound doctrine, but according to their own desires, because they have itching ears, they will heap up for themselves teachers; and they will turn their ears away from the truth, and be turned aside to fables" (2 Timothy 4:3, 4). Commenting on this passage, Ellen G. White said:

> "That time has fully come. The multitudes do not want Bible truth, because it interferes with the desires of the sinful, world-loving heart; and Satan supplies the deceptions which they love.
>
> "But God will have a people upon the earth to maintain the Bible, and the Bible only, as the standard of all doctrines and the basis of all reforms. The opinions of learned men, the deductions of science, the creeds or decisions of ecclesiastical councils, as numerous and discordant as are the churches which they represent, the voice of the majority—not one nor all of these should be regarded as evidence for or against any point of religious faith. Before accepting any doctrine or precept, we should demand a plain "Thus saith the Lord" in its support."[6]

Like the faithful Bereans, who "searched the Scriptures daily to find out whether these things were so" (Acts 17:11), we are to test everything by the Bible (Isaiah 8:20). We hear many false voices today, including from pastors and teachers. If the Bereans were commended for checking out the words of Paul, we would do well to do the same with teachings we hear in our day, when "every wind of doctrine" seems to be blowing (see Ephesians 4:14). Knowing—really knowing for ourselves—the teachings of the Bible and being able to share them with others is our only safeguard from being deceived. "None but those who have fortified the mind with the truths of the Bible will stand through the last great conflict."[7] This fact helps us to understand God's purpose in having revealed truth written down and passed on to subsequent generations.

WHY THE WRITTEN WORD IS IMPORTANT FOR DOCTRINE

Unlike spoken words, the written Word has permanence. God gave clear instructions to Moses (Deuteronomy 31:24-26), Joshua (Joshua 24:26), the prophets (e.g., Isaiah 30:8; Jeremiah 36:2; Habakkuk 2:2), and other Bible writers (1 Corinthians 14:37; Revelation 1:11), to record God's Word for the generations to come (cf. 1 Peter 1:13-15). We know it was put in writing very early, from later writers who refer back to previous portions of Scripture.[8] In fact, the king of Israel was commanded to "write for himself a copy of this law [*torah*] in a book" and to "read it all the days of his life, that he may learn to fear the Lord his God and be careful to observe all the words of this law and these statutes (Deuteronomy 17:18-20).[9] But the Scriptures were not just for the priests and rulers of Israel; parents also were to "teach them diligently" to their children, "to talk of them" when at home and when traveling, in family worship morning and evening ("when you lie down and when you rise up"), and even to write God's Word out in prominent places around their homes (Deuteronomy 6:6-9). The Bible and the teachings it contains were to be a perpetual divine influencer for His people.

That fact that God's Word is *in written form* helps prevent us from being led astray. We are to live, as Jesus said, quoting the Old Testament (Deuteronomy 8:3), "by every word that proceeds from the mouth of

God" (Matthew 4:4). In fact, right after quoting this text in response to Satan's first temptation, the devil himself quoted Scripture as part of his second temptation, but he omitted one key phrase. Transporting Jesus to the pinnacle of the temple, he said:

If You are the Son of God, throw Yourself down. For it is written:

> *"He shall give His angels charge over you," and,*
> *"In their hands they shall bear you up,*
> *Lest you dash your foot against a stone"* Matthew 4:6.

By checking Satan's quotation with the actual words of Psalm 91, we can see what he left out between the two quotes—"To keep you in all your ways." This is a promise that God's angels would help keep us from stumbling or falling into sin. From this incident we can see that, even when the Bible is quoted, we should (quoting a Russian proverb) "Trust but verify." It is possible for important texts to be overlooked, taken out of context, misquoted, or even deliberately left out and ignored in order to advocate a position or teaching that the Bible does not actually support.

Even apparently innocent questions, by raising doubts about God's Word, can be more deadly than outright lies, as Eve discovered only too late (Genesis 3:1). Paul actually uses this incident to warn us not to tolerate someone who "preaches another Jesus whom we have not preached, . . . or a different gospel which you have not accepted" (2 Corinthians 11:3, 4).

How will we recognize another Jesus or a different gospel unless we know clearly what the Bible teaches about these things? Truth must be based on "*all* the Scriptures," as the example of Jesus (Luke 24:27) and the rest of the Bible itself teaches us (Isaiah 8:20; 2 Timothy 3:16, 17). The whole Bible is trustworthy. "For *whatever things* were written before were written for our learning, that we through the patience and comfort of the Scriptures might have hope" (Romans 15:4). That includes doctrines of the Bible that, unfortunately, some Adventists have begun to doubt. As we look at a few examples, we will see how Jesus is at the heart of each one.

CHRIST—THE HEART OF EVERY BIBLE DOCTRINE

We are told that "Every true doctrine makes Christ the center, every precept receives force from His words."[10] Some might wonder if that can really be said about *every* doctrine of Seventh-day Adventists. Let us look at four doctrines as examples to show how Jesus is at the heart of each one: *the Remnant, the Sabbath, the Sanctuary, and Healthful Living.*[11]

The Remnant. Is Jesus really at the center of our doctrine of the remnant? Absolutely. We should keep in mind that the entire book of Revelation was revealed to John *by Jesus* (Revelation 1:1) and, therefore, Jesus teaches us what the two distinguishing characteristics of the remnant are—they "keep the commandments of God and have the testimony of Jesus Christ" (Revelation 12:17).

Several other passages describe in symbolic terms the events leading to the rise of the remnant (Revelation 10:1–11:1) and the message they proclaim (Revelation 14:6-12; 18:1-4).

In essence, that message, which includes "the everlasting gospel," applies Jesus' Great Commission, given to the early Christians (Matthew 28:18-20), to an end-time setting. It also makes clear that "the faith of Jesus" is the only way they can keep the commandments of God (Revelation 14:12). In fact, in this verse, Jesus answers a question He had asked but left unanswered at the time: "when the Son of Man comes, will He really find faith on the earth?" (Luke 18:8). There will be a people of faith on the earth.

Of the remnant who live to see Jesus come (cf. Revelation 14:14-16), John is told, "here are those who keep the commandments of God and the faith of Jesus" (Revelation 14:12).

The Sabbath. A crucial part of this final message is the Sabbath, because we are commanded to "worship Him who made heaven and earth, the sea and springs of water" (Revelation 14:7). This is an almost word-for-word quotation of the Sabbath Commandment (see Exodus 20:11). Who created all things? According to the New Testament, Jesus did (John 1:3).

"For by Him all things were created that are in heaven and that are on earth, visible and invisible, whether thrones or dominions or principalities or powers. All things were created through Him and for Him" (Colossians 1:16).

It was Jesus who finished the work of Creation in six days and rested on the seventh day (cf. Genesis 2:1-3). According to the Gospel of John, as Jesus completed His saving work on the Cross that Friday afternoon, "He said 'It is finished!'" and rested in the tomb over the Sabbath day (John 19:30, 31), only rising from the dead on "the first day of the week" (John 20:1).

So the Sabbath has been doubly blessed by Jesus—first at Creation and then at the Cross. Far from being legalistic, keeping the Sabbath is the most *Christ-centered, Gospel-oriented* thing we can do! It symbolizes that, just as we did not create ourselves (Psalm 100:3), we cannot save ourselves, either: "So then, there remains a Sabbath rest for the people of God, for whoever has entered God's rest has also rested from his works as God did from his" (Hebrews 4:9, 10, ESV). The Greek word translated "Sabbath rest" is *sabbatismos*, which literally means "keeping sabbath."[12] Our Sabbath observance actually affirms that we are saved by faith in Jesus and not by our own works (cf. Romans 3:28, 31).

The Sanctuary. We can see now that keeping the Sabbath is an important part of the everlasting Gospel. But how is it connected with Christ's ministry in the heavenly sanctuary and why is it singled out as part of the end-time message to be given just before He comes again? There are several reasons. First, as we have seen, this message results in a group who "keep the commandments of God and the faith of Jesus." Second, it directs our attention to Jesus' work of judgment (Revelation 14:7; cf. John 5:22) in the Most Holy Place of the heavenly sanctuary, where the commandments of God are enshrined (Revelation 11:19). Third, by that law all will be judged (James 2:12; Ecclesiastes 12:13, 14). When the issue of true versus false worship is brought clearly to the forefront, the saved at the end of time will be those who worship God "in spirit and in truth" (John 4:24), shown by their observance of the true Sabbath which is His seal (Revelation 7:2-4; 14:1), while the lost will worship the beast and receive his mark (Revelation 14:9-11). The fourth reason the Sabbath is singled out is that Jesus' work in the heavenly sanctuary corresponds to the work done by the high priest on the Day of Atonement. This was the only day of the year other than the weekly Sabbath, on which the Israelites were required to rest completely from all their work; otherwise, God would "destroy" them (Leviticus 23:26-32).

Just as the Sabbath points us to Jesus' work, so every phase of the ministry in the earthly sanctuary points to Jesus: the sacrifice, to Jesus' death on the Cross (1 Corinthians 5:7); the Holy Place, to Jesus' justifying righteousness (1 John 1:9; 2:1); the Most Holy Place, to the process of sanctifying His people and, finally, to His blotting out the record of our sins and purifying a people who are ready to meet Him. Every phase is *Christ's* work and *His* righteousness, NOT our own. The purpose of this third and final phase of Christ's heavenly ministry is summarized in the following statement:

> "The last rays of merciful light, the last message of mercy to be given to the world, is a revelation of His character of love. The children of God are to manifest His glory. In their own life and character they are to reveal what the grace of God has done for them."[13]

Healthful Living. A part of that witness of what God's grace has done for His people to prepare them for heaven is their healthy lifestyle. Jesus said He came that His people "may have life, and that they may have it more abundantly" (John 10:10). He wants to sanctify the *whole* person, including our bodies: "Now may the God of peace Himself sanctify you completely; and may your whole spirit, soul, and body be preserved blameless at the coming of our Lord Jesus Christ" (1 Thessalonians 5:23). Jesus wants the very best for us and, as our Creator, has already specified that the best, most nutritious, and healthiest food for us is a plant-based diet (Genesis 1:29). So, if we love Jesus, would we not want to live in harmony with what He has said is best for us? "Therefore, whether you eat or drink, or *whatever you do*, do all to the glory of God" (1 Corinthians 10:31). A lot is comprehended in those three italicized words. It involves caring for our bodies as the temple of the Holy Spirit (1 Corinthians 6:19), avoiding what would harm it, and living as healthfully as possible, including adequate rest, exercise, drinking plenty of water, and more. Even Jesus spoke of His physical body as God's temple (John 2:19-21) and, as part of His "new wine" ministry (Mark 2:22), seems to have abstained from alcohol (Matthew 27:34; cf. Proverbs 20:1). Faithful disciples will follow His example (1 Peter 2:21).

THE TRUTH AS IT IS IN JESUS

Some might call this presentation of Bible texts in support of each doctrine prooftexting. But it is really just what has been "taught by Him, as the truth is in Jesus" (Ephesians 4:21). Without a clear understanding of this "truth as it is in Jesus," we have only a superficial Christianity, shallow faith, and little genuine commitment. Worse, we are in danger of making Jesus in our own image. Are we creating a "christ" as we would like Him to be, instead of humbly accepting the Bible's own witness as to who Jesus truly is? That is why, on the road to Emmaus, rather than just *telling* the disciples who He was, Jesus *showed* them from the Scriptures (Luke 24:27). He cited texts from the Old Testament to prove His points, as did all the New Testament writers. Were Jesus and the apostles prooftexting? Of course not! Because they always quote Scripture in harmony with its original intention.

Prooftexting is quite different. Those who engage in it "ignore the historical context of Scripture and interpret the text by a loose association of certain aspects and words that are strung together without allowing the Bible to actually define its meaning in its original, historical and literary context."[14] In describing the Christ-centered focus of these doctrines, we have simply followed Jesus' method of interpreting

Scripture to show how they all revolve around Him—"These are they which testify of Me," He said (John 5:39).

The entire Bible, from first to last, is a witness as to who Jesus is. Genesis calls Him the Seed of the woman (Genesis 3:15). Balaam describes Him as the Scepter of Israel (Numbers 24:17). In Isaiah, He is the precious Cornerstone (Isaiah 28:16); "Wonderful, Counselor, Mighty God, Everlasting Father, Prince of Peace" (Isaiah 9:6). Daniel calls Him Messiah the Prince (9:25), the Prince of the Covenant (11:22), and the Prince of Princes (8:25). He is the True Vine (John 15:1), the Good Shepherd (John 10:14), the Bread of Life (John 6:35), and the Light of the World (8:12). John the Baptist proclaims Him "The Lamb of God who takes away the sin of the world" (John 1:29). He is the Son of man (Mark 13:26), "the Son of the living God" (Matt 16:16), our great High Priest (Hebrews 4:14), and our Advocate (1 John 2:1). Finally, in the book of Revelation Jesus is "the Faithful and True Witness" (Revelation 3:14), "the Root and the Offspring of David, the Bright and Morning Star" (Revelation 22:16), the Lion of the Tribe of Judah (Revelation 5:5), the Alpha and the Omega, the Beginning and the End, the First and the Last (Revelation 22:13), King of kings and Lord of lords (Revelation 19:16). This last book of the Bible even calls Him "The Word of God" (Revelation 19:13).

This is the Jesus of the Bible—the only true Jesus. We cannot separate Jesus from His teachings in Scripture any more than we can separate one side of a coin from the other. Jesus *is* the living Word to which His written Word witnesses. Everything else is fake.

But the devil specializes in the fake and is preparing his final deceptions to deceive, if possible, even the elect, including a future in-person appearance to "personate Christ" as "the crowning act in the great drama of deception."[15] Might he be already laying the great deception by spreading confusing and conflicting ideas about Christ within the Church? The only way now and always to distinguish the real Jesus from a fake Jesus is by "the word of truth" (Psalm 119:43; 2 Corinthians 6:7; Ephesians 1:13; 2 Timothy 2:15; James 1:18), inspired by the God of truth, "with whom is no variableness, neither shadow of turning" (James 1:17, KJV). That is why God urges us to be faithful to the Word:

> "Give diligence to present yourself approved by God, a workman who doesn't need to be ashamed, properly handling the Word of Truth" (2 Timothy 2:15, WEB).

ENDNOTES

1. Mark Witas (lead pastor of the Sunnyside Seventh-day Adventist Church in Portland, Oregon), "Jesus. Doctrine. Jesus and our beliefs," in *For the One: Voices from The One Project* (ed. Nathan Brown, with Alex Bryan and Japhet de Oliveira; Victoria, Australia: Signs Publishing, 2014), 61 (emphasis supplied).

2. See Clinton Wahlen, "Variants, Versions, and the Trustworthiness of Scripture," in *Biblical Hermeneutics: An Adventist Approach,* ed. Frank M. Hasel (Silver Spring, MD: Biblical Research Institute/Review & Herald Academic, 2020), 96.

3. Unless otherwise indicated, all Bible quotations are from the New King James Version, and any emphasis is supplied. Note that the Hebrew word translated *doctrine (leqach)* in Proverbs 4:2 is rendered differently by other versions, e.g., *teaching* (NAS95), *precepts* (NRSV, ESV), *learning* (NIV11), *instruction* (CSB).

4. The woes of Matthew 23 introduce Christ's final sermon, just as the Beatitudes of Matthew 5 introduce His first one.

5. W. Bauer, F. W. Danker, W. F. Arndt, and F. W. Gingrich, *A Greek-English Lexicon of the New Testament and Other Early Christian Literature,* 3d ed. (Chicago: University of Chicago Press, 2000), 881.

6. Ellen G. White, *The Great Controversy,* 595.

7. Ibid., 593, 594.

8. See Joshua 8:31; 1 Kings 2:27; 16:34; 22:38; 2 Kings 9:36; 10:10; 15:12; 23:15-17; 24:2; 1 Chronicles 11:3; 15:15; 2 Chronicles 34:21; 35:6; 36:21, 22; and the numerous quotations of the Old Testament by Jesus and the New Testament writers, often introduced with the authoritative phrase "It is written" which occurs sixty-seven times in the New Testament (e.g., Matthew 2:5; 11:10; 21:13; Mark 1:2; 14:27; Luke 2:23; 7:27; Acts 1:20; 7:42; Romans 1:17; 9:33; Galatians 3:13; 4:27; 1 Peter 1:16).

9. Since the word *torah* in Scripture often refers to the five books of Moses (e.g., Joshua 1:7; 23:6; 2 Kings 14:6; Isaiah 8:20; Nehemiah 8:1; Luke 24:44; Romans 3:21), this command may mean that the king was to write out a copy of the entire Pentateuch, though the Septuagint (the ancient Greek translation of the Old Testament produced in the third to second centuries BC) specifically limits this command to the book of Deuteronomy (Deuteronomy 17:18, LXX).

10. Ellen G. White, *Testimonies for the Church,* vol. 6, 54.

11. A description of twenty-eight Bible doctrines held by Seventh-day Adventists are available online: https://www.adventist.org/wp-content/uploads/2020/06/ADV-28Beliefs2020.pdf (accessed July 6, 2020). These four correspond to numbers 13, 20, 24, and 22.

12. Joseph Henry Thayer, *Thayer's Greek-English Lexicon of the New Testament,* 1889; reprint (Peabody, MA: Hendrickson, 2000), §4520.

13. Ellen G. White, *Christ's Object Lessons,* 415.

14. Cf. Clinton Wahlen, "John 2:10. What Kind of Wine Did Jesus Make at Cana?" In *Interpreting Scripture: Bible Questions and Answers,* ed. Gerhard Pfandl, Biblical Research Institute Studies in Hermeneutics 2 (Silver Spring, MD: Biblical Research Institute, 2010), 321-323.

14. Frank M. Hasel, "Factors for a Biblical Hermeneutic in Harmony with Scripture's Self-Claim," in *Biblical Hermeneutics: An Adventist Approach.*

15. Ellen G. White, *The Great Controversy,* 624.

AS YOU BEGIN THE NEXT CHAPTER...

A short quiz . . .

Question: What are the Bible's most "Adventist" books?

Answer: The Bible books of Daniel and Revelation.

True, if there are any two books in the Bible that would be most uniquely Adventist in the amount of attention they receive, would they not be Daniel in the Old Testament – and Revelation in the New Testament? Both contain much symbolism. Both contain many time prophecies. Both show not just theological *trees* but the whole theological *forest,* as well.

And both are ***apocalyptic*** in their focus.

As usually defined, apocalyptic is an adjective: (An *apocalyptic story* is one that deals with the destruction and end of the world.)

But Adventists are among the few for whom apocalyptic is also a noun: (*Apocalyptic* is a set of beliefs or teachings about the end of the world.)

As you page ahead now to the next chapter, you'll find some of the marks of apocalyptic: an historicist hermeneutic, prophecies centering on Jesus, and the presence of the "year-day" and recapitulation principles, for example.

Ellen White wrote often about Daniel and Revelation. So did Adventist pioneer Uriah Smith. In our own time, numerous scholars, pastors, and evangelists have written on and preached about these two books.

So in chapter 5, review for yourself the Bible's "True North" of prophecy—the fascinating, true end-time dramas penned by Daniel and John.

Elias Brasil de Souza is director of the Biblical Research Institute at the General Conference of Seventh-day Adventists, world headquarters of the Seventh-day Adventist Church. He previously served as a church pastor in the Southern Brazil Union. He was dean of the Theological Seminary at Northeast Brazil College in Bahia and also taught in the seminary as a professor of biblical studies. He holds a BA and MA in theology from the Latin American Adventist Theological Seminary at Brazil Adventist University in Engenheiro Coelho, Sao Paulo, and a PhD in Old Testament exegesis and theology from Andrews University in Berrien Springs, Michigan. His main areas of interest are the sanctuary and biblical theology. He has authored, co-authored, and published several academic publications in English, Spanish, and Portuguese.

ELIAS BRASIL DE SOUZA

CHAPTER 5

PROPHETIC INTERPRETATION OF DANIEL AND REVELATION

THE INTERPRETATION OF DANIEL AND REVELATION CAN BE BOTH EXCITING and challenging, and proper methods of interpretation make it possible to overcome the challenges and enjoy God's exciting messages of hope and salvation conveyed by these two apocalyptic[1] books. As one embarks on this adventure, one must bear in mind that Daniel and Revelation are apocalyptic books. As such, they focus on God's overarching plan to redeem creation and bring the great controversy to its resolution.

By contrast, certain biblical prophecies elsewhere in the Bible contain an element of conditionality that makes their fulfillment dependent on the response of the people to whom they were given. For example, although Jonah announced that Nineveh would be destroyed in forty days, that prediction did not come true, because the Ninevites repented.

In the same vein, some prophecies given to Israel in the context of the Old Covenant are conditional promises issued within the framework of the curses and blessings of the covenant (Deuteronomy 28). Thus, certain prophecies given to Israel portray the nation enjoying unimaginable prosperity, with Jerusalem as the center of the world (Isaiah 2). These prophecies are covenantal promises that never came to fruition, because God's people did not abide by the terms of the covenant.

The prophecies of Daniel and Revelation present a different picture. These two books convey prophetic predictions steeped in God's determination to overcome the powers of evil and establish His eternal kingdom. Such prophecies do not depend on human response but convey with divine authority what God has been doing and will do based on His foreknowledge and omnipotence.

So how should such prophecies be understood, proclaimed, and applied? The Bible itself provides the keys to open Daniel and Revelation. The following paragraphs provide four major principles to be used in the study of apocalyptic prophecy: First, Jesus as the center of apocalyptic prophecy; second, the historicist approach to biblical apocalyptic prophecy; third, the year-day principle; and fourth, the recapitulation principle.

JESUS: THE CENTER OF APOCALYPTIC PROPHECIES

Jesus stands at the center of apocalyptic prophecies. Indeed, the whole Bible bears witness of Jesus and conveys His message (John 5:39). But in a special way, Daniel and Revelation point to Jesus as the core of the apocalyptic message. Indeed, the book of Daniel presents Jesus as its main character.

Every prophetic sequence of Daniel brings Jesus to the foreground. As shown in the first major prophecy of the book (Daniel 2), the sequence of the four world empires represented by the image culminates with the establishment of the kingdom of God to be realized in the Second Coming of Jesus.

The vision of the heavenly tribunal (Daniel 7) reaches a culmination in the Son of man coming to the Ancient of Days to complete a work of judgment. In the next prophecy, Christ appears as the "Prince of the Host" and also as the heavenly High Priest (Daniel 8). Then Daniel utters a messianic prophecy that predicts exactly when the Messiah would appear to atone for the sins of His people (Daniel 9). The last prophetic section of Daniel opens with a man dressed in linen (Daniel 10) and concludes with Michael, the great Prince, who rises in the time of the end to save His people (Daniel 12).

Revelation also focuses on Jesus. Indeed, the book presents itself as "The Revelation of Jesus Christ" (Revelation 1:1). Among several designations for Jesus in Revelation area: Son of man (Revelation 1:13), the First and the Last (Revelation 2:8), the Son of God (Revelation 2 :18), Faithful and True Witness (Revelation 3:14), Lion of the tribe of Judah; the Root of David (Revelation 5:5), Lord of lords and King of kings (Revelation 17:14), Michael (Revelation 12:7), and Root and Offspring of David (Revelation 22:16).

However, by far the most common designation for Jesus in Revelation is that of Lamb"—which appears twenty-eight times in the book. By presenting Jesus as the Lamb, Revelation presents Jesus as the fulfillment of the types and shadows of the sacrificial system announced in the Old Testament; that is, Jesus as our Sacrifice.

On one occasion, John looks for a Lion, but then he sees the Lamb (Revelation 5:4, 5). The Lion of the Tribe of Judah was victorious precisely because He acted like a lamb in laying down His life for us. Therefore, He is worthy to open the sealed book and receive praises from many (Revelation 5:12, 13).

From this brief overview, it follows that the prophetic messages of Daniel and Revelation must be understood with a focus on Jesus. That said, the following principles, which emerge from the Bible, provide further guidance for our study and understanding of God's final messages.

THE HISTORICIST APPROACH

Historicism remains a fundamental tenet for the interpretation of Daniel and Revelation. Although the word may carry different connotations in different contexts in connection with prophetic interpretation, historicism "emphasizes a flow and continuity from the past through the present and into the as-yet-unfulfilled future. It is sometimes called the continuous historical view because it sees the prophecies as part of a continuum from the past to the future."[2] This means that the prophetic sequences of Daniel and Revelation are fulfilled throughout history. They tend to begin in the time of the prophet and lead up to the consummation of all things and the establishment of God's kingdom. Although the historicist approach has predominated throughout most of Christian history, it has been rejected by most denominations during the past 200 years.[3] It can be argued, however, that historicism emerges from the biblical prophecies themselves.

A natural starting point is Daniel 2. As the first long-range prophecy of the book, the image shown in a dream to Nebuchadnezzar sets the pattern followed by the subsequent prophetic sequences of Daniel and Revelation. Daniel conveys to the king the particulars of his dream, along with an interpretation given by divine Revelation. He then explains that the various parts of the statue symbolize a sequence of world powers, beginning with Babylon and leading to the establishment of God's eternal kingdom, represented by a stone.

The same pattern emerges in the parallel prophecy of Daniel 7. The angel interpreter explains that the sequence of animals represents kings, i.e., kingdoms that would emerge from the earth. This sequence of kingdoms would be followed by a heavenly judgment, leading up to the time when the saints of the Most High would possess the kingdom. Daniel 8, in turn, uses the symbolism of a ram, a goat, and a little horn to depict a sequence of world powers.

The vision reaches a climax, with the heavenly beings announcing the purification of the heavenly sanctuary after a period of 2300 evenings and mornings (for the year-day principle, see below). Again, the angel interpreter explains the vision in terms of a sequence of world powers that rise successively until the obliteration of the power represented by the little horn. A close reading of this chapter Revelation reveals that the angel interpreter explains the prophecy within an historicist framework.

The historicist approach also applies to the book of Revelation. Both books offer a long-range view of history and focus on the resolution of the great controversy between good and evil. In addition, Revelation alludes to the prophecies of Daniel in several places.[4] Although space limitations do not allow an in-depth study, a few remarks shall suffice to show the significance of historicism for the understanding of Revelation.

This book offers a broad view of church history from the time of John to the establishment of the New Jerusalem. As in Daniel, certain prophetic threads in Revelation indicate an historicist framework. A case in point focuses on the seven seals and the seven trumpets. The seven seals begin with the inauguration of the heavenly sanctuary services and extend until the Second Coming of Jesus. The scenes that unfold at the breaking of each successive seal "may be viewed as particularly significant of successive phases in the history of the church on earth."[5] The trumpets "emphasize outstanding political and military events during this period."[6] In addition, the time period of 42 months (Revelation 11:2; 13:5), its equivalents of 1260 days (Revelation 11:3), and "a time and times and half a time" point to the two and half times (years) referred to in Daniel 7:25. Thus, the long time periods required for the prophetic events to take place and the time frame of "two and half times" that occur at two crucial junctures in the book indicate that Revelation should be interpreted within a historicist framework.

THE YEAR-DAY PRINCIPLE

A significant point pertains to the timescale involved. Rather than measuring long timespans by years, as in normal everyday language, apocalyptic prophecy measures time by days (or weeks/months). For example, the time prophecy of 2300 evenings and mornings (Daniel 8:14) requires a longer time period than 2300 literal days. The time conveyed by the prophecy begins in the period of the Persian ram and extends over the time of the little horn, when the heavenly sanctuary would be purified. Obviously, such prophetic timespans must be calibrated to a different scale. In this matter also, Scripture provides the key. According to Numbers 14:34 and Ezekiel 4:5, 6, a given number of days can symbolize an equal number of years. Ample evidence exists that the concept of a day was often associated with that of a year. For example, in stating the age of the patriarchs, the biblical text says that "all the *days* that Adam lived were nine hundred and thirty *years*" (Genesis 5:5, emphasis supplied). In the first time prophecy of the Bible—the 120 years of grace that preceded the Flood—God spells the timespan thus: "My Spirit shall not strive with man forever, for he *is* indeed flesh; yet his *days* shall be one hundred and twenty years" (Genesis 6:3, NKJV, emphasis supplied). In both passages, the term *days* evokes a timespan measured in terms of years.

This pattern is repeated time and again in Scripture.[7] This time-scale is not arbitrary as it may seem. As one study argues, the timescale that takes a day for a year may be based on the principle of miniaturization. The basic idea is that since symbols in apocalyptic prophecy (e.g., animals) are miniature symbolizations of larger entities (e.g., kingdoms), so the time units (days) may symbolize larger time periods (years).[8] From this perspective, it appears that the year-day principle, rather than being an arbitrary imposition upon the biblical texts, follows the literary logic required by the imagery employed in prophecy. Therefore, as applied to apocalyptic prophecy, this timescale came to be known as the year-day principle, according to which one prophetic day equals one literal year.

The year-day principle, when applied to the apocalyptic prophecies, makes sense of time periods that otherwise would remain obscure. For example, the prophetic timespan of "a time and [two] times and half a time" (Daniel 7:25), when taken literally, amounts to three years and a half, or 1260 days. Revelation 11–13 gives the same period in three different ways: 1260 days, 42 months, and three and a half times (Revelation 11:2, 3; 12:6, 14; 13:5). This time element makes sense only if taken to represent a much longer time span. We do not know of any three-and-a-half-year period in church history that could make sense of this prophecy if taken literally. But once the year-day principle is applied, the corresponding historical period falls into place.

This period extends from AD 538 (time of Justinian) to 1798, when General Berthier invaded Rome and put an end to the 1260 years of papal domination.

Another example is the prophetic timespan of 2300 evenings and mornings (Daniel 8:14). This time period stretches from 457 BC to AD 1844, when the heavenly judgment begins in heaven and the Adventist movement is raised on earth to proclaim it. Finally, the prophecy of the 70 weeks (converted to 490 years) also provides a pragmatic test that shows the validity of the year-day principle. Beginning in 457 BC, this long prophecy leads up to the last week of years which begins in AD 27 with the baptism of the Jesus, stretches to His death in the middle of the week (AD 31), and finally to the spreading of the Gospel to the gentiles after the martyrdom of Stephen in AD 34 (Daniel 9:23–27).

Applying the year-day principle to the prophetic time periods of Daniel and Revelation makes evident the power of this timescale.

THE PRINCIPLE OF RECAPITULATION

Finally, the principle of recapitulation found in the prophecies of Daniel and Revelation deserves attention. Simply put, recapitulation consists of the fact that different visions can cover the same historical period but with different emphases and perspectives.[9] A close look at the threads of Daniel shows that the four visions of the book parallel one another. Taking Daniel 2 as the reference point, we can see that the prophetic sequences of Daniel 7, 8 and 11, 12 develop the prophecy of Daniel 2 and add significant details. As one scholar explains:

> "The fact that the four major lines of prophecy in this book go over the same outline of nations is called recapitulation, or parallelism. Just as the four Gospels go over the same events from different perspectives, so these four lines of complementary prophecies go over the same territory, filling in more details each time. The presentation starts out on the most broad scale in chapter 2, with the nations represented by different metals in an image. By the time we reach chapter 11, we are down to the individual kings of each nation and their personal actions. Chapter 2 starts out with the use of the telescope, while chapter 11 ends up with the use of the microscope."[10]

The principle of recapitulation helps explain certain critical aspects of the prophecy. For example, the reference to the sanctuary in Daniel 8:14 raises the question as to whether this is the temple of Jerusalem or the sanctuary in heaven Although many scholars point to the Jerusalem temple as the referent of this passage, the principle of recapitulation points in the opposite direction. Since Daniel 8:14 parallels the heavenly judgment depicted in Daniel 7:8–14, it is evident that the sanctuary mentioned in Daniel 8:14 must be the heavenly sanctuary. Of course, the parallels between these two chapters also show that the cleansing of the sanctuary and the heavenly judgment are the same event.

The book of Revelation also uses the principle of recapitulation or repetition. For example, both the seven seals and the seven trumpets describe events beginning in the first century AD. Also, Revelation 12–14 portrays the history of the Church from Jesus' first appearing (12:5) to His Second Coming (14:14). And within this section, recapitulation also occurs with smaller units of texts. For example, Revelation 12:6 and 12:13–16 stand in parallel and describe the same event. Revelation 13 provides a more detailed account of the war waged by the dragon against the woman of Revelation 12. Revelation 13:1–10 shows another case of recapitulation or parallelism, in that verses 1–4 and verses 5–8, rather than describing sequential events, parallel each other in content. In addition, Revelation 17 and 18 seem to portray parallel rather than sequential events.

As the above examples show, attention to the principle of recapitulation helps clarify significant elements in the prophecy and avoids the pitfall of reading parallel events as sequential.

SUMMARY AND CONCLUSIONS

To summarize, the apocalyptic books of Daniel and Revelation provide God's blueprint for the history of salvation and the resolution of the great controversy. However, these books must be studied with an interpretative approach provided by Scripture itself. First, Jesus is the center of Daniel and Revelation in that every prophetic sequence points to Jesus. Second, interpretation of the apocalyptic message must follow the historicist framework according to which the flow of prophetic events unfolds from the past through the present and into the future. Third, the time periods reported in such apocalyptic prophecies must be interpreted according to the year-day principle. Otherwise, no sense can be made of such prophetic timespans. Fourth, in studying Daniel and Revelation, the reader must pay close attention to the fact that different visions or passages can cover the same historical period but with different emphases. This is the recapitulation principle, which protects the reader from idiosyncratic interpretations that often contradict the intention of the inspired text.

To conclude, some significant implications must be drawn from the above study. First, we must beware of interpreting Daniel and Revelation according to news headlines. As one scholar advised,

> "Apocalyptic prophecy generally deals with the larger picture, with trends in history, not with one-day affairs, though one-day affairs may be significant in the overall development. Thus, the symbolic prophecies in Daniel and Revelation must be seen in the larger

context of the great controversy between Christ and Satan that has been going on for thousands of years."[11]

Second, given the fact that prophetic events depicted in Daniel and Revelation cover the broad sweep of history and focus on the resolution of the great controversy, the prophetic events predicted in these books find only one single fulfillment.

Third, such apocalyptic prophecies are unconditional. Unlike certain promises made to Israel within the framework of the Old Covenant, the prophecies of Daniel and Revelation express God's sovereignty over human affairs and His determination to guide history in a certain direction to fulfill His eternal purposes.

Finally, it follows from these considerations that we are not left in the dark as to the outcome of this world's history. Because God stands in control of human affairs, we can look to the future with hope.

ENDNOTES

1. In this chapter "apocalyptic" refers to the prophecies of Daniel and Revelation. For an in-depth study of this topic, see Gerhard Pfandl, "Understanding Apocalyptic," in *Biblical Hermeneutics: An Adventist Approach,* ed. Frank M. Hasel (Review and Herald Academic: Silver Spring, MD: Biblical Research Institute & Review and Herald Academic, 2020), 265–290.
2. William H. Shea, Daniel: *A Reader's Guide* (Nampa, ID: Pacific Press, 2005), 13.
3. Preterism, futurism, and idealism are the main alternative approaches to historicism. Preterism understands the apocalyptic prophecies of Daniel and Revelation as fulfilled in the past; futurism restricts prophetic fulfillment to the future. Idealism, in turn, understands such prophecies as conveying some general principles about God's dealings with the world rather than being a reference to specific historical events.
4. Although not an historicist himself, G. K. Beale—*The Use of Daniel in Jewish Apocalyptic Literature and in the Revelation of St. John* (Eugene, OR: Wipf & Stock, 2010),154–306—notes several interconnections between Daniel and Revelation.
5. Francis D. Nichol, ed., *The Seventh-day Adventist Bible Commentary* (Review and Herald, 1980), 7:775.
6. Nichol, 7:788.
7. See W. H. Shea, "The Year-Day Principle—Part 1," in *Selected Studies on Prophetic Interpretation,* DARCOM Series, vol. 1 (Washington, DC: Biblical Research Institute, 1982), 56–88.
8. For a detailed study of symbolic miniaturization, see Alberto Timm, "Miniature Symbolization and the Year-Day Principle of Prophetic Interpretation," *Andrews University Seminary Studies* 42, no. 1 (2004): 149–167.

9. For a detailed study on recapitulation, see Ekkehardt Mueller, *When Prophecy Repeats Itself: Recapitulation in Revelation*, Biblical Research Institute, Release 14 (Silver Spring, MD, 2015).

10. William H. Shea, Daniel: *A Reader's Guide* (Nampa, ID: Pacific Press, 2005), 16.

11. Gerhard Pfandl, "Understanding Apocalyptic," 290.

AS YOU BEGIN THE NEXT CHAPTER...

In the Sabbath School divisions for kindergarten and primary children, many contain a sandbox with items in it to help young minds understand Bible stories and truths and spiritual lessons.

Imagine what it would be like if God was the teacher. How big might His sandbox be? Well, we already have in the Bible the answer to that question. In the Old Testament, God made a very large sandbox to help illustrate His plan of salvation—and it spread out in the center of the encampment as the children of Israel dwelt in the Sinai Peninsula on their way to the Promised Land.

The sandbox illustrated justification, sanctification, judgment, sacrifices, atonement, forgiveness, the work of the Holy Spirit—and so much more!

Out there in the desert, God had Israel make a sanctuary so He could dwell in person with His people. The sanctuary, as most Adventists know, was divided into two compartments: the Holy Place and the Most Holy Place, each with its own symbolic furniture. Around the sanctuary was a courtyard, and the Israelites camped on all sides, extending outward from the courtyard.

Every day, sacrifices and services took place mostly in the Holy Place, illustrating various facets of God's salvation plan. And once a year, a special Day of Atonement took place in the Most Holy Place.

The sanctuary—whether the Old Testament one in the desert or the New Testament one located in heaven itself—can make wonderfully clear how the Father, Son, and Holy Spirit work together to save us. Enjoy the upcoming review of this fascinating topic, as you turn the page to begin reading "HOPE FROM ABOVE: The Good News of the Sanctuary."

Robert Costa has served as a pastor, departmental director and administrator since 1980 in South America and North America. A native of Uruguay, he received his higher education in Argentina and the United States. He is the volunteer Speaker-Director of the telecast It Is Written in Spanish, which is broadcast via satellite, cable, and local channels in more than 11,000 stations, reaching 138 countries. His passion being to share the Good News of God's Word, he's had the privilege of conducting more than 420 evangelistic series in the last twenty-one years on every continent. He and his wife, Nancy, reside in Maryland, USA, where both serve God—she as an assistant to Adventist World Radio, and he as Ministerial Associate of the General Conference, in charge of Evangelism and Church Growth for the Seventh-day Adventist Church.

ROBERT COSTA

CHAPTER 6

HOPE FROM ABOVE: THE GOOD NEWS OF THE SANCTUARY

AUGUST 5, 2010 WAS A COMMON, ORDINARY DAY IN THE MOST ARID PART OF our planet, where rain never falls—the Atacama Desert. That morning, thirty-three men went to work, as was their custom, in the gold mine near Copiapó, Chile.

As they descended deep into the bowels of the earth, the unexpected happened. At 2:05 p.m., the mine collapsed, blocking the exit and leaving the miners trapped beneath almost a mile of sand and solid rock.

Word of the disaster spread quickly. A drill was set up to try to rescue the men. But where to drill? There were no blueprints, and the mine's maintenance history was poor. Were the miners even alive? Was there hope of a rescue? Drilling began, with the machinery working nonstop day and night as families waited anxiously and tension mounted.

Finally, after several days, the operations engineer and the authorities informed the public that they would try to drill one more time, and if that didn't work, they would have no choice but to cancel the rescue.

It was then that someone whispered to the engineer that the drill had hit a rock and gone sideways. He almost cancelled the operation right then and there, but the world press was there, and he found himself saying, "Continue."

They continued at an angle until someone requested silence and the drill was stopped. Faint knocks could be heard. Could it be? Had they found the miners? They sent down a metal line, and from deep within the earth, a note came back which made world news: "We're fine in the shelter...the thirty-three."

Now the world knew where they were. The miners had managed to reach the emergency refuge shelter—a special chamber in the mine. They were alive, and there was hope!

Then began the most complex and costly rescue operation in the history of mining. Cameras were sent down to the miners, along with food, water, light, and everything else they might need to survive.

Above, on the surface, a camp was established. They named it "Camp Hope," and it looked more like a city than a camp. The families and the world press were there. NASA, Japan, Germany, and others united their talents for the rescue.

Carlos Parra, an Adventist pastor, gave hope to the miners by sending down thirty-three small Bibles. He instructed them to read certain passages. One of the miners later said, "We felt God's presence down there. We weren't thirty-three, we were thirty-four, because Jesus never abandoned us."

Finally, a special capsule was ready. Hours before the actual rescue, a specialist descended in that capsule to give instructions and show the miners how the rescue would take place. It would be during the night. By now, two months had passed, and the miners' eyes were not accustomed to the sunlight.

When all was ready, the rescue began. You probably watched it live on your television or computer screen. It was reported that one-third of the world watched as the greatest rescue ever attempted began to unfold.

One by one, the miners emerged. There were hugs and tears of joy. Some were sick or overwhelmed as the whole experience proved too much for them. Others just collapsed and thanked God, grateful to be out. It seemed like a dream. Families were finally reunited again. The men had been destined to die, but now they had risen to the surface. Their only hope had come from above. They were free. When the rescue was over, the access chute created for the rescue was closed and sealed forever. "Camp Hope" also closed. There was no longer a need for it. The rescue operation had ended, and the thirty-three men had been saved.

ANOTHER RESCUE

Another rescue is taking place right now—the largest and costliest operation the universe has ever seen—the rescue of Planet Earth.

When man sinned and our world fell captive, we all became buried in much more than a mile of sand and rock. We were doomed—lost and forever separated from our eternal family and heavenly home.

But God devised a plan—a rescue that could not fail. "Camp Hope" was erected in the heavenly sanctuary—the center of operations of this rescue plan. And when the moment arrived, Jesus encapsulated Himself in human nature and descended to this dark pit of a planet where we were imprisoned and destined to die forever. He did it to show us the way back home.

Did the plan of salvation end at the Cross with Jesus' sacrifice? Obviously not. We're still on this doomed planet, so the rescue must be ongoing. Then where is Jesus today, and what is He doing now?

The apostle Paul said:

> "For Christ did not enter a sanctuary made with human hands that was only a copy of the true one. He entered heaven itself, now to appear for us in God's presence" (Hebrews 9:24).

Ellen White wrote: "God's people should now have their eyes fixed on the heavenly sanctuary." (*Evangelism*, 223); "The sanctuary in heaven is the very center of Christ's work in behalf of men" (*The Great Controversy*, 488).

Our hope now is in the heavenly sanctuary—that special "Camp Hope" created for our rescue. What does that mean for us today? Understanding this truth is vital—our very lives depend on it!

THE PLAN OF SALVATION: UNDERSTANDING THE WHOLE MESSAGE

Why is the message of the sanctuary so important?

The rituals of the earthly sanctuary were instituted to help us understand God's plan of salvation. There were seven feasts/days associated with the earthly sanctuary service. They pointed to Jesus and His work of salvation in the heavenly sanctuary:

OLD TESTAMENT FEASTS	NEW TESTAMENT FULFILLMENT
Passover (Exodus)	Jesus, Our Sacrifice (Communion)
Unleavened Bread (Victory Over Sin)	Sanctification (Christian Living)
First-fruits (Early Harvest)	Resurrection Power/Early Rain/Baptism
Pentecost (Latter Early/Rain Harvest)	Pentecost (Spiritual Latter Rain)
Trumpets (Rosh H. Announced Judgment)	Three Angels' Messages (Revelation 14)
Day of Atonement (Cleansing of Sanctuary)	Judgment Begins (October 22, 1844)
Tabernacles (Celebration of Deliverance)	New Earth (Our Heavenly Home)

When we share the plan of salvation with others, we are—in essence—sharing what God outlined in the sanctuary service. If you don't believe it, compare the feasts of the sanctuary service with their fulfillment in the New Testament, and with our message today:

Jesus is our Sacrifice—our Passover. He died for us. We remember this through the communion service.

He has promised to sanctify us and free us of slavery to sin (leaven) in our lives. This is the work of the Holy Spirit as we grow in the Christian life and prepare for heaven.

Jesus' resurrection from the dead is the first-fruits—our guarantee of eternal life. He also gives us a new birth experience through baptism.

He promises us the outpouring of the Holy Spirit in the latter rain.

He gave us a special message—the present truth to proclaim—in the Three Angels' Messages.

We are now living in the time of the Day of Atonement, and it's been happening since October 22, 1844, when Jesus entered the Most Holy Place in the heavenly sanctuary and began the work of cleansing and judgment. It's a time of soul searching and heart cleansing in preparation for the Second Coming of Jesus.

Jesus will come to take us home, and we will rejoice as He clothes us with the finishing touch of immortality and we enter into eternity.

There you have it. If this is not studied and understood, then we don't fully understand the plan of salvation and are sharing an incomplete message.

David understood it when he said:

> "They have seen thy goings, O God; even the goings of my God, my King, in the sanctuary (Psalm 68:24).

Ellen White said:

> "The correct understanding of the ministration in the heavenly sanctuary is the foundation of our faith" (*Evangelism*, 221). And again, "The intercession of Christ on man's behalf in the sanctuary above **is as essential to the plan of salvation as was His death upon the cross**" (*The Great Controversy*, 489, emphasis supplied).

Jesus has been working in our behalf since His return to heaven. But what is He doing today in the heavenly sanctuary?

HEAVEN'S "CAMP HOPE"

Something big was about to happen in heaven. The last prophecy with a date indicated that the end of time would arrive when Jesus began His last phase of the rescue plan for all humanity—and the world had to know about it!

For that reason, God raised a people in a prophetic moment, to give the world the most solemn warning ever given to mortals. This special people—God's Church—is symbolized by three angels who fly with urgency, announcing in a loud voice: "Fear God and give Him glory, **for the hour of his judgment has come**" (Revelation 14:6, 7, emphasis supplied).

While here on earth, humanity was confronting calamities, disease, suffering, economic collapse and much more, as up in heaven—at the precise prophetic moment—God would begin a work of such magnitude and importance as was Christ's death on the Cross. It would affect every human being—and the world had to be told!

The Bible speaks clearly and with chronological precision about this judgment: "For He has set a day when He will judge the world" (Acts 17:31).

The Bible mentions an exact day when the judgment would begin. God revealed this to the prophet Daniel centuries ago: "For two thousand three hundred days; then the sanctuary shall be cleansed" (Daniel 8:14).

We know that in Bible prophecy, a prophetic day equals a literal year. We see this in Numbers 14:34 and Ezekiel 4:6. Therefore, we know that the 2,300 prophetic days of Daniel 8:14 span 2,300 literal years.

If you're a student of Bible prophecy, then you know this period began in 457 BC (Ezra 7:12, 13). When you add 2,300 years, you arrive at the key date of October 22, 1844. It is here that Daniel saw Jesus in prophetic vision as He entered the Most Holy Place in the heavenly sanctuary to accomplish His final work of judgment and purification.

> "I watched till thrones were put in place, and the Ancient of Days was seated. His garment was as white as snow, and the hair of his

> head was like pure wool. His throne was a fiery flame, its wheels a burning fire; a fiery stream issued and came forth from before him. A thousand thousands ministered to Him; ten thousand times ten thousand stood before Him. The court was seated, **and the books were opened**" (Daniel 7:9, 10, emphasis supplied).

In the Old Testament, the cleansing of the sanctuary was a day of judgment for Israel, a symbol of the final judgment—the Day of Atonement. How do we know for certain that it symbolized a real event? God said it:

> "We do have such a high priest, who sat down at the right hand of the throne of the Majesty in heaven, and **who ministers in the sanctuary and true tabernacle** set up by the Lord, not by man" (Hebrews 8:1, 2, KJV, emphasis supplied).

> "And let them make me a sanctuary; that I may dwell among them. According to all that I shew thee, after the pattern of the tabernacle, and the pattern of all the instruments thereof, even so shall ye make it. And thou shalt rear up the tabernacle according to the fashion thereof which was shewed thee in the mount" (Exodus 25:8, 9; 26:30).

In other words, the earthly sanctuary was a miniature model of the original one in heaven, and God commissioned Israel to show the world His amazing rescue plan.

So why does most of the Christian world not fully understand this when there are large parts of various books in the Bible that talk about it? And do we ourselves—as a Church—grasp the importance of this truth for our time?

THE GOOD NEWS ABOUT THE JUDGMENT

If there is something that makes many Adventists uncomfortable, it's the subject of the judgment, symbolized by the Day of Atonement in the

Old Testament, or what is described in the current day as the "investigative judgment." But while many Adventists are queasy, most of the Christian world is completely unaware of it. Why is this?

Unless the plan of salvation, as detailed in the Old Testament, is studied and understood, then what Jesus did as recorded in the New Testament—and what He is doing in the sanctuary today—cannot be fully understood.

Jesus said, "Search the Scriptures, for in them ye think ye have eternal life: and they are they which testify of me" (John 5:39, KJV).

Yet the only Scripture that existed in Jesus' day was the Old Testament. The New Testament had not yet been written. It's impossible to fully understand the New Testament without studying the Old. In fact, much of the Old Testament finds its fulfillment in the New.

It's like enrolling in a university without ever attending school: a sure recipe for failure. That's also why many Christians confuse the ceremonial laws, written by Moses in a scroll, with the Ten Commandments written in stone by the finger of God.

The ceremonial laws of Moses ended with Christ's crucifixion—they pointed to the Lamb who would die for our sins. The Ten Commandments continue—they're eternal, a reflection of God's character—yet many Christians believe they were abolished by Jesus at the Cross and are no longer valid. What a lack of understanding of the gospel! If there is no law, then there is no need for grace or a judgment.

Yet James is clear, "So speak and so do as those who will be judged by the law of liberty" (James 2:12).

That's the first piece of good news about the judgment: it's not a law of bondage, but of liberty. It's meant to set us free. It will vindicate God's children from the accusations of Satan, "Who accuses them before God day and night" (Revelation 12:10).

We have believed Satan for a long time, because we know his accusations are true. He has good reason to accuse us, not only for what we have done, but for who we are—simply for being born on this planet.

But how can the judgment be good news when there are texts

that alarm us, such as, "For God will bring every work into judgment, including every secret thing, whether good or evil" (Ecclesiastes 12:14), as well as, "For we must all appear before the judgment seat of Christ" (2 Corinthians 5:10).

Yes, those are sobering texts, especially if we would need to "appear before the judgment seat of Christ" on our own merits, without a defender.

Thank God! There's more good news in our favor: Jesus invites us to "Come boldly to the throne of grace, that we may obtain mercy and find grace to help in time of need" (Hebrews 4:15, 16).

The amazing good news is that Jesus is both our Judge and our Defender in the judgment! That's unheard of—almost laughable. The trial is rigged in our favor, because Jesus has never lost a case. That's why the psalmist said, "Mercy and truth are met together; righteousness and peace have kissed each other" (Psalm 85:10). He understood. And the good news keeps coming, because He "demonstrates His love for us, in that while we were still sinners, Christ died for us. . . . we shall be saved by His life. And not only that but we also rejoice in God through Christ, through whom we have received the reconciliation" (Romans 5:8-11).

We may study this for years and hear it over and over, until one day we finally see the light: the judgment is truly for the benefit of God's children—for those who are in Christ—to declare them free from guilt as heirs to the kingdom of heaven.

Everything is ours if we accept Jesus as our Savior. Our name is written in the Book of Life, and Jesus declares us perfect, because He is perfect.

But there is no hope for us—not a chance—to make it through this trial on our own merits. If we refuse the precious gift of salvation and have not accepted Jesus as our Savior and Defender, then we are doomed to die forever, sealed in the dark pit that is this planet.

> "But there is a promise for those who accept Him: "He who overcomes will thus be clothed in white garments; and I will not erase his name from the book of life" (Revelation 3:5).

What a wonderful promise! If that isn't good news, I don't know what is!

How do we overcome sin? Jesus said, "Therefore if the Son makes you free, you shall be free indeed" (John 8:36). "If we confess our sins, He is faithful and just to forgive us our sins and to cleanse us from all unrighteousness" (1 John 1:9). The spiritual weapons God gives us are "mighty . . . , bringing every thought into captivity to the obedience of Christ" (2 Corinthians 10:4, 5).

THE FINAL REWARD

I began by sharing the story of the thirty-three miners. Shortly after their rescue, I had an opportunity to visit the site of the now-abandoned mine and interview one of the miners, Jorge Galleguillos: miner number eleven. What a story he had to tell!

And while the mine is now abandoned, it's not neglected. At the sealed entrance stands the monument of a giant cross—an acknowledgment of God's intervention in that rescue. On the horizon, thirty-three flags wave in the breeze—a reminder of the lives that were saved.

Camp Hope is history; it is closed forever. The rescue was completed, and at the foot of the cross, there is a plaque engraved with the famous words: "We are fine in the refuge, the thirty-three." What a message!

Now imagine this: what would the world have thought if one of the miners had said, "I don't want to be rescued. I am too busy down here, so I'll just remain behind."

There would have been a collective gasp of amazement and horror that would have traveled around the world. Everyone would have been appalled and said, "Surely, he's lost his mind. He must be crazy or inhaled some toxic fumes!"

And yet, that's what millions are saying today when confronted with the rescue that Jesus is offering—of cleansing our lives and taking us out of the pit and into His light, and into our universal family.

The question remains: why don't we preach this more? There are many who tell only part of the story—what Jesus did on the cross. But the story doesn't end there. Jesus is not on the Cross now. He lives and intercedes for us and, through the Holy Spirit, helps us when we are tempted (see Hebrews 2:18). Our security is not only in what He did then, but in what He is doing today.

If something distracts us from presenting this special message for our time—of what Jesus is doing in the heavenly sanctuary—and we don't proclaim this truth to the world, then we're in negligent disregard of what God has asked us to do.

We have the rest of the story. Are we sharing this message, or are distractions keeping us from our mission? There are sincere, searching people waiting to hear it. They, too, want to be rescued. Thousands perish every day—their cases close forever without having this opportunity that we have.

The long Day of Atonement that began on October 22, 1844, will soon end. Jesus will cease His intercession in the heavenly sanctuary. The day of opportunity will have ended. Each case will have been decided. There will be only two groups: those who by faith are saved and those who refuse the gift of salvation and freedom from sin. Soon the heavenly sanctuary will close and Jesus will remove His High Priest's robe and don His brilliant garment as the King of kings.

He will leave His place in the heavenly sanctuary and close His intercession forever. The heavenly Camp Hope will be closed, and He will pronounce that solemn decree that will paralyze the world and seal every case:

> "He that is unjust, let him be unjust still: and he which is filthy, let him be filthy still: and he that is righteous, let him be righteous still: and he that is holy, let him be holy still. And, behold, I come quickly; and my reward is with me, to give every man according as his work shall be" (Revelation 22:11, 12, KJV).

Then He'll gather his billions of angels and say, "Let's go! Let's gather my children—those who have accepted My gift of righteousness and want to live with Me forever."

What a joy that will be as we participate in last great celebration planned through "Camp Hope"—our rescue from Planet Earth!

May we all be there.

Let our prayer today be: "Father, thank You for the good news of the judgment. There are so many injustices in the world, but You are just. There are so many things twisted and broken, but You have promised to right and heal all things. There is a pending accusation against all of us, because we have sinned and deserve death. But today we accept Jesus as our Savior and Defender, so He can declare us free from guilt, keep us free from sin, and make us heirs to His eternal kingdom. We accept the challenge to share this message with the world. Give us the power of your Holy Spirit in the promised latter rain, so we may proclaim the good news with power. In Jesus' name, Amen."

AS YOU BEGIN THE NEXT CHAPTER...

- Of all the nearly eight billion people on this planet, no one is ***exactly like you.***
- In all the history of Earth, no one has ever been ***exactly like you.***
- And no matter how long time lasts, no one will ever be ***exactly like you.***

You are the only one with your exact DNA, personality, opinions, temperament, strengths and weaknesses, preferences, and life experiences.

You are unique. One of a kind.

But it's not just you that God has made to be unique. So is everyone else. And God has delighted in making so much of His creation to be unique—absolutely one of a kind!

Something else of God's making also stands alone in being incomparable and unparalleled. A church. A church that is the final, remnant (last stretch of cloth on the roll!) church God calls to a special work just before Jesus returns to Earth. Well, more than just another church—a movement He called into existence back in the mid-1800s that He gave a, yes, unique task, a unique and urgent message to share with the world.

This movement, known early on as the Great Second Advent Movement, God gave the task of sharing with the world three vital messages, found in the 14th chapter of the Bible's last book, Revelation. God's unique movement in the early 2020s has about 22 million members in more than 200 countries around the world.

If you belong to this movement—the Seventh-day Adventist Church—God wants to use your uniqueness to do something for Him that no one else can do. He needs you. Isn't that amazing? The God who Created this universe and called the remnant movement into existence needs ***you!*** What a joy to answer His call!

Doug Batchelor is president of Amazing Facts, an international evangelistic radio, television, and publishing ministry. Author of fourteen books, including *At Jesus Feet,* and *Christ in all the Bible,* pastor Batchelor and his wife, Karen, reside in Northern California, where he also serves as lead pastor of the Granite Bay Hilltop Seventh-day Adventist church.

CHAPTER 7

"WHAT HATH GOD WROUGHT!"

AN END-TIME MOVEMENT WAS RAISED UP BY GOD IN 1844 IN FULFILLMENT OF Bible prophecy, to proclaim to all the world the message of Christ's soon return.

An amazing fact: On May 24, 1844, inventor Samuel F. B. Morse sent the first long-distance telegraph message in U.S. history. Over an experimental forty-mile line between Washington D.C. and Baltimore, he successfully transmitted, in a new electronic alphabet made up of dots and dashes (aptly named Morse Code), a sentence from the Bible: "What hath God wrought!" (Numbers 23:23, KJV). Now cross-country messages that once took weeks, months, or years could be delivered in seconds. Historians have marked the invention of the telegraph as a turning point in world history.

Balak was deeply agitated. The ancient Midianite king was determined to prevent the nation of Israel from marching through his territory en-route to their promised land in Canaan. Balak even paid a fortune to a backslidden prophet of Yahweh named Balaam to come and pronounce a curse on the Israelites so Balak could defeat them. But the cursing ritual backfired miserably.

Instead of a wicked hex, a stream of blessings poured from the reluctant lips of the wayward prophet. Prompted by the Holy Spirit, Balaam then stated, "For there is no enchantment against Jacob, no divination against Israel; now it shall be said of Jacob and Israel, 'What has God wrought!'" (Numbers 23:23, ESV).

Human words could hardly express the miraculous works God had performed in delivering His people from Egypt, inspiring the first electronic words transmitted by Samuel Morse,

Little did Morse realize that in the very year of his successful 1844 transmission, one of the Bible's greatest time prophecies—the 2,300-day prophecy of Daniel 8:14—would come to fruition. It was a far greater turning point in world history, for it not only marked the beginning of Christ's work of investigative judgment in the Most Holy Place of the heavenly sanctuary, but it set in motion on earth the beginnings of an end-time movement—a remnant called to restore and transmit Jesus' final message to all the world.

Just as Satan tried to keep Israel from entering Canaan, the enemy is working today to derail Christ's Church, the Israel of God in the last days, from entering the heavenly Promised Land. It is the devil's wicked scheme to cause Seventh-day Adventists to forget "what God has done" in raising up this amazing movement.

One of the greatest challenges facing the Adventist Church today is a diminishing belief in our unique identity. Many Adventists have lost a sense of who we are and why we are here. This chapter highlights what I believe is the most important contribution of the Seventh-day Adventist Church to the world. Through Bible prophecy, you will discover that Adventists are not just another denomination but a prophetic movement specially raised up by God to prepare the world for the return of Christ.

As we briefly consider the rise of this prophetic people, found in Revelation 10, the characteristics of these believers in Revelation 12, and the message they are called to proclaim to the world in Revelation 14, you will not only see Satan's efforts to destroy God's Church, but you will stand in awe of what God has wrought in these last days.

REVELATION 10—THE RISE OF A PROPHETIC MOVEMENT

A turning point in earth's history was forecast in the book of Daniel, which would mark the beginnings of a new movement; but its true meaning was "shut up ... until the time of the end" (Daniel 12:4). Daniel's time prophecies were sealed, including the 1,260-day prophecy (7:25), and the 2,300-day prophecy (8:14, 26). Both reached their fulfillment in the last days, for the prophet was told, "Go your way, Daniel, for the words are closed up and sealed till the time of the end" (12:9).

If we fast forward to the book of Revelation, we discover how these prophecies would be opened and understood. In fact, Revelation 10 marks a change in this apocalyptic book, by making frequent references and strong allusions to the book of Daniel. The context of Revelation 10 shows how "a little book open" (v. 2) in the hand of a mighty angel is the opening of the prophecies of Daniel. From Revelation 10 forward we can see many points of contact with Daniel (e.g., a beast with "ten horns" in Daniel 7:7 and a similar beast with "ten horns" in Revelation 12:3).

Notice this connection: Just as the angelic being who spoke to Daniel "held up his right hand and his left hand to heaven, and swore by Him who lives forever" (12:7), so John saw that a mighty angel "raised up his hand to heaven and swore by Him who lives forever and ever ... that there should be time no longer" (Revelation 10:5, 6). It's a clear indication that these two sealed time prophecies of Daniel had reached their fulfillment.

Students of prophecy who use the historicist method of interpretation and the day-year principle of prophetic time, endorsed within the Bible itself, have determined that the end of the 1,260-day prophecy was completed in AD 1798, and that the 2,300-day prophecy was fulfilled in AD 1844, marking a transition in the heavenly ministry of Jesus as our High Priest.

Let's consider some history that highlights the fulfillment of these prophecies.

A GREAT AWAKENING

In the early 1800s, a number of dedicated Christians around the world began to rediscover and explore the prophecies of Daniel. After considering Daniel 8:14—"For two thousand three hundred days; then the sanctuary will be cleansed"—many came to the same conclusion: The most momentous event in history was about to take place. They believed the "cleansing of the sanctuary" foretold the return of Jesus, who would cleanse the earth with fire.

These believers came to be known as "Adventists," since they were convicted about the soon advent (coming) of Christ. ("Adventists" here should not be conflated with Seventh-day Adventists that were not formed as a denomination for another thirty years.) Because of the prophecy in Daniel 8, William Miller, a farmer and widely read captain from the war of 1812 turned Baptist preacher, and his following, known as the Millerites, believed that Jesus would return in October, 1844. Between 1833 and 1844, more than a million people attended his revivals, and a large number of believers from many Christian denominations agreed with his conclusion that Christ was about to return. A number of them even sold or gave away property in their eager expectation of Jesus' soon coming.

However, when the anticipated date came and went uneventfully, it became known as the "Great Disappointment." But what they saw as a crushing letdown was actually a striking fulfillment. They did not realize their experience would become the catalyst for a powerful new Christian movement.

Revelation 10 describes the experience of the early Adventists through John's vision:

> Then the voice which I heard from heaven spoke to me again and said, "Go, take the little book which is open in the hand of the angel who stands on the sea and on the earth." So I went to the angel and said to him, "Give me the little book." And he said to me, "Take and eat it; and it will make your stomach bitter, but it will be as sweet as honey in your mouth." Then I took the little book out of the angel's hand and ate it, and it was as sweet as honey in my mouth. But when I had eaten it, my stomach became bitter. And he said to me, "You must prophesy again before many peoples, nations, tongues, and kings" (Revelation 10:8–11).

The prophecy of Daniel, the "little book," was sweet to the Millerite Adventists, but the great disappointment was bitter. Yet the text goes on, "You must prophesy again before [to] many peoples, nations, tongues, and kings" (v. 11, see Revelation 14:6). As we will see, God was raising up an end-time movement in 1844 to carry forth the prophetic messages of Daniel and Revelation to prepare the world for Christ's soon return.

As foretold, following this prophetic period, God began to *lift up the truth* found in His Word, turning a bitter disappointment into a worldwide movement to restore Bible teachings that had been obscured by the rubbish and dust of human tradition and the garb of pagan rituals.

RIGHT DATE, WRONG EVENT

When Christ did not return in 1844, the Millerite movement fragmented into several categories.

Some returned to their former churches. Some abandoned their faith in Scripture or became Deists. Some continued to set new dates for Jesus' coming. But another group humbly continued to pore over the prophecies word-by-word to discover their error in interpretation.

Eventually, they realized they had the dates right but the event wrong. Nothing in Scripture said that the earth was the sanctuary to be cleansed. Instead, they realized that Scripture teaches there are in fact two sanctuaries: one in heaven, where Christ now ministers as our High Priest and a temple on earth, better known as the church (Ephesians 2:19–22; 1 Peter 2:4–6).

It should not surprise us that God was leading in a movement where His people managed to misunderstand the main event of the prophecy. This very same thing happened with the apostles at the crucifixion. They thought the prophecies taught that Jesus was going to overthrow the Romans and establish an earthly kingdom immediately after the resurrection (Acts 1:6). But their great disappointment was turned to joy when they finally understood the true meaning of Christ's sacrifice.

DISCOVERING THE TRUTH

When Adventists studied the subject of the sanctuary more deeply, they realized the Scriptures clearly taught that Jesus is our High Priest who ministers for us in a very real heavenly sanctuary (Hebrews 8:1, 2). The earthly sanctuary of the Jewish people was patterned after the heavenly (Hebrews 8:5). In a similar way, in 1844 Christ had entered a final phase in His heavenly intercession, sometimes referred to as the pre-Advent judgment.

For the Israelites, the most sacred final event in the religious calendar was the Day of Atonement (Yom Kippur), or cleansing of the sanctuary, when the High Priest entered into the very presence of God within the Holy of Holies, performing a special work that would represent a cleansing of sin from the nation. (Leviticus 16:1-34).

The inner sanctum of the temple, where the High Priest ministered, held the ark of the covenant, containing the original Ten Commandments. The Jewish nation knew that this was a time of judgment, and they would forgive one another, settle their grievances, right any wrongs, and put away their sins through repentance.

They saw that on the earthly Day of Atonement, the sanctuary was filled with the smoke of incense, and no man was allowed to enter the temple while the High Priest ministered (Leviticus 16:13, 17).

Revelation taught that this event would be repeated in heaven just before the end of the world: "The temple was filled with smoke from the glory of God and from His power, and no one was able to enter the temple till the seven plagues of the seven angels were completed" (Revelation 15:8). They realized that in 1844 they had entered the last period in the history of the church, Laodicea, which means "a judging of the people."

RESTORING TRUTH

While many studies explain the final phase of Christ's heavenly ministry in more detail, I'd like to suggest that a fulfillment of Daniel 8:14 can also be clearly seen in events that occurred on the earth. The cleansing of the heavenly sanctuary correlates with a special cleansing of the hearts of God's people on earth—His body, the Church—which began in 1844.

Not only does the Bible teach that God has a very real temple in heaven, the Church is referred to as His temple on earth. "Do you not know that you are the temple of God and *that* the Spirit of God dwells in you? If anyone defiles the temple of God, God will destroy him. For the temple of God is holy, which *temple* you are" (1 Corinthians 3:16, 17).

You may have studied how, contained within the 2,300-day prophecy, another time prophecy is found—of 1,260 years of persecution by the apostate church (AD 538 to 1798). This was the time when the Bible itself was obscured from the people, its truths hidden from humanity; this was the time when the antichrist power, as described by Daniel, "exalted himself as high as the Prince of the host; and by him the daily sacrifices were taken away, and the place of His sanctuary was cast down. Because of transgression, an army was given over to the horn to oppose the daily sacrifices; and *he cast truth down to the ground*. He did all this and prospered" (Daniel 8:11, 12, emphasis added).

A CLEANSING FROM ERROR

Following the Great Disappointment, when Christ did not return in 1844, several believers came together committed to setting aside doctrinal differences in order to study the Bible with open minds, comparing Scripture with Scripture. They were determined to follow its teachings without denominational bias. Through intense study, many times lasting all night, this small group was stunned to discover a number of practices and teachings that had crept into Christianity, having no foundation in the Bible.

Among many other findings, they rediscovered the truth of baptism by immersion, seeing that there are no biblical grounds for baptizing babies. Some rediscovered that salvation was by faith alone through grace; that the Ten Commandments had not been annulled; that the seventh day, Saturday, was still the Sabbath; that the Bible teaches that the dead will sleep unconsciously until the resurrection; and that the wicked will not be eternally tormented in hellfire but will instead be consumed by it and ultimately perish. They also learned that a believer's body is the temple of the Holy Spirit and that we should eat and drink to God's glory.

Just as in the Day of Atonement, the message of the 2,300-day prophecy calls each of us to seek a cleansing of our own hearts from any false teachings, which inevitably lead to wrong behaviors. In this way, the work of Jesus in the heavenly sanctuary has a corresponding response on earth in the sanctuary of God's Church. This movement, which resulted from the Great Disappointment, not only identifies the last-day apostate church but also lifts up Christ as the true High Priest and head of the Church, the One who calls all people out of the darkness of spiritual Babylon (which means "confusion") and into the light of Bible truth. "Come out of her, my people, lest you share in her sins, and lest you receive of her plagues" (Revelation 18:4; see also Daniel 12:4, 9; Revelation 10:6, 9–11).

At the end of the 2,300-year prophecy of Daniel, Jesus began cleansing His sanctuary, both in heaven and on earth, the Church. Since 1844, the Adventist movement that discovered and announced this event has become the fastest-growing, most widespread, and racially diverse Protestant church in the world.

It seems more than coincidental that 1844 was marked by many significant events, not just in the Church but in the world. For instance:

OTHER SIGNIFICANT EVENTS IN 1844

- Karl Marx wrote *The Economic and Philosophical Manuscripts* of 1844, forming the foundation of The Communist Manifesto.
- Charles Darwin completed his "Essay" on natural selection, the first of his major manuscripts to espouse the theory of evolution.
- German philosopher Friedrich Nietzsche was born (October 15, 1844) and would later teach that "God is dead."
- As already noted, Samuel F. B. Morse sent the first official telegram from Washington, D.C. to Baltimore, which read, "What hath God wrought!" It is the dawn of electronic communications.
- Charles Goodyear received a U.S. patent for vulcanization, a process to strengthen rubber, transforming the industrial world.
- The Edict of Toleration was passed, the catalyst by which Jews were allowed to resettle in the Holy Land.
- Persian prophet "the Báb" began preaching, and his teachings eventually formed the foundation of the Bahá'í Faith, which is partly based on prophecies found in Daniel 8 and 9.
- Joseph Smith, founder of Mormonism, was killed. Brigham Young, their next president, led followers to the Utah Territory and founded The Church of Jesus Christ of Latter-day Saints, which eventually grew into a worldwide movement.
- The *Codex Sinaiticus* (the Sinai Bible), one of the world's oldest-known handwritten Bibles, was uncovered in Egypt by Constantin von Tischendorf.

A SHIFT IN LOCATION

The Bible gives clear identifying marks of this remnant. A brief overview of Revelation 11 tells of the persecution of God's people during the 1,260-day (year) prophecy, from AD 538 to 1798, including the role of the French Revolution in driving people to search the Scriptures. While we won't go into the details of this prophecy, I'd like to focus on an interesting passage at the end of Revelation 11 that segues into Revelation 12 and the characteristics of this remnant church. Notice, "Then the temple of God was opened in heaven, and the ark of His covenant was seen in His temple. And there were lightnings, noises, thunderings, an earthquake, and great hail" (Revelation 11:19).

It's important to understand that all the references up to this point in the book of Revelation refer to the first apartment of the sanctuary—the Holy Place, where Jesus is pictured standing among the seven golden candlesticks. But from this point on, allusions to the sanctuary point to the Most Holy Place, where the ark of the covenant is located. The ark not only represents the throne of God (see Exodus 25:10–22) but also contains "the Testimony" (v. 21), which is God's law, the Ten Commandments.

The focus of the Old Testament sanctuary on the ark of the covenant took place on the Day of Atonement (Leviticus 16), which pointed forward to the great work of atonement by Christ in the Most Holy Place, a work that was prophetically foretold and began in 1844. How does all of this connect with identifying God's people?

REVELATION 12—CHARACTERISTICS OF THE PROPHETIC MOVEMENT

Revelation 12 begins with a description of God's people, the Church, described as "a woman clothed with the sun, with the moon under her feet, and on her head a garland of twelve stars" (v. 1). Then it describes a brief Christian history beginning with Christ's birth (including a reference to the original conflict between Jesus and Satan in heaven) down to the last days of earth's history.

After the dragon (Satan, v. 9) attempts to destroy the Child (Christ, v. 5) and the woman (the Church) flees into the wilderness for "a time and times and half a time" (v. 14, the 1,260-year period completed in 1798), John makes this telling statement: "And the dragon was enraged with the woman, and he went to make war with the rest of her offspring, *who keep the commandments of God and have the testimony of Jesus Christ*" (v. 17, emphasis supplied).

Two identifying marks are given for the "rest [remnant or remainder] of her offspring," a group of Christian believers who arise after the year 1798. They are known for keeping God's commandments and having the testimony of Jesus. Why these two specifications?

The final issue in the great controversy between Christ (and His people) and Satan (and his followers) will center on obedience to God and His commandments, with a particular focus, as we will see in Revelation 14, on the fourth commandment of the Sabbath.

This same identification of the remnant is repeated at the end of Revelation 14, which states, "Here is the patience of the saints; here are those who keep the commandments of God and the faith of Jesus" (v. 12). Obviously, keeping God's commandments through faith in Jesus is important enough to mention more than once. Let's look more closely at these two characteristics.

The Commandments of God. To have true faith in Jesus, a follower of Christ will walk in His steps. John wrote, "He who says he abides in Him ought himself also to walk just as He walked" (1 John 2:6). Jesus kept God's commandments. "If you keep My commandments, you will abide in My love, just as I have kept My Father's commandments and abide in His love" (John 15:10). Christ promises us strength to obey Him (Philippians 4:13), including keeping His eternal moral law (Romans 7:12).

The Faith of Jesus. God's last-day people will have faith like that of Christ. They also believe that Jesus is the divine Son of God and the Savior of the world. This remnant church will teach the everlasting Gospel, that salvation comes through faith in Christ's sacrifice for sin and that Jesus will return to this earth to save the redeemed and destroy sin.

The Testimony of Jesus Christ. In addition, Revelation 12:17 says that believers in this last prophetic movement will not only keep God's commandments but also will "have the testimony of Jesus Christ." John explains that the testimony of Jesus "is the spirit of prophecy"

(Revelation 19:10). This gift of prophecy will be a hallmark that helps guide and guard the remnant in their final work. Prophecy is not only how God's last Church was established and is guided but will be a significant part of the messages given to the world in preparation for Jesus' soon coming.

REVELATION 14—THE MESSAGES OF THE PROPHETIC MOVEMENT

In sequence with the rise of God's last-day church (Revelation 10) and the characteristics of this movement (Revelation 12), Revelation 14 outlines three important messages that the remnant will proclaim to the world.

THE FIRST ANGEL'S MESSAGE

The first message is to carry the everlasting Gospel to the world. The Bible predicts that the Gospel will be preached to everyone on earth before Jesus comes again (Matthew 24:14). This has happened in successive eras since Jesus' declaration, but it is particularly fulfilled in the last days by this message:

I saw another angel flying in the midst of heaven, having the everlasting gospel to preach to those who dwell on the earth—to every nation, tribe, tongue, and people (Revelation 14:6).

Jesus has commissioned His followers to be messengers who preach the Gospel to every person (Mark 16:15). For God's people living in these last days, the prophecy of Revelation 14 indicates that this commission will be completed through sharing the Three Angels' Messages with everyone everywhere. This is our great privilege and responsibility.

What are the elements of this gospel message? Notice what the first angel broadcasts:

Fear God and give glory to Him, for the hour of His judgment has come; and worship Him who made heaven and earth, the sea and springs of water (Revelation 14:7).

Four distinctive points are covered in this first angel's message:

1. **It tells us *whom* to worship.** God alone deserves worship. To "fear God" does not mean to be frightened of Him. The Greek word actually means "to reverence." So we are to adore, trust, and obey God. Doing so is for our own good: "By the fear of the LORD one departs from evil" (Proverbs 16:6).

2. **It tells us *how* to worship.** The language used here denotes a fullness in the worship of God—mentally, physically, and spiritually. When you "fear God," you receive "wisdom" (Job 28:28). You also "keep His commandments" (Ecclesiastes 12:13). When you "give glory to Him," you honor the body He gave you: "Whether you eat or drink, or whatever you do, do all to the glory of God" (1 Corinthians 10:31). When you "worship Him," you "worship Him ... in spirit and truth" because God Himself "is Spirit" (John 4:24). We are to worship God unreservedly, with our whole being. "He that loveth me not keepeth not my sayings: and the word which ye hear is not mine, but the Father's which sent me" John 14:24.

3. **It tells us *when* this message is being proclaimed.** "The hour of His judgment has come"—the days approaching the final judgment are here! Jesus is coming soon, and we must tell to the world this lifesaving message! The fact that the first angel relays his message "with a loud voice" emphasizes its importance.

4. **It tells us the *reason* to worship.** God is deserving of worship for this crucial reason: He created you. No other creature—not the devil, not the beast of Revelation 13, not the false prophet (see Revelation 16:13)—can claim this. The fourth commandment states: "In six days the LORD made the heavens and the earth, the sea, and all that is in them, and rested the seventh day" (Exodus 20:11). This is undeniable evidence of the Sabbath's imperative role as the sign or seal of God's authority in these last days.

THE SECOND ANGEL'S MESSAGE

The second angel comes directly after, accompanying the first:

> And another angel followed, saying, "Babylon is fallen, is fallen, that great city, because she has made all nations drink of the wine of the wrath of her fornication" (Revelation 14:8).

The ancient city of Babylon was originally known as Babel, where more than four millennia ago, its inhabitants decided to build a tower. Their objective was to "make a name for [themselves]," to become great and famous; they intended for their edifice to reach into "the heavens" (Genesis 11:4). This might sound familiar to you, for Satan also plotted to "ascend above the heights of the clouds" (Isaiah 14:14). Scripture refers to the devil as the real power behind "the king of Babylon" (v. 4).

But the Tower of Babel was never finished. Babylon soon fell into ruin before it was gloriously reconstructed by its most famous king, Nebuchadnezzar. During his reign, Babylon became known as a lap of luxury, a mecca of domination.

But by divine judgment, Babylon was eventually destroyed, never to be inhabited again (Isaiah 13:19, 20). Symbolically, though, it has lived on. The first Christians were known to have called ancient Rome *Babylon* due to its seductive power and its determined persecution of Christians (see 1 Peter 5:13).

Thus, Babylon in Revelation signals a satanic counterfeit religion aimed at taking God's place through a system that enforces false worship by confusing and deceiving the masses. Its ultimate goal is the complete destruction of God's people. In essence, Babylon contains within it every apostate form of religion, symbolized by the dragon, the beast, and the false prophet.

Later, in eighteenth chapter of Revelation, another angel expands on the second angel's message:

> And he cried mightily with a loud voice, saying, "Babylon the great is fallen, is fallen.".... And I heard another voice from heaven saying, "Come out of her, my people" (18:2, 4).

This is a clarion call to "search the Scriptures" (John 5:39) and to examine our own beliefs in the light of Bible truth. Each person should humbly ask God to "see if there is any wicked way in me, and lead me in the way everlasting" (Psalm 139:24). By so doing, we may answer the call to come out of Babylon before it is too late, instead of perishing along with Babylon (Revelation 18:8).

THE THIRD ANGEL'S MESSAGE

In the rise of God's last-day prophetic movement, the solemn message of the third angel is of special interest.

> Then a third angel followed them, saying with a loud voice, "If anyone worships the beast and his image, and receives his mark on his forehead or on his hand, he himself shall also drink of the wine of the wrath of God, which is poured out full strength into the cup of His indignation. He shall be tormented with fire and brimstone in the presence of the holy angels and in the presence of the Lamb. And the smoke of their torment ascends forever and ever; and they have no rest day or night, who worship the beast and his image, and whoever receives the mark of his name" (Revelation 14:9–11).

This final message has a direct relation to the language and events of Revelation 13, a chapter that warns of two end-time powers that will join hands in persecuting God's people.

This establishes the messages of the three angels as a warning and response to the coming confederacy of the first and second beast powers that Revelation 13 describes.

That chapter, which leads up to Revelation 14, describes how the United States, partnering with the papacy, will enforce a counterfeit sabbath and enact a religious law that when, not obeyed, will be punishable by death. The devil will stop at nothing to completely exterminate God's remnant people who have His Sabbath seal.

But God saves His people at the Second Coming (Revelation 14:14). Those having His seal will escape death, while those who perpetrated satanic principles will reap what they have sown. This should be a source of great joy! Sin will be eradicated for all eternity; "affliction will not rise up a second time" (Nahum 1:9).

This sobering message is not a threat—it is a merciful warning from God. He is "not willing that any should perish but that all should come to repentance" (2 Peter 3:9). God has disclosed the whole of this three-point message to us so that we can be saved and be used by Him to save others!

TRUE WORLDWIDE REVIVAL

God has raised up a people who are now proclaiming the Three Angels' Messages throughout the earth. When the time comes for the United States, with the catalyst of spiritualism, to join hands with the papacy, the three angels will do their culminating work, and the Gospel that illuminates the world will bring in true revival. People from all nations will decide to step under Christ's banner of love and truth and receive God's Sabbath seal.

Satan will be enraged by this and will "make war with" those "who keep the commandments of God and have the testimony of Jesus Christ" (Revelation 12:17). God's people will have to undergo the greatest test of their faith. They will be accused, slandered, derided, "hated by all nations" (Matthew 24:9); they will be seen as divisive, radical, unpatriotic, and above all, dangerous. But in this darkest of times, the Bible again gives us hope:

> Here is the patience of the saints; here are those who keep the commandments of God and the faith of Jesus (Revelation 14:12).

The original Greek word for *patience* means "cheerful endurance." Through the trials of these last days, God's people will not only stand steadfast for Him, they will do it with "the peace of God, which surpasses all understanding" (Philippians 4:7). They will do so by having God's commandments—and yes, God's seal—written on "their minds" and in their "hearts" (Jeremiah 31:33).

They will do so by faithfully "[following] the Lamb wherever He goes" (Revelation 14:4), constantly "looking unto Jesus, the author and finisher of our faith" (Hebrews 12:2). Just as Jesus, "who for the joy that was set before Him endured the cross, despising the shame," so too they will endure.

CONCLUSION

The year 1844 marked the beginning of high-speed electronic communication by telegraph in the United States; it also marked the end of the longest time prophecy in Scripture—the 2,300-day prophecy of Daniel 8:14—and the beginning of a great last-day movement to carry the Three Angels' Messages to the world.

Prophecy also tells us that Satan, the dragon, is enraged toward God's last-day Church (Revelation 12:17). The ancient enemy is intent on stopping the advancement of the remnant, spiritual Israel—a people raised up by the Lord, delivered from sin, and illumined with Bible truth. The devil is doing everything in his power to distract, discourage, divide, and defeat them.

But to those who keep God's commandments and have strong faith in Jesus, nothing will stop them, not even the threat of death. Looking back over how God has led them through disappointment and trial, they will confidently proclaim the prophetic end-time warning to the world.

Scripture undeniably points to activities both in the heavens and on earth in 1844. It reveals a time of prophecy fulfilled, when the Lord raised up the great Advent movement, a movement with a unique message that will be proclaimed by no other denomination; a movement that will lead a people to the Promised Land and into eternity; a movement that will cause the entire universe of intelligent beings to exclaim, "What hath God wrought!"

Have you chosen to be part of this movement?

AS YOU BEGIN THE NEXT CHAPTER...

Every few years, among the most-viewed disciplines of the global Olympic games is the sport of gymnastics. And for gymnasts, perhaps the most-needed skill is balance. Watching a top medalist on, say, the balance beam is to witness a demonstration of precision and courage.

If balance is important for gymnasts, it's also indispensable for tight-rope walkers (see the beginning of this upcoming chapter for a true story about this one!). But perhaps nowhere is balance more needed than for those of us who seek to live the Christian life.

Achieving balance requires avoiding the extremes. On either side of a road—to the left or the right—danger is found: a ditch, a steep cliff, a rushing torrent of water. These days, it seems as if balance is becoming increasingly hard to find.

The writer of this next chapter mentions the experience of Peter as he walked on the water toward Jesus. So long as he kept his eyes on Jesus, he was just fine. But when he yielded to either of two extremes, he began to sink. When he let himself look at the huge waves headed his way, he sank. And when he looked back at the boat to see if his fellow disciples were suitably impressed with his water-walking, he sank.

It's the extremes that do us in. We need to seek to avoid those and stay balanced, lest we fall.

We won't find Jesus in the extremes. That's where fanaticism is found. That's where arguments break out. We so need to keep our eyes on Jesus—in doing this, we will be kept from the ditches on either side of the road. We'll avoid both the fire of fanaticism and the ice of indifference. Instead of Christians becoming polarized and abrasive, we'll be God's peacemakers.

How to stay balanced? For plenty of ideas, just turn the page!

Phil Mills, MD is a graduate of Loma Linda School of Medicine and is double boarded in both Physical Medicine and Dermatology. Throughout his professional life, he has been active in comprehensive medical evangelism on a local and national level. He is past president of AMEN and past editor of The AMEN journal. He has served on the NAD Health Committee and the GC Health Medical Missionary Committee. In addition to writing and speaking, He currently serves as Chairman of the Weimar University Board of Trustees. His experience as medical director of a rehabilitation hospital with patients who had difficulty standing/walking gives him a unique perspective on the importance of balance at the end times.

PHIL MILLS

CHAPTER 8

SPIRITUAL FUNAMBULISTS

A FUNAMBULIST IS A PERSON WHO WALKS ON TIGHTROPES. FUNAMBULISTS must stay balanced at all times. It took careful balance for the funambulist Blondin to walk across the Niagara Gorge on a high wire in 1859. One misstep, one wrong move to the right or to the left would have cost him his life. In a small way this illustrates the importance of balance in the Christian life. But even this illustration fails to show the widespread damage that one unbalanced person can cause.

"One fanatic, with his strong spirit and radical ideas, who will oppress the conscience of those who want to be right, will do great harm. The church needs to be purified from all such influences."[1] Fires kindled by arson and raging out of control, better illustrate this (James 3:5). Satan was able to light a destructive fire in Germany through the fanaticism of Thomas Müntzer,[2] which resulted in a civil war with great loss of life and property. Little wonder that "as the end draws near, the enemy will work with all his power to bring in fanaticism among us."[3] Fanaticism is like a firebomb that can severely damage or destroy a church or community. It starts with imbalance.

"Truth is sensible, genuine; it bears the signature of Heaven,"[4] but fanaticism is falsehood that bears a forged signature of heaven. It causes people to lose their balance. "Our work is to teach men and women to build on a true foundation, to plant their feet on a plain "Thus saith the Lord."[5]

THOMAS MÜNTZER

Thomas Müntzer[6] "was a man of considerable ability."[7] But Müntzer did not fix his gaze on Jesus. He kept his eyes on himself. Like Judas, Müntzer was ambitious for position, power, and honor. He first espoused belief in Lutheranism, but when he realized this made him second to Luther, he abandoned it, using friendship with Luther only to advance his own interests and career. He was a well-educated and gifted speaker who could attract and hold audiences of thousands. Though unwilling to reform his own life, he thought he was called to reform the world.[8]

Although Müntzer used Bible texts that superficially appeared to support his views, he taught that once a Christian had received the Holy Spirit,[9] the Bible became unnecessary because the inner light of the Holy Spirit would give guidance. This is mysticism; it opens the door to receiving communication from demons.[10] Müntzer followed impressions and dreams.[11]

Peter's instruction to "Honor all people. Love the brotherhood. Fear God. Honor the king" (1 Peter 2:17) was lost on Münster. True, there was injustice in Germany. For that matter, peasants had been oppressed for generations. Müntzer railed against this injustice and the nobles who not only permitted it but profited from it. He believed that he was called to give a prophetic end-time message. He failed to understand that

Christ's kingdom would be cut out of the mountain "without hands" (Daniel 2:34), and he taught his followers to overthrow their present oppressive government and set up God's end-time kingdom, where all would share equally in the wealth. "He attempted to establish by force an ideal Christian commonwealth, with absolute equality and a community of goods."[12] It has been said that what Luther was to Germany's Protestants, Thomas Müntzer was to East Germany's Marxists. Müntzer was depicted as an early hero who stood for the workers, the proletariat, while Luther was portrayed as a villain standing for the bourgeoisie.[13]

His preaching inflamed the peasants against the landowners, and riots followed. However, we should not miss the difference in the riots associated with Müntzer and the riots associated with Christ, the Apostles, and the reformers. Müntzer's *followers* started riots. Jesus' *opposers* started riots. The Peasant War that Müntzer incited brought death to a hundred thousand people and worsened the plight of the peasants Müntzer claimed to be trying to help.[14]

A FIRST KEY TO BALANCE—A STEADY GAZE

The Anchor Point. A funambulist does not look at himself, his feet, or the dangers below him. He fixes his gaze on a point called the anchor point. The balanced Christian also has such an anchor point. "I have set the Lord always before me; because He is at my right hand I shall not be moved" (Psalm 16:8). "When once the gaze is fixed upon Him, the life finds its center.... To honor Christ, to become like Him, to work for Him, is the life's highest ambition and its greatest joy."[15]

Disciplined Practice. "The more they discipline their minds to dwell upon the character of Christ, and the nearer they approach to His divine image, the more clearly will they discern its spotless perfection, and the more deeply will they feel their own defects."[16]

Overconfidence. Overconfidence will mean a fall for both funambulists and Christians. Paul reminds us, "Let him who thinks he stands take heed lest he fall" (1 Corinthians 10:12). The story of Peter walking on water reminds us of this truth. The instant he took his eyes off his anchor point, Jesus, he began to sink into the water.[17] Like the pilot in a fog who ignores his instruments and trusts his senses, the Christian who takes his eyes off Jesus is in extreme danger (Proverbs 28:26).

Wavering. A funambulist who is about to fall begins to waver. This is just as true for the Christian. "To be wavering and halfhearted in allegiance to truth is to choose the darkness of error and satanic delusion."[18]

> "He that wavereth is like a wave of the sea driven with the wind and tossed. For let not that man think that he shall receive any thing of the Lord. A double minded man is unstable in all his ways" (James 1:6-8, KJV).

A SECOND KEY TO BALANCE—THE BIBLE

Balance pole. The funambulist needs a balance pole. The Christian's balance pole is the Bible, and there is nothing more stabilizing than this. "Take God's word to balance the mind."[19] And the *entire* Bible is needed (Matthew 4:4). "As the end draws near, the enemy will work with all his power to bring in fanaticism among us.... Our work is to teach men and women to build on a true foundation, to plant their feet on a plain "Thus saith the Lord."[20]

We should notice several important ways the Bible keeps Christians balanced.

Proper Timing. Timing is an important component of balance. "It is the very essence of all right faith to do the right thing at the right time."[21] The Bible gives us proper timing with prophetically revealed *present truth*. As Peter said, "I will not be negligent to remind you always of these things, though you know and are established in the *present truth*" (2 Peter 1:12). The leaders of Issachar understood *present truth* for they "were men that had understanding of the times, to know what Israel ought to do" (1 Chronicles 12:32).

THE GENOME

The genome helps us understand present truth. The genome is our entire DNA. It contains all the instructions necessary to go from a one-cell fetus to a completed adult human. Every living cell of our body contains the full genome with its encyclopedic instructions.

How is it that the cells that build the eye, know to make eye material? How is it that the cells that build the ear know to make material for the ear? Why don't the cells in the brain make fingernails in the brain?

In a poorly understood but marvelous process, a cell is enabled to selectively activate only the parts of the genome's DNA that are needed for that cell, at that time, location, and situation. That is the cell's present truth.

When a cell becomes confused about its mission—its purpose in the body—it becomes extreme, and begins activating the DNA instruction in ways that were never intended. It produces substances in improper amounts or locations. It may become cancerous.

Properly understood, prophecy helps us understand *present truth*—the right message at the right time in the right way.

The prophecies of Daniel 7–9, Revelation 14:6-13, and Matthew 24-25 reveal that we are in the time of God's judgment. The *present truth* today is the judgment-hour message found in the Three Angels' Messages.

THE THREE ANGELS' MESSAGES—BALANCE AT THE END OF TIME

Fear God. The first angel's message is the Gospel in the context of the judgment. It calls the world to fear God (Revelation 14:7). "'The fear of the Lord is the beginning of wisdom.' It is the mainspring, *the balance wheel* of character."[22] This is why "the preaching of the first angel's message and of the 'midnight cry' tended directly to repress fanaticism and dissension."[23]

Babylon's Instability. The Second Angel's Message is a message warning of the lack of balance in Babylon. When we are unbalanced, we fall—and Babylon has fallen (Revelation 14:8). We can't obtain balance from Babylon.

Balanced Emphasis. "Significant figures" is often an early lecture in science classes. Students must learn about significant figures and how to avoid being distracted by measurements and amounts that are too insignificant to matter.

> "We are to proclaim the third angel's message to a perishing world, and we are not to permit our minds to become diverted by minutiae that practically amount to nothing."[24]

Balanced Priorities. The Third Angel's Message, accompanied by the outpouring of the Holy Spirit in the Early Rain, balances our priorities.

> "If you are balanced by the Holy Spirit, you will seek first the kingdom of God and His righteousness...and your experience will be in complete harmony with the message of the third angel."[25]

CENTERED BY PRACTICAL RELIGION

Knowing and Doing. Bible balance requires not only devotional study, but practical application of the Bible's instruction to the daily life. Extremes may cause the fanatic to cease either practical work or careful study. Paul had to meet such fanaticism in his day.[26] Fanatics associated with Thomas Müntzer's brand of Christianity quit their jobs, claiming that they had received the Holy Spirit and needed no further study.[27] Following the Disappointment, fanatics emerged, teaching that we must cease working.[28] But spirituality cannot remain balanced when it is separated from life. Our spiritual exercises will either cease or become an empty formality.[29] Monasteries have proved this over and over.

The Third Angel's Message shows that we need thorough education and training. "It is the most solemn message ever given to mortals, and all who connect with the work should first feel their need of an education, and a most thorough training process for the work, in reference to their future usefulness."[30] Of course this also needs balance.

"Religion can never safely be disconnected from the intellectual training. But manual training is to be combined with the study of books, to correctly balance the mind and give solidity to brain, bone, and muscle."[31]

Counsel. While the Bible's balance includes God's instruction personally to us through His Word, it also includes the wisdom and restraint that God gives us through others.[32] Solomon admonished, "Listen to counsel and receive instruction, that you may be wise in your latter days" (Proverbs 19:20).

Counseling together is an essential part of God's system of balanced government. Even the Godhead counsel together.[33] This promotes balance. This is why institutions and churches have boards and why each quinquennium there is a General Conference with worldwide representatives to deliberate, select leaders, and determine world policies.

A RED FLAG

We should recognize rejection of counsel as waving a red flag. When evaluating a messenger of so-called truth, always watch to see whether they are teachable or instead, they just come back and argue their view with renewed energy. To follow such an individual is dangerous. Fanatics are almost always uncorrectable. They "refuse the counsel of their brethren, and press on in their own way until they become just what Satan would desire to have them—unbalanced in mind."[34] "It is not a good sign when men will not unite with their brethren, but prefer to act alone."[35] They desire "to take an independent course, and to lead instead of yielding to be led."[36]

The Church Body. One of the most famous psalms begins, "The Lord is my shepherd" (Psalm 23:1). A shepHERD has a "herd"—a flock. God led His people out of Egypt "like a flock' (Psalm 77:20). Just *one cloud* led all the people together. There wasn't a little cloud over each individual, leading each in his or her own separate way. Even now, there is "one fold and one shepherd" (John 10:16). "God is leading a people, not one or two upon a track, peculiar and separate from the body."[37] God designed the Church to protect members from fanatics.

Health Reform. After medical missionaries work to open doors, fanatics come along after them and undo what they have done, effectively closing those doors. "Health reform becomes health deform, a health destroyer, when it is carried to extremes."[38] And the Church helps protect from extremes. "It is time that something was done to prevent novices from taking the field and advocating health reform. Their works and words can be spared; for they do more injury than the wisest and most intelligent men, with the best influence they can exert, can counteract. It is impossible for the best-qualified advocates of health reform to fully relieve the minds of the public from the prejudice received through the wrong course of these extremists."[39] Even worse, "the door is also closed in a great measure, so that unbelievers cannot be reached by the present truth upon the Sabbath and the soon coming of our Saviour."[40]

Science. God would have His people, like Daniel and his three companions, known for "understanding science" (Daniel 1:4). "God is the author of science. Scientific research opens to the mind vast fields of thought and information."[41] This equips us to better evaluate the validity of health claims, determine the strength of underlying statistics, and recognize "junk" science. This protects us from extremes based on unsound data, bogus claims, or the latest "health" fad.

But Bible balance is essential for true scientific knowledge. "To many, scientific research has become a curse; their finite minds are so weak that they lose their balance. They cannot harmonize their views of science with Scripture statements, and they think that the Bible is to be tested by their standard of 'science falsely so called'."[42] The Bible keeps us balanced in every area of study from sociology to psychology, from history to archeology, from science to philosophy.

Because "some who think that they have scientific knowledge are by their interpretations giving wrong ideas both of science and of the Bible,"[43] one of the primary purposes for the establishment of our colleges was to provide an opportunity for Adventist young people to learn both science and the Bible.[44]

A THIRD KEY TO BALANCE—AVOIDING THE DESTABILIZING WINDS OF FALSE DOCTRINE

False Doctrine. Just as a funambulist faces dangers from gusts of wind, the Christian faces destabilizing gusts of false doctrine (Ephesians 4:14). Like a parasite, fanaticism feeds off and saps the energy generated by true spiritual awakenings. It is important to study past revivals and the fanaticism that invariably appeared soon after.[45]

Because Satan "is satisfied when men rest their faith on spurious doctrines and religious enthusiasm,"[46] he sends false revivals with "an emotional excitement, a mingling of the true with the false, that is well adapted to mislead."[47] These gusts will increase in intensity at the end. "We shall meet with false doctrines of every kind, and unless we are acquainted with what Christ has said, and are following His instructions, we shall be led astray."[48]

> "'A great wave of excitement is an injury to the work....' Under great excitement, strange work is done. There are those who improve this opportunity to bring in strange and fanciful doctrines. Thus the door is closed to the proclamation of sound doctrine."[49]

SAMPLING OF END-TIME FALSE DOCTRINES

We can only give a sampling of fanatical doctrines we will see, for "Every wind of doctrine will be blowing.... Watchfulness and prayer must be our safeguards in these days of peril."[50] "Scriptures are brought in in such a way that error is made to appear as truth."[51]

FALSE PROPHETS

Jesus' warning against false prophets (Matthew 7:15) remains relevant. "There will be those who will claim to have visions.... People are going to be led more and more astray in foreign countries and in America."[52]

EXTREMES IN JUSTIFICATION AND SANCTIFICATION

False sanctification:

"One of the most dangerous of these doctrines is that of false sanctification. There are those who claim to be holy, and yet are breaking God's commandments. Their assertion that they are sinless is false and should not be received."[53]

Justification makes sinning impossible:

"Another doctrine that will be presented is that all that we have to do is to believe in Christ—to believe that He has forgiven our sins, and that after we are forgiven, it is impossible for us to sin."[54]

REJECTION OF THE SANCTUARY DOCTRINE

No Sanctuary:

"The enemy will bring in false theories, such as the doctrine that there is no sanctuary. This is one of the points on which there will be a departing from the faith."[55]

FALSE AND SPECULATIVE IDEAS ABOUT GOD AND THE TRINITY

Jesus' final commission to His disciples was to "make disciples of all the nations, baptizing them in the name of the Father and of the Son and of the Holy Spirit" (Matthew 28:19). Satan hates this divine trinity—"the eternal heavenly dignitaries—God, and Christ, and the Holy Spirit."[56] Throughout its history the Church has faced fanatics "seducing souls by presenting speculative theories regarding God"[57] and explaining away the plainest statements of the Bible on the reality and personality of each of the members of the Godhead. We will have to face such fanaticism in the future.

"Again and again we shall be called to meet the influence of men who are studying sciences of satanic origin, through which Satan is working to make a nonentity of God and of Christ."[58]

The Holy Spirit. Satan seeks to keep people in ignorance of the Holy Spirit and His work. In Ephesus Paul had to instruct those who did not know there was a Holy Spirit (Acts 19:2). Early in Ellen White's experience she encountered those that "would have me believe that there was no Holy Spirit."[59] Satan will continue to press this fanatical deception just before the Holy Spirit falls in Latter Rain abundance.

Pantheism. There have been and will be panentheistic and speculative doctrines of "an impersonal God, diffused through nature."[60] Such "spiritualistic theories regarding the personality of God, followed to their logical conclusion, sweep away the whole Christian economy,"[61] and leave their victims in "the mist and fog of spiritualism and fanaticism."[62]

PAGAN MEDITATION

Mysticism. This has been a key component of false religions from ancient times.[63] Mysticism, whether defined by some as a prayer-like state linking one with God—or, as others have it, as connecting one instead with devils, can indeed connect humans with demons and even provide a gateway to spiritualism for Seventh-day Adventists.

We are told that it "will get the hall-room of the heart all ready for these miracles that Satan will come to work *right in our midst.* Some shall depart from the faith, giving heed to seducing spirits and doctrines of devils."[64]

FEAST KEEPING

Judaizers. With their emphasis on keeping the pre–Cross ceremonies, Judaizers were destructive fanatics in Paul's day (Galatians 2:14). Though "Paul and the other apostles laboured to show" that "all the sacrificial offerings and services were to be abolished,"[65] Christian history remains littered with accounts of this heresy through the centuries. Despite the clarity of the Spirit of Prophecy that "to continue these rites would be an insult to Jehovah,"[66] it has its adherents still.

UNBALANCED PROPHETIC INTERPRETATIONS

Laodicean Message. Heaven designed the Laodicean message to "rid the church of ... fanatical influence."[67] Fanatical members have misused the expression "I will spew thee out of my mouth" (Revelation 3:16, ASV) and applied it in an extreme and overbearing manner to sensitive Christians, shunning those whom they felt had been spewed out.[68]

Time-Setting Messages. The last message of time God's people will ever be given was the Midnight Cry, calling attention to the beginning of the Judgment, October 22, 1844. Ellen White has clearly warned:

> "Again and again have I been warned in regard to time setting. *There will never again be a message for the people of God that will be based on time.* We are not to know the definite time either for the outpouring of the Holy Spirit or for the coming of Christ."[69]

Jesus said, "It is not for you to know times or seasons which the Father has put in His own authority" (Acts 1:7).

Despite these plain statements . . .

> "there will always be false and fanatical movements made by persons in the church who claim to be led of God—those who will run before they are sent and will give day and date for the occurrence of unfulfilled prophecy. The enemy is pleased to have them do this, for their successive failures and leading into false lines cause confusion and unbelief."[70]

Help the deluded followers, particularly their children if you can, but categorically reject all such messages.

STANDARDS PERVERTED OR IGNORED

Fanaticism on the right. Satan tries to link a position so extreme as to disgust reasonable people with every timely message of truth. Extremists may focus on some point such as dress, which becomes the test by which all others are judged. Like the Pharisees, fanatics make their own preference and practice the scale by which others are judged. Extremists drive away souls by their "harsh, censorious, condemnatory spirit."[71] They have such an obsession with their rigid beliefs that sensible reformers can no longer address the topic.

Fanaticism on the left. The opposite extreme is often ignored, but it is as easy to fall to the left as the right, and it is *not* somehow safer to fall on one side than another. Omitting an essential element is just as extreme and harmful as over-emphasizing it. God's Word *does* contain commands and prohibitions that separate us from the world in finances, diet, dress, adornment, amusement, music, work, and worship (2 Corinthians 6:17).

Those who ignore this instruction not only fall themselves, but by word and example are a stumbling block that causes others to lose their balance and fall also. Speaking of such extremists, we are told that "others go to an extreme in their conformity to the world. There is no clear, distinct line of separation between them and the worldling."[72] This causes the loss of souls just as certainly as the previous extremists.

> "If in one case men are driven away from the truth by a harsh, censorious, condemnatory spirit, in this they are led to conclude that the professed Christian is destitute of principle and knows nothing of a change of heart or character."[73]

PROTECTION FROM FANATICAL WINDS

"A man will be as a hiding place from the wind, and a cover from the tempest" (Isaiah 32:2). That hiding place is the man Christ Jesus. When we fully surrender and keep our gaze fixed on Him while we seek to faithfully follow the instructions in His Word, He keeps us from falling (Jude 24). And He can keep our homes from falling into these delusive extremes.

> "Therefore whoever hears these sayings of Mine, and does them, I will liken him to a wise man who built his house on the rock: and ... the winds blew ... and it did not fall" (Matthew 7:24).

ENDNOTES

1. *Historical Sketches of the Foreign Missions of the Seventh-day Adventists*, 212.
2. Thomas Müntzer's fanaticism is discussed in more detail later in this chapter.
3. *Gospel Workers*, 316.
4. *Manuscript Releases*, vol. 14, 55.
5. *Gospel Workers*, 316.
6. Also spelled Munzer, Münzer, Monczer, and Monetarius.
7. *The Great Controversy*, 191.
8. Ibid.
9. He is listed as part of the Pentecostal tradition in Protestantism. *Christian History Magazine–Issue 58: The Rise of Pentecostalism*. Carol Stream, IL: *Christianity Today*, 1998.
10. Mysticism is a method for "listening to the seducing spirits and doctrines of devils." Manuscript 241, 1902.
11. Similar fanaticism will be seen in the future. See *Signs of the Times*, March 27, 1884.
12. Daniel K. Cassel, *History of the Mennonites* (Philadelphia: Daniel K. Cassel, 1888), 327.
13. Harvard trained Mark Edwards, Jr., past President of St. Olaf College. See https://www.pbs.org/wgbh/pages/frontline/shows/apocalypse/explanation/muentzer.html accessed 6/15/20.
14. Marian Goldberg, *Encyclopedia Britannica*, https://www.britannica.com/event/Peasants-War, accessed 6/12/2020.
15. *Education*, 296.
16. *The Sanctified Life*, 7.
17. *The Desire of Ages*, 381.
18. *The Desire of Ages*, 312.
19. *Signs of the Times*, March 4, 1889.
20. *Gospel Workers*, 316.
21. *General Conference Daily Bulletin*, March 2, 1899, Art. B.
22. *Review and Herald*, April 23, 1889.
23. *The Great Controversy*, 398.

24. Letter 16, 1903.
25. *Medical Ministry*, 50.
26. See *Acts of the Apostles*, 348.
27. See *The Great Controversy*, 187.
28. https://www.ellenwhite.info/ellen_white_life_10a.htm accessed 6/15/2020.
29. *Steps to Christ*, 101.
30. *The Review and Herald*, June 21, 1887.
31. Manuscript 135, 1898.
32. Consider Josiah's failure when he "did not heed the words of Necho from the mouth of God" (2 Chronicles 35:22).
33. See *Counsels to Parents, Teachers, and Students*, 438.
34. Manuscript 139, 1901.
35. Manuscript 56, 1898.
36. *Testimonies for the Church*, vol. 1, 230.
37. Letter 10, 1870.
38. Letter 37, 1901.
39. *Testimonies for the Church*, vol. 2, 386.
40. Ibid.
41. *Counsels to Parents, Teachers, and Students*, 426.
42. *Spirit of Prophecy*, vol. 4, 345.
43. *Medical Ministry*, 96.
44. *Testimonies for the Church*, vol. 5, 21.
45. See *Ellen G. White, The Early Years*, 73-89, where the history of some of these fanatical movements is recounted. Also see *The Great Controversy*, "Modern Revivals," 461-478.
46. Manuscript 59, 1899.
47. *The Great Controversy*, 464.
48. Manuscript 27, 188.6
49. *Gospel Workers*, 316.
50. *The Review and Herald*, November 6, 1883.
51. *Selected Messages*, vol. 1, 202.

52. *The Review and Herald*, May 25, 1905. Also see *Selected Messages*, bk. 2, . 72-100.
53. Manuscript 27, 1886.
54. Ibid.
55. *Review and Herald*, May 25, 1905.
56. Manuscript 130, 1901.
57. Letter 262, 1903.
58. *Testimonies for the Church*, vol. 9, 68.
59. *Testimonies for the Church*, vol. 1, 71.
60. *Manuscript* 145, 1903.
61. *Selected Messages*, bk. 1, 203.
62. *Spiritual Gifts*, vol. 2, 103.
63. *Patriarchs and Prophets*, 248.
64. Manuscript 138, 1906.
65. *Bible Echo*, April 16, 1894.
66. Manuscript 19, 1897.
67. *Life Sketches of James and Ellen White 1888*, 333.
68. Letter 19, 1859.
69. *Selected Messages*, bk. 1, 188.
70. Letter 28, 1897.
71. *Testimonies for the Church*, vol. 5, 305
72. Ibid.
73. Ibid.

AS YOU BEGIN THE NEXT CHAPTER...

Extremists.

Fanatics.

Is it even possible to check the daily TV, radio, or Internet news without yet another recitation of global extremism and fanaticism—of a world out of balance, as noted in the chapter just ended? And the media reports far more beside—worldwide suffering, misery, violence, and death.

Conflict everywhere. Between couples and political parties and nations. Even between those who claim the name of followers of Christ. From the rebellion of the angel Lucifer, to Adam and Eve in Eden, to their sons Cain and Abel—right on down through unending pain to this very day, the universe has been one long unbroken story of wars large and small.

Hollywood's science fiction wars? Think much bigger! Behind all wars of earth, real or imagined, is the War Behind All Wars. In the chapter coming up, it's called the Great Controversy.

It's the story of the titanic struggle between . . .

- Light and darkness
- Truth and lies
- Love and selfishness
- Life and death
- It's the story of Michael versus Lucifer . . .

And ***you.***

Pastor John Bradshaw is the President of *It Is Written,* a media evangelism ministry based in Collegedale, Tennessee. An author, pastor,and speaker, John is blessed to work as part of a dedicated team committed to hastening the return of Jesus. His programs, sermons, and devotionals can be viewed at itiswritten.tv.

CHAPTER 9

BEHIND THE SCENES: THE GREAT CONTROVERSY

MANY YEARS AGO, I SAW A MOVIE AT A THEATER IN LEICESTER SQUARE, London, that left me totally confused. It was an "artsy" sort of movie. The more I watched, the more bewildered I became. No matter how hard I tried, I simply couldn't figure out what the movie was about. And it was evident that many others in the audience felt much the same way. As people exited the theater the confusion was palpable. "What in the world was that?" one man asked his wife." I overheard a woman tell her friend, "If I'd known it was going to be like this, I wouldn't have bothered." The comment of another moviegoer stayed with me. "It's not worth it when you have no idea what it's about."

I didn't know back then in my pre-Christian days that I would later meet so many people who feel that way about the Bible. "I have no idea what it's about."

UNDERSTANDING THE BIBLE'S CENTRAL THEME

The Bible contains some truly incredible stories. The Creation of the world. The sin of Adam and Eve. The lives of Abraham and Joseph. Captivity in Egypt. The Ten Commandments given on Mt Sinai. Leviticus, with sacrifices and blood and offerings and regulations. Deuteronomy with an almost bewildering array of details about various laws. Numbers with, well, numbers. An array of prophecies and symbols and types and shadows. War and death and betrayal and history. Many people are really confused trying to understand it all. Trying to work it all out has caused many people's head to spin. Like the movie I watched when I wore a younger man's clothes, people have been heard to say of the Bible "I just can't figure it out."

Although the Bible is made up of 66 different books and 1189 separate chapters, it is in reality ONE book with a certain thread running through it. Miss that thread, and it's like building a model without using glue. It's virtually impossible to make it all hold together. Many people are missing the "glue" that allows them to see the Bible's big picture. If we can identify the missing piece of the puzzle, the mysteries of the Bible become much clearer.

The Bible starts with Moses' account of Creation. "In the beginning God created the heavens and the Earth" (Genesis 1:1). After a description of the Creation week in Genesis chapters 1 and 2, the Bible's third chapter finds us listening to an unlikely conversation between a woman—50 percent of the global population at the time—and a snake. I'd excuse anyone who said, like the moviegoers in Leicester Square, "What is going on here?"

Understanding what is going on in Genesis 3 is the glue that makes sense of the other 1188 chapters of the Bible. And to really understand what is happening there in the first book of the Bible, it is necessary to read the last book of the Bible. It's there that we clearly see the thread running all the way through Scripture.

The book of Revelation is described by its author, the apostle John, as "the revelation of Jesus Christ" (Revelation 1:1). It includes the revelation given by Jesus, a revelation about Jesus, and the revelation of Jesus' plans to unmask the devil and reveal the plans of God. The 22 chapters of the book of Revelation reveal the plan of salvation, the conflict between sin and righteousness, the end of sin and the Creation of a new Earth. But mention of sin gives rise to another question. Where in the world did *sin* come from? Why does sin—and all its attendant complications—exist?

Sin cost Jesus His life. It made the plan of salvation necessary. Sin is why there will one day be a lake of fire and an earth made new. And we see the genesis of sin in the book of Revelation.

After referencing the birth of Jesus, Revelation 12 takes us directly to the origin of sin.

> "And war broke out in heaven: Michael and his angels fought with the dragon; and the dragon and his angels fought, but they did not prevail, nor was a place found for them in heaven any longer. So, the great dragon was cast out, that serpent of old, called the Devil and Satan, who deceives the whole world; he was cast to the earth, and his angels were cast out with him" (Revelation 12:7-9.)

We're used to paradise being tainted here on Earth. Although an advertising slogan in use at the time said the South Pacific island nation of Fiji was "the way the world should be," it was never a complete shock when the democratically elected government of Fiji was overthrown by a coup d'etat in 1987. These things happen here on Earth. But in heaven? How can things go wrong in heaven?

That war in heaven spoken of in Revelation provides the backdrop for every episode of sin and sadness that has ever darkened our Earth. And understanding that war unlocks some of the most puzzling mysteries of the Bible.

A BATTLE FOR THE THRONE OF THE UNIVERSE

The prophet Isaiah allows us to understand something of the mind and motivation of Satan himself, when he writes:

> "How you are fallen from heaven, O Lucifer, son of the morning! How you are cut down to the ground, you who weakened the nations! For you have said in your heart: 'I will ascend into heaven, I will exalt my throne above the stars of God; I will also sit on the mount of the congregation on the farthest sides of the north; I will ascend above the heights of the clouds, I will be like the Most High'" (Isaiah 14:12-14.)

Ezekiel gives us this insight in Ezekiel 28:

> "You were the seal of perfection, full of wisdom and perfect in beauty. You were in Eden, the garden of God; Every precious stone was your covering... The workmanship of your timbrels and pipes was prepared for you on the day you were created. You were the anointed cherub who covers; I established you; You were on the holy mountain of God; You walked back and forth in the midst of fiery stones" (Ezekiel 28:14).

It is evident Satan is being referred to in this passage. And given what follows in the next few verses, it is fascinating that he is described as "full of wisdom" and "perfect in beauty." His own apparent knowledge of his wisdom and beauty seems to have led in large part to his ultimate downfall.

> "You were perfect in your ways from the day you were created, till iniquity was found in you. By the abundance of your trading, you became filled with violence within, and you sinned; therefore, I cast you as a profane thing out of the mountain of God; And I destroyed you, O covering cherub, from the midst of the fiery stones. Your heart was lifted up because of your beauty; You corrupted your wisdom for the sake of your splendor" (Ezekiel 28:15-17).

Compare what Isaiah wrote with what we find in Ezekiel, and some illuminating details emerge. Satan came to a place in his life where he desired the worship that belonged only to God. While it's not possible to completely understand his motives, it is clear he desired to "ascend into heaven" and "exalt [his] throne above the stars of God." Satan stated plainly that he wanted to "be like the Most High" (Isaiah 14:13, 14). In short, Satan—an angel created by God—came to the place where He wanted worship.

This brought him into conflict with the government of heaven. After a "war" in heaven—a dispute during which Satan's desire to receive worship was opposed by God—one third of the angels of heaven sided with history's first rebel and along with their chosen leader were evicted from heaven. And since arriving on Planet Earth thousands of years ago, Satan has not forsaken his original desire to receive worship. His behind-the-scenes attack on the government of heaven clearly manifests itself today in society, in politics, and—perhaps especially—in the Church.

Revelation's narrative of this cosmic conflict between good and evil reveals that Satan was cast out of heaven to this earth (Revelation 12:9). Since the earth was created perfect by God, Satan's arrival must have been shortly after the Creation of our perfect world. Soon Adam and Eve fell prey to his seductive temptations. Shortly after, Cain killed Abel—murder had come to Paradise—and in just the seventh chapter of the Bible, the Earth is destroyed by a Flood sent from God. The highs and lows of the history of God's people announce that although you can't see it, there's something dangerous going on behind the scenes, much like glassy calm water at a beach hiding a deadly rip current just beneath the surface. The turmoil seen in society today points to a vast spiritual battle raging behind the scenes.

Perhaps the most graphic depiction of the behind-the-scenes war between Satan and the government of God is found in the book of Job. Likely the first book of the Bible written, the opening verses of Job introduce us to a "blameless and upright" man "who feared God and shunned evil" (Job 1:1). Satan accused Job of serving God merely because of the blessings he received from God, prompting God to say,

"Behold, all that he has is in your power; only do not lay a hand on his person" (Job 1:12).

After sweeping away Job's possessions and children in a single day, Satan then afflicted Job physically.

"Behold, he is in your hand," God said, "but spare his life. So, Satan went out from the presence of the Lord, and struck Job with painful boils from the sole of his foot to the crown of his head" (Job 2:6, 7).

This began Job's painful, debilitating journey with suffering. His wife advised him to "curse God and die" (Job 2:9), and his friends heaped upon him condemnation and criticism.

The reader of the book of Job sees what Job could not. Behind the scenes, there is a spiritual battle raging, Often referred to as the "great controversy," this spiritual battle is spearheaded by an angry devil desperate to usurp God's authority and to receive the worship due to God alone. This selfish desire for the world's worship comes to a head in Earth's last days.

EARTH'S FINAL CONFLICT

Revelation chapter 13 introduces us to Earth's final conflict, in which the issue of the mark of the beast confronts all humanity before the return of Jesus. When viewed through the lens of the great controversy, the mark of the beast is seen to be the single issue that ultimately divides those who have surrendered their lives to God from those who have not. The verses explaining this drama would be perplexing if not for an understanding of what is going on behind the scenes.

While in Rome, Italy, I had the opportunity to visit the Sistine Chapel. It was named in honor of Pope Sixtus, who restored the chapel in the fifteenth century. Its walls and ceilings are lined with magnificent art. Its famous ceiling—featuring portrayals of nine different stories found in the book of Genesis—was painted by Michelangelo, one of history's greatest artists. Five million tourists visit the Sistine Chapel each year.

It's easy to forget that the Sistine Chapel is part of the Apostolic

Chapel, the official residence of the pope. When visiting the Sistine Chapel, you're essentially visiting part of the pope's home.

During my visit, chapel officials were slow to open the exit doors to let us out. While they waited, people wondered why they weren't being permitted to exit. Officials didn't seem to be in any mood to provide an explanation.

When the doors finally opened, and we were ushered out, we were told the reason we had been kept in the Sistine Chapel longer than expected. Pope Francis had accompanied a head of state through the Apostolic Palace and walked through the hallway into which the Sistine Chapel emptied. Which meant that while we waited, the pope himself had walked about six feet from where we were standing, on the other side of the exit doors. Behind the scenes, arguably the most famous and most powerful person in the world walked past us.

You can't always know what is going on behind the scenes. But when you do, it helps makes sense of what is going on around you. The same is true when it comes to reading and understanding the Bible.

In Revelation 13, "all the world" marvels and follows the beast (Revelation 13:3), worships both the dragon (which is Satan) and worships the beast itself. Revelation 13:8 says, "All who dwell on the earth shall worship him," and those that do so receive the mark of the beast (Revelation 13:16, 17; 14:9-11).

The last great conflict to engulf Planet Earth can only be understood when viewed through the lens of the great controversy, the thread that runs through the Bible. A jealous devil is seeking the world's worship. He works through people, organizations, and churches to separate people from God by undermining faith in God and His Word.

THE ENTIRE WORLD IS INVOLVED

Everyone in the world is embroiled in a fierce spiritual battle. The apostle Paul echoed the experience of Job when he wrote to the Ephesians, "Finally, my brethren, be strong in the Lord and in the power of His might. Put on the whole armor of God, that you may be able to stand against the wiles of the devil" (Ephesians 6:10, 11). In Greek, the "methodeia" of the devil, is closely related to the word *methods*. What are these "wiles" or "schemes" of the devil?

Paul continues in verse 12:

> "For we do not wrestle against flesh and blood, but against principalities, against powers, against the rulers of the darkness of this age, against spiritual hosts of wickedness in the heavenly places."

The warfare in which God's people are embroiled isn't against other people. It isn't against things that we can see. What happened in the book of Job is happening all around us. We wrestle with principalities and powers, with the rulers of the darkness of this age. We war against spiritual hosts of wickedness. There is a spiritual battle raging. The great controversy between light and dark, between good and evil, between righteousness and unrighteousness, between Christ and Satan, is real.

While he was still a covering cherub in heaven (see Ezekiel 28), Satan coveted the place that only God had the right to occupy. He desired the worship that belonged (and belongs) only to God. Whereas God—"who cannot lie" according to Titus 1:2—can only counter Satan with truth, Satan has chosen to use both truth and lies in his battle against God's throne. Misrepresenting God's character in heaven so expertly and deviously as to persuade one third of heaven's angels to relinquish their place in glory, Satan began his campaign of equivocation, obfuscation, and disinformation in the Garden of Eden. When Eve announced she and Adam were forbidden by God to eat the fruit that grew on the Tree of the Knowledge of Good and Evil, Satan subtly led Eve to choose his lies over God's truth.

> ""Has God indeed said, 'You shall not eat of every tree of the garden'?" he asked in Genesis 3:1. After being told by Eve that eating the fruit would mean certain death for the world's first inhabitants, Satan responded by saying, "You will not surely die. For God

knows that in the day you eat of it your eyes will be opened, and you will be like God, knowing good and evil" (Genesis 3:4, 5).

Utter lies but presented in such a way that Eve felt attracted and not repulsed, intrigued, and not appalled. "I will be like God?" she said to herself, as she noticed how attractive the fruit appeared. The devils tactics have changed little over the years.

During the Cold War, it was the practice of both western and Soviet governments to influence the thinking of foreign governments and citizens. Soviet agents operating in western countries, for example, expertly insinuated themselves into the confidence of individuals and institutions, which at times were entirely unsuspecting of what was taking place. While some people were recruited as spies, more frequently individuals would be maneuvered to use their influence in a way that favored Soviet interests and advanced Moscow's cause. Journalists would be courted and almost imperceptibly encouraged to write articles sympathetic to socialism or the aims of the Soviet government. Government officials who weren't outright recruited to subvert western interests could be gently led to use their influence to promote policies that served the interests of Russia. The intention was that over time Soviet principles would take hold, and through interventions small and large entire nations would adjust key policies to the advantage of the Soviet Union and disadvantage the west.

Moscow was playing the long game, hoping that over decades the playing field of the world would tilt in its direction. The Soviets ultimately failed to meaningfully advance eastern European communism into the west. Following a series of revolutions across central and eastern Europe, the iron curtain fell in the early 1990s. Communism met its demise.

In a similar fashion, Satan has been slowly but surely advancing his cause over the last 6,000 years and has made such dramatic progress that Jesus was able to describe him as "the ruler of this world" (John 12:31; 14:30; 16:11). But just as the Soviet Union crumbled and the communist regimes of eastern European fell, Satan will be ultimately destroyed. The death of Jesus on the Cross assures His complete triumph over the powers of evil. (Isaiah 14:16; Revelation 20:9, 10).

Satan's intention in the great controversy is to separate people from faith in God and lead them to disobey His commands by choosing not to surrender their lives fully to Jesus. We see this played out spectacularly in society. While the Bible opens with the words, "In the beginning God created" (Genesis 1:1), masses of people today deny the Creation account of Scripture and believe in the entirely implausible theory that life on earth spontaneously generated. They have accepted the lie that the unfathomable intricacies of the created world resulted from nothing more than chance. They assume that the beauty and complexity of the natural world resulted from an ages-long series of mutations.

It took almost 6,000 years for evolution to become widely accepted. But knowing evolution would eventually produce spiritual chaos in the Christian church, Satan bided his time working slowly but surely to replace a glorious truth—Creation—with a pestilential error.

While it seemed for decades that the enemy of souls had committed himself to the destruction of the nuclear family, it has become strikingly evident in recent years that his plans were far more broad, contemplating instead the dissolution of the traditional family altogether. And when Cain killed Abel, intolerance for the ending of a life was such that "the Lord set a mark on Cain, lest anyone finding him should kill him."

Today, according to one pro-abortion group, somewhere in the region of 850,000 abortions are performed in the United States every year. That's almost two and a half thousand every single day. Society has very evidently become far more charitable in its view of murder than it was shortly after Creation.

The fact that there will be people reading this who maintain, *What's wrong with abortion on demand?* demonstrates how incredibly successful Satan has been in shifting the world—and the Church—away from biblical values.

SATAN'S STRATEGY: DECEPTION, LIES, AND FALSEHOOD

It is in the Church where the progress of the great controversy is most clearly seen. Evolution is today widely accepted among Christians, despite God's Word being unambiguous in its support of Creation (see Genesis 2:1, 2; Psalm 33:6, 9; John 1:3; Romans 1:20; Colossians 1:16; Hebrews 11:3). Even though Satan's first lie was with regard to death—"you shall not surely die" (Genesis 2:17)—the overwhelming majority of Christians stand on the side of the fallen angel rather than the plainly revealed will of God. The Christian Church, inexplicably, is virtually unanimous in its opposition to the keeping of all the commandments of God.

The fourth commandment—the commandment that deals with worship and starts with the word *remember*—has been almost entirely forgotten. How is it possible that the Christian faith outright rejects one of the Ten Commandments? It's the result of thousands of years of conditioning. Satan has been leading people of faith to consider the Ten Commandments unnecessary.

The plan of salvation has become almost hopelessly confused in many areas. While the message of the Gospel seems to be abundantly clear in Scripture, many prominent voices present the Gospel as little more than a theory, something to be believed but not necessarily experienced.

While by most Christians the Cross is valued, the high priestly ministry of Jesus in the heavenly sanctuary is almost forgotten. A sentimental Christianity has usurped the place of an experiential Christianity. The Christian Church presents a Christ who wants all believers to be rich and to prosper materially; a Christ who grants ecstatic utterances as the sign of true conversion; a Christ who grants faulty human beings the privilege of dispensing forgiveness to their fellow men and women; and a Christ who claims the entire Old Testament is of no consequence to today's Christian Church.

Little wonder Jesus' Himself describes the vast majority of Christianity as "Babylon" (Revelation 14:8; 17:1-7; 18:1-4). How did we get here? These stunning developments did not come about overnight. Instead, a well-studied enemy of God has for millennia bided his time, slowly and deliberately preparing the world for the great deceptions that are soon to come upon Planet Earth. There is a battle raging. For thousands of years Satan has been setting up the planet and all who live on it to be swept away in his great last-day deceptions.

Which begs the question: If Satan and his angels are arrayed against fallen sinners, what hope is there for any believer successfully navigating the troubled waters of earth's last days? As if to answer the question, David wrote this in Psalm 24:3, 4:

> "Who may ascend into the hill of the Lord? Or who may stand in His Holy Place? He who has clean hands and a pure heart, who has not lifted up his soul to an idol, nor sworn deceitfully."

In speaking to the Church of earth's last days, Jesus bride is portrayed as being "arrayed in fine linen, clean and bright." That fine linen is said by God to be "the righteousness of saints" (Revelation 19:8).

VICTORY IN CHRIST

Rarely does an army win when it faces an opposing force with superior numbers. Yet the human family has for thousands of years been confronted by an enemy with more power, more wisdom, and a greater determination to win. But in the great controversy, God offers His people the companionship of angels (Psalm 34:7), the power of the Holy Spirit (Luke 11:13) and the presence of Jesus Himself (John 15:5). And He offers His Son's own righteousness. As God clothed Adam and Eve after their fall into sin (Genesis 3:21), He offers us "white garments"—the righteousness of Christ—"that [we] may be clothed" (Revelation 3:18).

When faced by a mighty opponent and with an army reduced by God to number only 300 men, Gideon was triumphant in his battle against what appeared to be an unconquerable enemy. In the same way, when our battles are so great that we are forced to rely only upon God for strength and deliverance, we can be confident that He is with us and not against us.

In the great controversy that rages mostly unseen, in the grand conflict between Christ and Satan being fought out in our very midst, God's promise is that we may stand triumphantly with Jesus in this world as we prepare for the world to come.

Wars, famines, disease outbreaks, soaring crime rates, uncontrollable drug problems, faithless believers and compromised belief systems are simply a revelation of the clarity of the issues we face. There is an unseen battle raging. A jealous devil is seeking to take the place of God. He has succeeded in doing so in the world. He has had unthinkable success in the church. The only battleground that is yet to fall to one or the other of the two protagonists in this great controversy is the battleground of your heart.

Where will you be when the great controversy comes to its conclusion? The decision is yours. By God's grace, you may be clothed in the righteousness of Jesus Christ. Open your heart to God and believe by faith that He accepts you and loves you.

The Christ who has already won the war against sin and unrighteousness will hold you and keep you, so that when Jesus returns to this earth, you will be found with the redeemed on a journey to the heavenly Canaan. Allow God to clothe you in the righteousness of Jesus today. And let each new today find you consecrating yourself to God, allowing Jesus to work "in you both to will and to do for His good pleasure" (Philippians 2:13).

Christ's kingdom will triumph. Christ's plans and purpose for this world will be fulfilled. One day there will be a new heavens, and a new earth wherein righteousness dwells. (2 Peter 3:13) Sin and sinners will be no more. Disease and death will be over. Worry, want and war will be gone forever. With no tempter to deceive we will rejoice around God's throne in the glory of His presence, walking in the light of His truth through the ceaseless ages of eternity.

AS YOU BEGIN THE NEXT CHAPTER...

No matter what we human beings plan for, we almost always have a backup plan—a Plan B.

Plan A: *A road trip across the country to visit family—but just before leaving, the car breaks down.*
Plan B: *A rental car, travel by air, or perhaps the trip rescheduled.*

Plan A: *Become a doctor—but alas, math and science courses are beyond me.*
Plan B: *Become a musician, or better yet, learn what God wants me to do.*

When Jesus gave the Great Commission to His Church, charging them with the task of reaching the entire world with the Good News of His plan of salvation, He had no Plan B.

On a Galilee morning 2,000 years ago, Jesus gave His Church their marching orders. He gave them the most important mission ever given to the world.

Go...teach...baptize, Jesus said in Matthew 28:18-20. This is God's Plan A for sharing the Gospel—the Good News—with those around us. Are we faithful in sharing the Gospel as Jesus opens the doors for us to do so?

Listen carefully for God's "still, small voice" urging you to personally "Go, teach, and baptize."

As you turn the page, Jesus will share with you how you can personally share His Plan A with your family, your friends, and many you will meet as God sets up "divine appointments" with them.

Mark Finley and his wife, Ernestine "Teenie," have teamed up in ministry throughout the years. Teenie is known worldwide for teaching natural lifestyle cooking. Together they have been involved in Christian ministry for over 40 years-preaching, teaching and offering spiritual growth workshops, and conducting over 100 evangelistic series that have spanned the globe with sermons translated into over 50 languages. Today, Pastor Finley and Teenie continue their ministry at the Living Hope School of Evangelism Training Center in Haymarket, Virginia.

CHAPTER 10

FAITHFULNESS IN MISSION: PARTICIPATING WITH CHRIST IN HIS WORK

IMAGINE JESUS ARRIVING IN HEAVEN IMMEDIATELY AFTER HIS ASCENSION. He is welcomed by millions of angels and representatives from unfallen worlds. The scene is one of joy and celebration. The entire heavenly host bursts into a rapturous song of praise:

> "Saying with a loud voice, 'Worthy is the Lamb that was slain to receive power, and riches, and wisdom, and strength, and honour, and glory, and blessing'"(Revelation 5:12).

In my imagination I see the mighty angel Gabriel approach Jesus, "Lord, you poured out your life on the Cross to redeem every person on Planet Earth. Your suffering was incomprehensible even to the angels. Your death provides eternal life for all who will accept it and believe.

Does everyone on Planet Earth know about the great sacrifice that has been made to save them? Have they all heard of your great love and the incredibly good news of salvation?'"

'"No, Gabriel, they have not all heard," the Savior responds. "Right now, there are "just a few of My followers in Jerusalem and Galilee who know of My great love.'"

"'Well, Master," continues Gabriel, 'what is your plan for everyone to know the story of salvation?"'

The Master replies, "I have commissioned all of my followers—- each believer—to carry the message of salvation into the entire world. I told them to tell others, who will in turn tell others, until the last person in the farthest corner of earth has heard the story."'

Gabriel's countenance changes. He detects a possible flaw in the Master's plan. "What if after awhile Peter forgets or grows weary of telling the story of the Cross and goes back to his fishing in the Sea of Galilee? What if James and John and Andrew join him? Suppose Matthew returns to his tax booth , and all the others lose their zeal and just don't tell others. What then? Or suppose these disciples die off, and the task is not complete, and your Church grows large and comfortable, and the hearts of your people no longer burn to tell the incredible story of your love. What if they are no longer faithful to the great commission you have given them? What is your backup plan?"'

After a pause the calm voice of the Lord Jesus says: "Gabriel, I have no other plan. I am counting on them to be faithful to the mission I have given them."

The scene, of course, is imaginary, but the lesson it teaches is for every generation: Christ has no other plan for spreading the Gospel. If the mission could have been completed by angels, it would have been completed long ago. But He invites us to cooperate with Him in His mission. The Great Commission to "make disciples of all nations" was given to His Church. The charge to preach the Gospel to every nation, people, and language was given to His Church. The call to be His witnesses was given to His Church.

CHRIST'S DIVINE PRIORITY

Christ clarifies His priority for His Church in His last message to them on a hillside in Galilee just before ascending to heaven. Matthew's Gospel tells the story in these words: "Then the eleven disciples went away into Galilee, into a mountain where Jesus had appointed them" (Matthew 28:16).

This divine appointment was of paramount importance. The meeting in Galilee was a crucial moment in the history of the Christian Church. It was so important that Jesus Himself set the appointment to meet with His disciples before He returned to heaven. It was so important that the angel at the tomb reminded the women who came to embalm Jesus body:

> "And go quickly, and tell his disciples that he is risen from the dead; and, behold, he goeth before you into Galilee; there shall ye see him: lo, I have told you" (Matthew 28:7).

When angels at the site of the resurrection confirm an appointment with Jesus, it must be important. But there is more. As the women return rejoicing to tell the story of their resurrected Lord to the disciples, Jesus Himself appears to them and declares, "Be not afraid: go tell my brethren that they go into Galilee, and there shall they see me" (Matthew 28:10).

The appointment at Galilee is so vitally important—it is so crucial for the entire future of the Christian Church—that it is one of the first things Jesus says to the women who came to the tomb and are now running to tell the story of His resurrection.

The disciples grasped the significance of this meeting with their Lord. They traveled over ninety miles on foot from Jerusalem to Galilee, braving the elements as well as hostile Jewish and Roman forces arrayed against them. They traversed desert sands, climbed rough mountain paths, walked miles on dusty dirt roads and crossed rivers to gather at the appointed time with their Master. It likely took them the better part of a week to get there. The word spread to Jesus' followers throughout the land, and around five hundred believers assembled that day in Galilee. They sensed that this day was to be one of the most significant in their lives. Jesus had something of overwhelming importance to tell them.

Suddenly, Jesus appeared in their midst. They were overwhelmed with joy. They now knew that He was the Messiah, and they fell at His feet to worship Him; but Matthew's Gospel records something quite strange: "And when they saw Him, they worshipped Him but some doubted" (Matthew 28:17).

Some doubted.... They doubted then, and they doubt now. They doubted there, and they doubt here... They doubted in the first century, and they doubt in the twenty-first century. Ellen White makes this insightful statement about doubt: "The obstacles that hinder our progress will never disappear before a halting, doubting spirit" (Ellen G. White, *Patriarchs and Prophets*, 290).

Christ's commission to His disciples was to go, advance, and conquer in My Name. Doubters never accomplish anything great for God. There are those who criticize the Church for the evangelistic methods it is using, but they themselves do very little to win souls to Jesus. These armchair critics writing from the comfortable convenience of their studies often direct their darts at those who are giving their lives in soul-winning ministry.

In a speech in the Sorbonne in Paris, Theodore Roosevelt made this poignant statement:

> "It is not the critic who counts; not the man who points out how the strong man stumbles, or where the doer of deeds could have done them better. The credit belongs to the man who is actually in the arena, whose face is marred by dust and sweat and blood; who strives valiantly; who errs, who comes short again and again, because there is no effort without error and shortcoming; but who

does actually strive to do the deeds; who knows great enthusiasms, the great devotions; who spends himself in a worthy cause; who at the best knows in the end the triumph of high achievement, and who at the worst, if he fails, at least fails while daring greatly, so that his place shall never be with those cold and timid souls who neither know victory nor defeat" (Theodore Roosevelt Speech, April 23,1910, in the Sorbonne in Paris, France).

It is the man or woman in the arena who really counts for God. The work of God on earth is not going to be finished by critics. It is not going to be finished by skeptics. It is not going to be finished by doubters. It is not going to be finished by people who undermine the integrity of God's end-time message and erode confidence in His last-day Church.

Jesus is not looking for critics, He is looking for Christians filled with the Holy Spirit who, armed with the Word, go out to change the world. It takes little courage to criticize what others are doing. It takes a lot of courage to witness to your friends and neighbors of the matchless charms of Christ, to distribute literature, give the sharing book of the year to a working associate, conduct a small group in your home, or hold a community outreach seminar or a lay evangelist meeting.

A DOUBTER CHANGED BY GRACE

When you think of one of the disciples who was a skeptical doubter, who do you think of first? Thomas, of course! But Thomas was not doubting now. He had seen his resurrected Lord. His faith was strong. All of us from time to time have our doubts. We all have moments of discouragement. Each one of us fails at times.

Thomas is the one disciple who is remembered because he doubted. In fact, Thomas the disciple is often known as "doubting Thomas." But if you study Thomas' life carefully, the opposite is true. Thomas was filled with courage. He is first mentioned in the Gospels when Jesus' life was in danger. Jesus had left Jerusalem, crossed the Jordan, and was in a much safer environment in the district of Galilee. The Jewish leaders were already plotting His death. It was at this time that Jesus learned of Lazarus' death. Jesus said to His disciples, "Let us go into Judaea again."

"Let us go to him" (John 11:7). Many of Jesus' disciples may have thought that it was foolhardy to risk the very real threat of arrest and execution for the sake of visiting the tomb of a dead friend. But Thomas was so loyal to Jesus that he was willing to die with his Lord..."Let us also go that we may die with Him" (John 11:16). What courage! What faith! What loyalty!

Although Thomas was not with the disciples when Jesus first appeared to them in the Upper Room, Jesus did appear to him later, and Thomas fell on his face and declared, "My Lord and My God!" John 20:28. All of Thomas' hopes and dreams were fulfilled in the resurrected Christ. Thomas was with the disciples on the Sea of Galilee when Jesus prepared them breakfast in the morning, and Thomas was awestruck with Peter, James, and John when Jesus filled their nets with fish after they had toiled all night and caught nothing.

Thomas was with the disciples on Pentecost and was filled with the Holy Spirit and participated in the baptism of 3,000 (Acts 1:17).

And Christian tradition tells us that Thomas became one of the Church's most courageous missionaries and planted the seed of the Gospel in India.

Can you identify with Thomas? Maybe you have doubted whether God can use you. Possibly you too have failed your Lord. Maybe you have made mistakes, compromised your conscience, and disappointed your Lord. Or possibly you have become complacent and lost your passion for sharing your faith. Here is the incredibly good news: Christ restores people who have fallen. He restored Thomas, and He can restore you.

His Spirit can awaken within each of us a renewed passion for His mission. He can shake us out of our Laodicean lethargy. He has plans for your life that you cannot yet imagine. He has not given up on you. He wants to use you powerfully in His closing work. He has no other plan but to use forgiven people, saved and transformed by His grace. He has no other plan but to empower His Church through the mighty working of the Holy Spirit to reach the world with His eternal truths for this crisis hour of earth's history.

THE DISCIPLES' DIVINE IMPERATIVE: THE LITTLE BIG WORD

On that morning in Galilee 2,000 years ago, Jesus gave His Church their marching orders. He outlined their priority. He gave them the most important mission ever given to the world. Matthew's Gospel records it in these words:

> And Jesus came and spake unto them, saying, "All power is given unto me in heaven and in earth. Go ye therefore, and teach all nations, baptizing them in the name of the Father, and of the Son, and of the Holy Ghost: Teaching them to observe all things whatsoever I have commanded you: and, lo, I am with you always, even unto the end of the world. Amen" (Matthew 28:18-20).

This commission was given to men and women, young and old , rich and poor, educated and uneducated. There were fisherman and farmers, tax collectors and merchants, carpenters and stone masons, sheep herders and weavers, in the crowd that day. These were lay people who were the future of the Christian Church. And Jesus said "Go." He did not say, " Wait."—Wait until you feel more comfortable about witnessing—He said Go. He did not say wait until the religious leaders give you permission He said Go. He did not say Wait until you have more training. He said Go. He did not say wait until the church board votes it, He said Go. He did not say wait until the conditions are right, He said Go. He did not say wait until a more convenient time, He said Go.

The truth of the matter is simply this: no one must give you permission to witness;you are a witness commissioned by Jesus to tell the story of His love and truth. Ellen White urges us that "The work of God in this earth can never be finished until the men and women comprising our church membership rally to the work and unite their efforts with those of ministers and church officers (Ellen G. White, *Testimonies* vol. 9, 116).

THE GREAT COMMISSION: A COMMAND TO BE OBEYED

James Hudson Taylor, founder of the Inland China Mission, spent fifty-one years sharing the Gospel in China. He once made this thought-provoking statement: "The Great Commission is not an option to be considered; it is a command to be obeyed."

Pastor Taylor recounts a remarkable experience that profoundly impacted his life. While traveling by boat one day, he entered conversation with a Chinese man who had once visited England, where he went by the name of Peter. The man listened attentively to the missionary's account of Christ's saving love and was even moved to tears, but refused the immediate acceptance of salvation. A little later, evidently in a mood of great despondency, Peter jumped overboard and sank into the dark, cold waters. In agonized suspense Taylor looked around for assistance and saw some fishermen in a fishing boat close by with a net.

"Drag over this spot. A man sank here and is drowning!"

"It is not convenient," was the unfeeling reply.

"Don't talk of *convenience*," cried the missionary. "A man is drowning."

"We are busy fishing and cannot come" they responded.

When Taylor urged them to come at once and offered to pay them, they demanded to know how much. His offer of five dollars was refused. He then said: "Do come quickly, and I will give you all the money I have—about fourteen dollars" Finally, the boat was brought and the net let down. Less than a minute was required to bring up the body, but all efforts at resuscitation failed. His body was lifeless. He had no pulse. His breath was gone. He died within reach of help.

To Hudson Taylor this incident was profoundly sad and pathetic in its significance. Were not those fishermen guilty of the death of the Chinese man, in that they had the opportunity and means of saving him but refused to use them? Most assuredly they were guilty. "And yet," says Taylor, "let us pause ere we pronounce judgment against them, lest a greater than Nathan answer, "*Thou art the man.*"

The Lord Jesus commands *me,* commands *us:* 'Go into *all* the world and preach the gospel to *every* creature.' Shall we say to *Him,* 'No, it is not convenient? 'Shall we tell *Him* that we are busy at other business and cannot go? In the light of eternity, souls are perishing. There are people all around us who are receptive to the Gospel if they only knew the truths of Scripture. While we often seem secure in the comfort of our churches, Christ's heart is broken over the lost. He sees what we often do not see, men and women lost without a Savior who might be saved if only someone would share the good news of Christ's redemptive love with them. There are also tens of thousands of committed Christians who are studying God's Word, seeking God's truth, and longing for answers about the future of our world.

Commenting on the story of Philip's encounter with the Ethiopian on the Gaza road, Ellen White says,

> "This Ethiopian represented a large class who need to be taught by such missionaries as Philip—men who will hear the voice of God and go where He sends them. There are many who are reading the Scriptures who cannot understand their true import. All over the world men and women are looking wistfully to heaven. Prayers and tears and inquiries go up from souls longing for light, for grace, for the Holy Spirit. Many are on the verge of the kingdom, waiting only to be gathered in" (Ellen G. White, *Acts of the Apostles*, 109).

Did you catch the significance of this statement? The Holy Spirit is at work stirring up hearts, enlightening minds, and leading people to search the Scriptures for truth. Just as the Ethiopian was studying the prophecies of the first coming of Christ in Isaiah 53, people all over the world are studying the prophecies of the Second Coming of Christ. They are praying for someone to explain the prophetic Word to them.

In the divine drama of destiny God providentially leads us to people who are looking for answers regarding life's deepest questions. If we are in tune with the Spirit's working, He will use us in powerful ways to witness for the Master. He will do for us "exceedingly, abundantly, above all that we ask or think" (Ephesians 3:20). God does not necessarily call the qualified, He qualifies those He calls. He is not necessarily looking at our ability, He is looking at our availability. God is not necessarily looking for those who believe they are knowledgeable, He is looking for people who know they don't know so they depend totally, absolutely, completely on Him.

WILLIAM CAREY: THE FATHER OF MODERN MISSIONS

William Carey, the father of modern missions, was called by God to go to India when he was in his 20s. As a young pastor of a small Baptist church at Mouton, England, he attempted to persuade the association that they should engage in world evangelization. He was told, "Sit down young man, and respect the opinions of your elders. If the Lord wants to convert the heathen, He will do it without your help"

William Carey never gave up on his conviction that God had called Him to India. He had a burning passion in His heart to reach a lost world with the love of Christ and the truths of Scripture. He began work as a shoe cobbler in England but put a map of the world on the wall of his shop with these words under the map, "I cobble shoes to pay expenses but soulwinning is my business." His longing to win lost souls to Jesus never left him, and in 1792 he sailed to India. In his lifetime of service, thousands were won to Christ and His kingdom. William Carey's motto, "Attempt great things for God and expect great things from God" became the motto of missionaries around the world. Like both William Carey and Hudson Taylor, we have a story to tell, a mission to accomplish, and divine truths to share. Jesus is longing to use each one of us in this crisis hour of earth's history.

DIVINE PROVISION

In Christ's great commission, He said, "all authority is given unto me, go you therefore..." Matthew 28:18, 19. The Greek word for *authority* or *power*, as the King James Version of the Bible puts it, is *Exousia*. It can be translated *authority, power*, or *divine privilege*. In His death on the Cross, Jesus triumphed over all the forces of evil, including evil spirits, the elements, disease, and death. He is the One who has absolute control of every situation.

Let's study some ways the Gospel writers used this word, *exousia*, to grasp its significance. Just before Jesus sent His disciples out on their first missionary journey, Matthew's gospel records—"And when He had called His twelve disciples to Him, He gave them power over unclean spirits, to cast them out, and to heal all kinds of sickness and all kinds of disease" (Matthew 10:1). The word *power* might also be translated "authority." Jesus has authority over the principalities and powers of hell, so success in His service is guaranteed. The messenger of the Lord assures us that

> "Christ gave His disciples their commission. He made full provision for the prosecution of the work and took upon Himself the responsibility for success. So long as they obeyed His Word and worked in connection with Him, they could not fail." (Ellen G. White, *Desire of Ages*, 811)

When we are faithful to His command and step out in faith to share Jesus' love with others, He supplies the power. We go in His strength, not ours. We go by His authority. He provides us with wisdom, strength, and courage. He has triumphed over the forces of evil. There is no situation too difficult for Jesus. When we accept His commission and witness for Him, we will see miracles, for He is the God of miracles. He will pour out His Holy Spirit through us.

A REMARKABLE ABOUT-FACE IN ADVENTIST HISTORY

In its early years, the Seventh-day Adventist Church grew rapidly. Pastors and members sensed they were called of God to participate in

Christ's mission of proclaiming the Three Angels' Messages to their friends, neighbors, and working associates. Adventist pastors devoted their energies to evangelism and planting new churches.

In 1886, Adventist evangelist G. B. Starr was interviewed by a writer for the Wabash, Indiana newspaper, the *Plain Dealer*. The reporter asked Elder Starr this fascinating question, regarding the past forty years of the Advent movement: "By what means have you carried forward your work so rapidly?" In other words, Why is the Seventh-day Adventist Church growing so rapidly?

Starr answered, "We have no settled pastors. Our churches are taught to take care of themselves, while nearly all our ministers work as evangelists in new fields." In this era of Adventist Church history, pastors were largely church planters entering new areas to build up the work of God. Some of our larger churches had full-time pastors, but this was the exception, not the norm. Following the New Testament model, lay people were committed to care for the church and witness in their communities. The members were committed to mission, and pastor/evangelists preached the Gospel in new areas.

> "In 30 years, from 1870 to 1900, the church grew in membership 430 percent, with a ratio of one new church planted each year for every three to four fulltime paid gospel ministers." (Fredrick Dana, *Adventist Review,* May 29, 2020).

The annual growth rate from 1870 to 1880 was a whopping 12 percent a year. But by 1900, with institutional development, organizational concerns, and theological challenges, the growth of the church slowed dramatically. Institutional development and administrative issues overshadowed missional focus. In 1909, the President of the General Conference, A. G. Daniels, reported that since 1901, 500 persons had been brought into church administration. This is astonishing, since there were only 1,200 ministerial workers in the field. The results were seen in a dramatic downturn in the growth of the

Church. From 1906 to 1909 the Adventist Church in North America grew by only 1 percent per year, while the annual national population growth rate was approximately double during the same period.

Ellen White was alarmed. She sent message after message to her colleagues in church leadership. In 1909 she made a powerful appeal to the General Conference administration and department leaders. She urged leadership on all levels of church organization to set the example by becoming actively involved in reaching the lost, especially in reaching the large cities. Her earnest appeals moved the hearts of church leadership. She said,

> "When I think of the many cities still unwarned, I cannot rest. It is distressing to think that they have been neglected so long.... Oh! that we might see the needs of these great cities as God sees them!" (Ellen G. White, *Manuscript*, talk to the General Conference Committee, June 11, 1909).

The response to Ellen White's solemn appeal was mixed. There was a verbal commitment to focus on evangelism and reach the massive populations in America's burgeoning cities, but very casual follow-through. Very little initial change occurred. Evangelistic meetings were conducted in a few places, but nothing significant happened. The church languished in Laodicean complacency.

A. G. Daniels himself was a proven soulwinner and effective evangelist. By 1910 he was beginning to powerfully sense the leading of the Holy Spirit to redirect the Adventist Church to its initial focus of proclaiming God's last-day message to the world. On a visit to California, it was his intent to visit Ellen White and share his convictions and a report of the growing emphasis on evangelism. He was stunned when she refused to see him. She was convinced that the Lord had spoken through her to Elder Daniels, and unless he heeded her counsel to wholeheartedly lead this movement into a major thrust in reaching the cites, there was little purpose in meeting him. God had spoken through her to him, and now it was up to him to implement the counsel given by God. It was his responsibility to lead the Adventist Church into a renewed emphasis on soulwinning and evangelism. Ellen White had nothing more to say to the president of the General Conference.

Elder Daniels was greatly humbled by this rebuke, accepted the counsel of the Lord, and wrote to Ellen White regarding his commitment to carry out the Lord's counsel. He conducted evangelistic meetings in major cities across America, held ministerial institutes, wrote articles on the necessity of reaching the cities, and used his influence among administrators, pastors, and members to redirect the Adventist Church to its original purpose of faithfulness to Christ's mission mandate. His influence, along with the influence of other godly leaders, made a dramatic difference. Pastors accepted the challenge. Church members heard God's call. Budgets were allocated. Outreach activities of all kinds were planned for the great cities of America.

At the 1913 General Conference Session the delegates heard an encouraging message read from God's messenger, now 85 years old. She expressed her deep satisfaction at the new direction the Church was taking as it re-engaged in active evangelism, using varied methods to reach people with God's last-day message. She wrote,

> "It has brought great rejoicing to my heart to see the marvelous transformations that have been wrought in the lives in some who chose to advance by faith in the way of the Lord...When they heeded the instruction that was sent and sought the Lord, God brought them into full light and enabled them to render acceptable service and bring about spiritual reformations.... He will never forsake or leave in uncertainty those who follow His leadings with full purpose of heart" (General Conference Bulletin, May 19, 1913, 34).

This statement is insightful. Our lives *are* transformed when we are committed to share Christ's message with others. Our witness to the world brings revival to the Church. Revival leads to evangelistic proclamation, and involvement in Christ's mission fosters, sustains, and nourishes revival.

At a crucial time in the history of the Seventh-day Adventist Church, God sent messages through His prophet to refocus our energies on mission. As a result, the Church made a dramatic about-face. God honored that commitment, and the Church grew rapidly in the ensuing years. Adventism at its heart is a mission movement. We are a witnessing community. We have been raised up by God to prepare a world for the soon return of our Lord. If we would ever lose this mission-driven passion, we would merely become another denomination on the landscape of churches.

We have a mission mandate echoing down the centuries given by Christ to the last of the living apostles. Here are John's words written from a rocky, barren outcrop on the Island of Patmos:

> "And I saw another angel fly in the midst of heaven, having the everlasting gospel to preach unto them that dwell on the earth, and to every nation, and kindred, and tongue, and people" Revelation14:6. The preaching of the everlasting Gospel leaps across geographical boundaries; it penetrates earth's remotest areas,; it reaches people of every language and culture. It impacts the entire world. The foundations of hell are shaken, and the forces of evil tremble. The Church will rise to its destiny. It will fulfill its purpose. It will accomplish Christ's mission.

> "Servants of God, with their faces lighted up and shining with holy consecration, will hasten from place to place to proclaim the message from heaven. By thousands of voices, all over the earth, the warning will be given" (Ellen G. White, *The Great Controversy* 670).

The power of Christ is greater than the power of the evil one. The love of Christ is a stronger motivation than the world's cheap allurements. The appeal of the eternal is greater than the appeal of the transitory pleasures of this life. In the blazing light of eternity, Christ invites us to readjust our priorities. The one thing that really matters is people saved by His grace, redeemed by His power, informed by His Word, and prepared for His soon return.

> "The salvation of sinners requires earnest, personal labor. We are to bear to them the word of life, not to wait for them to come to us. Oh, that I could speak words to men and women that would arouse them to diligent action! The moments now granted to us are few. We are standing upon the very borders of the eternal world. We have no time to lose. Every moment is golden and altogether too precious to be devoted merely to self-serving. Who will seek God earnestly and from Him draw strength and grace to be His faithful workers in the missionary field?" (Ellen G. White, *Testimonies*, vol 9, 117.)

Our witness will impact people for all eternity. Life and death hang in the balance. We can make a difference. Jesus will open divine doors for us. The "moments are few." This is our day of "golden opportunity." God is calling us to faithfulness in His mission of winning the lost now!

DIVINE PRESENCE

Jesus' priority is saving lost people. God had only one Son, and He sent Him on a rescue mission. Luke writes, "the Son of Man came to seek and save the lost." (Luke 19:10) Our Savior invites us to join Him in His mission of reaching the lost. As we partner with Him in His work, He promises us His power and His presence. In Matthew 28:20, He declares, "I am with you always, even to the end of the world." We are assured that:

> "It is in doing Christ's work that the church has the promise of His presence.... The very life of the church depends on her faithfulness in fulfilling the Lord's commission. To neglect this work is surely

to invite spiritual feebleness and decay. Where there is no active labor for others, love wanes and faith grows dim" (Ellen G. White, *The Desire of Ages*, 815).

When you share Jesus with a colleague at work, Jesus is there by your side. When you pass out literature from house to house, Jesus is by your side. When you give Bible studies or are actively involved in some health or family life, youth ministry, or children's ministry witnessing for Jesus, He is by your side. His presence is there to impress your thoughts, guide your words, and empower your witness.

Imagine that scene in heaven again., Jesus speaks to Gabriel "I have no other plan, if my people do not share the message of salvation with others, they may never know. If my people are not faithful to accomplish my mission, they will be in this sinful world much longer than necessary."

What a tragedy to disappoint our Lord in this critical hour of earth's history! What a tragedy to slumber on the knife edge of eternity. Will you open your heart to Jesus right now and make a renewed commitment to be His witness in this final generation? Will you pray, "Lord, use me? I accept the challenge. I will go in your power to tell the story of Your love and truth." Will you make an all-out commitment to be faithful to the call of Christ?

Together as we are actively involved in His mission to the world, His promise in Mathew 24:14—"And this gospel of the kingdom will be preached in all the world as a witness to all nations and then the end will come"—will be fulfilled. Together as we accept the challenge of faithfulness to His mission, Jesus will come, and we will go home because He has no other plan to finish His work.

A TIME OF CONSECRATION

Why not open your heart to Him wherever you are and rededicate your life to be faithful to His last day message and mission? Spend a few moments in prayer, speaking to Jesus about your renewed commitment to faithfulness. If He impresses you to make changes in your life, say "yes" to the prompting of the Holy Spirit. Ask Jesus to deeply impress you with a new passion for the salvation of those people within your sphere of influence and make the practical changes in your life to reach them for Him. Listen for His still small voice, impressing your mind, as you pray right now.

AS YOU BEGIN THE NEXT CHAPTER...

For certain, this book will avoid getting sidetracked by any focus on the polarity of partisan politics currently monopolizing attention in America. However, let us note that three words in the current partisan bickering are: "The Big Lie."

As we prepare to move forward now to the next chapter on "Spiritualism," might we suggest replacing that phrase with "The Bigger Lie"? Then again, let's go all the way to "The Biggest Lie." Yes, the Biggest. The Oldest. The ***First Lie Ever!***

Let's find that lie and notice what it says. When God made Adam and Eve and gave them their beautiful Garden of Eden home, He gave them also a warning about a certain tree in the middle of the Garden: "Of the tree of the knowledge of good and evil you shall not eat, for in the day that you eat of it ***you shall surely die"*** Genesis 2:17, NKJV, emphasis supplied.

Later, the fallen angel Lucifer, in the form of a serpent, said to Eve: "You will **NOT** surely die" Gen 3:4, NKJV, emphasis supplied. The first lie. The biggest lie. The lie that nobody would ever really die. Oh, a person's body might temporarily die, but their spirit—their conscious personhood—would live on.

As if to prove this, Lucifer, renamed Satan, would employ his fellow fallen angels to impersonate the dead friends and loved ones of the living left behind. These "living spirits" of the dead would imitate their appearance, voice, and personality and would convincingly know the events of their past lives.

Through time, "spiritualism" would take many forms. For some, it would be their primary religious experience. For others, it would involve them in seances, in seeking answers from "the beyond" through such media as the supposedly harmless parlor game Ouija™, or assuming that the souls of the departed guide the living through personal spirit "guides" or even through a connection with the world of astrology.

But what if the first great lie is just that—a total, utter, satanic lie? What if the dead do not appear to us, speak to us, guide us? Want to learn the truth? It begins with another turn of the page!

John Lomacang is pastor of the Thompsonville, Illinois, SDA Church located at the 3ABN Worship Center. John and his wife, Angela, have been with 3ABN for seventeen years. Pastor Lomacang attended Oakwood University in Huntsville, Alabama, as well as Manhattan College in New York and Valencia College in Orlando, Florida. A professional Christian singer-songwriter for more than thirty-five years, he sang with the Heritage Singers and has three CDs and a DVD available. Their singing and speaking ministry has taken John and Angela to more than sixty-four countries and to nearly every state in the U.S. Recently, Pastor Lomacang presented four program series called "Anchors of Truth" on 3ABN, including "Unclean Spirits" and "Unclean Spirits Unplugged" (on the occult and the entertainment industry). Pacific Press has published his life story, titled *Abandoned But Not Alone.* Pastor Lomacang believes that the Lord called him and Angela to the ministry. He loves his wife, he loves the Lord, and he plans on spending eternity with both!

CHAPTER 11

SPIRITUALISM

"THE SHOT HEARD 'ROUND THE WORLD," BEGAN BOTH THE BATTLE OF CONCORD on April 19, 1775, and the American Revolutionary War—and propelled the rise of the United States of America.

"The lie heard around the world," began the earthly battle between God and Satan, between truth and lies, and between Spirituality and Spiritualism, as chronicled in Genesis 3:1-3:

> "Now the serpent was more cunning than any beast of the field which the LORD God had made. And he said to the woman, 'Has God indeed said, "You shall not eat of every tree of the garden"'? And the woman said to the serpent, 'We may eat the fruit of the trees of the garden; but of the fruit of the tree which is in the midst of the garden, God has said, "You shall not eat it, nor shall you touch it, lest you die."'"

In the Garden of Eden, Satan planted the lie, "You will not surely die" (Genesis 3:4, NKJV). This, the exact opposite of what God said to Adam:

"But of the tree of the knowledge of good and evil you shall not eat, for in the day that you eat of it you shall surely die" (Genesis 2:17, NKJV).

Spirituality—God's statement.
Spiritualism—Satan's statement.

Which statement do you believe?

"You will not surely die... you have an immortal soul," is a 6,000-year-old lie that refuses to die.

SPIRITUALISM IS PREDICATED ON THE BELIEF THAT MAN *HAS* A SOUL

With an immortal soul, some portion of a person lives on after death and allows the living to communicate with the dead. Dead relatives can contact you, or the deceased are now your guardian angels. Internet posts wish dead relatives, "Happy birthday in heaven." The dead are asked for advice, the living believing the dead respond.

Following a surgical operation, some report having died, floating above their bodies before returning. Some even say they went to heaven and returned to earth with a message from God.

Mediums claim the ability to conjure up the spirits of the dead and to stand between the living and the dead. Finally, some supposedly have dead relatives physically reappear to them. Songs have been written claiming to have friends in high or heavenly places.

But all these claims are misleading, for David the psalmist wrote, "The dead praise not the LORD, neither any that go down into silence" (Psalm 115:17, NKJV). The dead go down into silence, not up into praise.

Unfortunately many pastors teach that the deceased go to heaven at the time of death; they teach it with such conviction that one would think it's based on the Bible. Why is it important to trust God's Word over experiences and speculation? By turning to God's Word we can see how it counteracts Satan's false claims.

"And the LORD God formed man of the dust of the ground, and breathed into his nostrils the breath of life; man became a living soul" (Genesis 2:7, KJV). Adam *became* a "living soul." Adam was *not* given *a soul*. The soul is created by the combination of the "dust of the ground" and God's "breath of life."

In Genesis 2:7 the word *soul* is the Hebrew word, *nephesh*. Translated from the Hebrew, it means, Adam became a "breathing creature." Job clarifies the relationship between the breath and the spirit. "All the while my breath is in me, and the spirit of God is in my nostrils" (Job 27:3, KJV). The "spirit" that returns to God (see Ecclesiastes 12:7) is synonymous with the breath of life that He gave Adam when creating him. The soul does not exist apart from the body.

SPIRITUALISM IS PREDICATED ON THE BELIEF THAT MAN IS NATURALLY IMMORTAL

The Bible says only God has immortality; God exists in a light that no one can approach, no one has seen, or even can see (1 Timothy 6:15, 16, NKJV). When people say that they died and went toward a light, according to Paul that supposed light could not be God's presence or heaven.

The prophet Ezekiel confirms man's mortality, "Behold, all souls are Mine; The soul of the father as well as the soul of the son is Mine; The soul who sins shall die" (Ezekiel 18:4, NKJV).

The word *soul* refers to the complete person, not a part of the person, not a separate entity that exists inside the body that is immortal.

SPIRITUALISM IS PREDICATED ON THE BELIEF THAT THE DECEASED ARE LIVING IN HEAVEN, NOT IN THE GRAVE

"Homegoing Services" is a new term in Christian circles to suggest that as soon as we die, we go "home" to heaven, so we celebrate their leave-taking with a "homegoing service" at a church. But the Bible teaches, "If I wait, the grave is mine house: I have made my bed in the darkness" (Job 17:13, KJV). Job also writes, "As the cloud disappears and vanishes away, so he who goes down to the grave does not come up. He shall never return to his house, nor shall his place know him anymore" (Job 7:9, 10, NKJV). The *grave* is the only *home* that we will be in until the resurrection.

It is amazing that people are taken to the cemetery and buried, but the minister says that the deceased is going "home." It is an appendage to Satan's first lie. When we reject the truth that death is the end of life, we have to keep creating seductive lies to justify our false belief in spiritualism.

How much better would it be if the grieving family were given Job's comforting words:

> "But man dies and is laid away; indeed he breathes his last and where is he? As water disappears from the sea, and a river becomes parched and dries up, So man lies down and does not rise. Till the heavens are no more, they will not awake nor be roused from their sleep. Oh, that You would hide me in the grave, that You would conceal me until Your wrath is past, that You would appoint me a set time, and remember me! If a man dies, shall he live again? All the days of my hard service I will wait, till my change comes" (Job 14:10–14, NKJV).

SPIRITUALISM IS PREDICATED ON THE BELIEF THAT THE DEAD ARE INVOLVED IN LIFE

The wise man Solomon reiterates what God already said about death.

> "For the living know that they shall die: but the dead know not any thing, neither have they any more a reward; for the memory of them is forgotten. Also their love, and their hatred, and their envy, is now perished; neither have they any more a portion for ever in any thing that is done under the sun" (Ecclesiastes 9:5, 6, KJV).

- The dead don't know what the living know.
- The memories that they had are no longer there.
- Affections that were good or evil perish at death.
- The dead are no longer involved in the transactions of the living.

Taking into account the finality of death, Solomon encourages us with the following words, "Whatever your hand finds to do, do it with your might; for there is no work or device or knowledge or wisdom in the grave where you are going" (Ecclesiastes 9:10, NKJV). The psalmist David wrote, "His breath goeth forth, he returneth to his earth; in that very day his thoughts perish" (Psalm 146:4, KJV).

SPIRITUALISM IS PREDICATED ON THE BELIEF THAT THE DEAD ARE AWAKE, NOT ASLEEP

The Old and New Testaments both teach that death is a sleep. Let's begin with the Old Testament. When the kings and leaders of Israel died, they *slept*: "So David slept with his fathers, and was buried in the city of David" (1 Kings 2:10, KJV).

The key term in the phrase, *slept with his fathers* is the Hebrew word *shakhav,* which means, "to lie down to sleep" or "to be deceased."

When speaking of the fate of King David, the apostle Peter said:

> "Men and brethren, let me speak freely to you of the patriarch David, that he is both dead and buried, and his tomb is with us to this day" (Acts 2:29, NKJV).

"For David did not ascend into the heavens" (Acts 2:34, NKJV). David is still in his grave awaiting the resurrection.

Jesus also used the word *sleep* when speaking to Martha and His disciples about Lazarus' death:

> "'Our friend Lazarus sleeps, but I go that I may wake him up.' Then His disciples said, 'Lord, if he sleeps he will get well.' However, Jesus spoke of his death, but they thought that He was speaking

> about taking rest in sleep. Then Jesus said to them plainly, 'Lazarus is dead. And I am glad for your sakes that I was not there, that you may believe. Nevertheless let us go to him'" (John 11:11-15).

Notice what Jesus said when He called Lazarus to life: "Now when He had said these things, He cried with a loud voice, "Lazarus, come forth!" (John 11:43, NKJV.) Jesus did not say, "Lazarus, come down."

There are those who teach that Lazarus was in heaven and that then, Jesus called him back to earth. But imagine how disappointed Lazarus would be if he were in heaven and had to return to this sinful world! That suggestion is just another link in the chain of falsehoods about death.

SPIRITUALISM IS PREDICATED ON THE BELIEF THAT WE CAN SEE THE SPIRIT OF OUR LOVED ONE

People report seeing spirits, even spirits of dead relatives! From all we have learned about death, what are these apparitions? Let's look at the Bible story of King Saul visiting the witch of Endor, hoping to talk to the dead prophet Samuel.

> "Then said Saul unto his servants, seek me a woman that hath a familiar spirit, that I may go to her, and enquire of her. And his servants said to him, Behold, there is a woman that hath a familiar spirit at Endor" (1 Samuel 28:7, KJV).

The word *familiar* is associated with the word *family,* meaning someone who is recognizable. These apparitions are evil spirits appearing in the form of one who was known. God warned against consulting the dead, because it gives Satan an opportunity to deceive through "familiar spirits." "Give no regard to mediums and familiar spirits; do not seek after them, to be defiled by them: I am the LORD your God" (Leviticus 19:31, NKJV).

The Bible makes clear that Saul did not actually see the dead prophet Samuel, but rather, a familiar spirit:

> "And the king said to her, 'Do not be afraid. What did you see?' And the woman said to Saul, 'I saw a spirit ascending out of the earth.' So he said to her, 'What is his form?' And she said, 'An old man is coming up, and he is covered with a mantle.' And Saul perceived that it was Samuel, and he stooped with his face to the ground and bowed down" (1 Samuel 28:13, 14, NKJV).

One of the first things Jesus said concerning signs of the end was, "Take heed that no one deceives you" (Matthew 24:4, NKJV). One of the most effective ways of deception is thinking that you are communicating with your dead relative, when in fact you are communicating with a demon.

> "A man or a woman who is a medium, or who has familiar spirits, shall surely be put to death; they shall stone them with stones. Their blood shall be upon them" (Leviticus 20:27, NKJV).

As we approach the end of the world, these apparitions will become more prevalent. "Now the Spirit expressly says that in latter times some will depart from the faith, giving heed to deceiving spirits and doctrines of demons" (1 Timothy 4:1, NKJV). Our only safeguard against the influence of evil spirits is to believe God's Word.

SPIRITUALISM OVERLOOKS THE NEED FOR A RESURRECTION

Just as Jesus cried, 'Lazarus, come forth!' in John 11:43, NKJV, He will again cry,

> "All who are in the graves will hear His voice and come forth—those who have done good, to the resurrection of life, and those who have done evil, to the resurrection of condemnation" (John 5:28, 29, NJKV).

Important in the exchange between Jesus and Martha is the statement that those who believe in Him "shall never die." Jesus was saying that even though the Christian may experience the *first death*, they are exempted from the *second death*, because that one only affects the wicked. The apostle John mentions the second death in the book of Revelation.

> "Blessed and holy is he who has part in the first resurrection. Over such the second death has no power, but they shall be priests of God and of Christ, and shall reign with Him a thousand years" (Revelation 20:6, NKJV).

The second death involves the judgment of the lake of fire. It is the final judgment on sin and on those who have not accepted Jesus as their Lord. Even in this teaching, the Bible does not support an immortal, eternally burning soul. "And do not fear those who kill the body but cannot kill the soul. But rather fear Him who is able to destroy both soul and body in hell" (Matthew 10:28, NKJV). In the final judgment sin and sinners will be eternally destroyed.

In pulpits of the world where ministers teach that the deceased are now in heaven, the resurrection has been largely omitted. However, Jesus did not exclude the resurrection from His teachings.

He taught two resurrections—two destinations—the Resurrection of Life or the Resurrection of Condemnation. The destinations do not become apparent until Jesus returns. "And behold, I am coming quickly, and My reward is with Me, to give to every one according to his work" (Revelation 22:12, NKJV).

Simply put, our dead relatives don't go to heaven before us, and we don't go to heaven before them. We are caught up *together* so that we can *meet* the Lord together.

> "For the Lord Himself will descend from heaven with a shout, with the voice of an archangel, and with the trumpet of God. And the dead in Christ will rise first. Then we who are alive and remain shall be caught up together with them in the clouds to meet the Lord

in the air. And thus we shall always be with the Lord. Therefore comfort one another with these words" (1 Thessalonians 4:16-18, NKJV).

SPIRITUALISM'S "WHAT-ABOUTS"

Absent from the Body: What about the belief, *to be absent from the body is to be present with the Lord?* This belief is commonly used to refer to dying and going immediately to heaven, but it does not mention the word *death* at all. An important point is, a single passage cannot override what the Bible collectively teaches about death. Here is the full context of Paul's statement:

"For we know that if our earthly house, this tent, is destroyed, we have a building from God, a house not made with hands, eternal in the heavens. For in this we groan, earnestly desiring to be clothed with our habitation which is from heaven, if indeed, having been clothed, we shall not be found naked. For we who are in this tent groan, being burdened, not because we want to be unclothed, but further clothed, that mortality may be swallowed up by life. Now He who has prepared us for this very thing is God, who also has given us the Spirit as a guarantee. So we are always confident, knowing that while we are at home in the body we are absent from the Lord. For we walk by faith, not by sight. We are confident, yes, well pleased rather to be absent from the body and to be present with the Lord. Therefore we make it our aim, whether present or absent, to be well pleasing to Him" (2 Corinthians 5:1-9, NKJV).

We long for the day when the trials of life will end eternally. This life is one of despair. That's why Paul wrote, "We are confident, yes, well pleased rather to be absent from the body and to be present with the Lord." The body that Paul is desiring to be *absent from,* is this mortal body. That is why he was looking forward to the day when "mortality may be swallowed up by life." Mortality will be swallowed up when, as Paul wrote in 1 Corinthians 15:53, "This mortal must put on immortality." This change takes place at the return of Jesus, not at death. The apostle Paul did not promote conflicting views about life and death. When we combine what he wrote on the subject of life, death, the resurrection, and the change from mortal to immortal, the confusion ends.

Heaven is the ultimate home for those who trust in Jesus. But going to that home does not happen at death. Paul wrote:

> "For our citizenship is in heaven, from which we also eagerly wait for the Savior, the Lord Jesus Christ, who will transform our lowly body that it may be conformed to His glorious body, according to the working by which He is able even to subdue all things to Himself" (Philippians 3:20, 21, NKJV).

Jesus wrote:

> "Let not your heart be troubled; you believe in God, believe also in Me. In My Father's house are many mansions; if it were not so, I would have told you. I go to prepare a place for you. And if I go and prepare a place for you, I will come again and receive you to Myself; that where I am, there you may be also" (John 14:1-3, NKJV).

The only means of going to heaven is, as Jesus said, "I will come again and receive you."

THE THIEF ON THE CROSS

What about the promise that Jesus made to the thief on the Cross? Didn't the thief go to heaven the same day that Jesus made the promise? Let us look at the full statement surrounding the event.

What did the thief ask Jesus?

> "Then he said to Jesus, 'Lord, remember me when You come into Your kingdom.' And Jesus said to him, 'Assuredly, I say to you, today you will be with Me in Paradise'" (Luke 23:42, 43, NKJV).

The thief implored Jesus, "Remember me when you come."

This is the same request that Job asked in the Old Testament:

> "Oh, that You would hide me in the grave, that You would conceal me until Your wrath is past, that You would appoint me a set time, and *remember me!*" (Job 14:13, NKJV, emphasis supplied.)

Jesus did not go to heaven the same day that He made the promise to the thief. He went to heaven after His resurrection. On the day of His resurrection Jesus met Mary at the tomb.

> "Jesus said to her, 'Do not cling to Me, *for I have not yet ascended* to My Father; but go to My brethren and say to them, "I am ascending to My Father and your Father, and to My God and your God"'" (John 20:17, NKJV, emphasis supplied).

The misunderstanding behind the thief on the Cross is *punctuation,* not *theology*. When the comma is properly placed, it harmonizes with the rest of the Bible's teaching on the topic of death and resurrection. The thief did not go to heaven on crucifixion day.

He was given the assurance that when Jesus returned, he would be taken to Paradise. When the Bible was written, it did not have punctuation marks. Correctly written, it should have been, "And Jesus said to him, 'Assuredly, I say to you today, you will be with Me in Paradise'" (Luke 23:43, NKJV, punctuation alteration supplied).

SPIRITUALISM LAYS THE FOUNDATION FOR THE FINAL TEST

The birth of spiritualism in America opened the door for Satan's end-time deceptions. Ellen White describes the rise of modern spiritualism like this:

> "I saw that the mysterious knocking in New York and other places was the power of Satan, and that such things would be more and more common, clothed in a religious garb so as to lull the deceived

> to greater security and to draw the minds of God's people, if possible, to those things and cause them to doubt the teaching and power of the Holy Ghost."

The spirit manifestations were mostly confined to the city of Rochester, known as the "Rochester knockings." The heresy spread beyond the expectations of anyone. See *Early Writings*, 83.

In 1848 mysterious rappings were heard in the home of the Fox family at Hydesville, a community about thirty-five miles east of the city of Rochester, New York. At a time when there were various conjectures as to the cause of the rappings, Ellen White announced, on the authority of the vision given to her, that they were a manifestation of spiritualism, that this phenomenon would develop rapidly, and in the name of religion would gain popularity and deceive multitudes, developing into Satan's last-day masterpiece of deception. (From the Appendix to *Early Writings*, 300.)

How amazing that while God was establishing truths that had been lost, Satan was seeking ways to interrupt the resurgence of truth by the introduction of spiritualism in America.

Ellen White also explained how the false teaching on death lays the foundation for spiritualism:

> "The doctrine of man's consciousness in death, especially the belief that spirits of the dead return to minister to the living, has prepared the way for modern spiritualism. If the dead are admitted to the presence of God and holy angels, and privileged with knowledge far exceeding what they before possessed, why should they not return to the earth to enlighten and instruct the living? If, as taught by popular theologians, spirits of the dead are hovering about their friends on earth, why should they not be permitted to communicate with them, to warn them against evil, or to comfort them in sorrow? How can those who believe in man's consciousness in death reject what comes to them as divine light

communicated by glorified spirits? Here is a channel regarded as sacred, through which Satan works for the accomplishment of his purposes" (*The Great Controversy*, 551).

The false claims of spiritualism laid the foundation for the final coalition against God and against those who stand on God's Word. Through spiritualism Satan (*the dragon*—Revelation 12:9) forms a three-way coalition by uniting with *the Beast*—the religious leaders of Rome, and *the False Prophet*—Christian leaders who reject the truths of God's Word. In Revelation 16:13, 14, NKJV, we read:

> "And I saw three unclean spirits like frogs coming out of the mouth of the dragon, out of the mouth of the beast, and out of the mouth of the false prophet. For they are spirits of demons, performing signs, which go out to the kings of the earth and of the whole world, to gather them to the battle of that great day of God Almighty."

Satan has seen the power of God displayed, and he will produce a counterfeit, such as bringing fire down from heaven to capture the human imagination and lead many to believe that God is behind these spectacular displays. "He performs great signs, so that he even makes fire come down from heaven on the earth in the sight of men" Revelation 13:13, NKJV).

Ellen White describes Satan's "concern" for God's people:

> "As the people of God approach the perils of the last days, Satan holds earnest consultation with his angels as to the most successful plan of overthrowing their faith. He sees that the popular churches are already lulled to sleep by his deceptive power. By pleasing sophistry and lying wonders he can continue to hold them under his control. Therefore he directs his angels to lay their snares especially for those who are looking for the second advent of Christ and endeavoring to keep all the commandments of God" (*Testimonies to Ministers*, 472).

Ellen White's description clearly describes the Seventh-day Adventist movement. Through obedience to God's Word they are safeguarded against Satan's aim to lead the world to false worship:

> "And he deceives those who dwell on the earth by those signs which he was granted to do in the sight of the beast, telling those who dwell on the earth to make an image to the beast who was wounded by the sword and lived" (Revelation 13:14, NKJV).

> "We need not be deceived. Wonderful scenes, with which Satan will be closely connected, will soon take place. God's Word declares that Satan will work miracles. He will make people sick, and then will suddenly remove from them his satanic power. They will then be regarded as healed. These works of apparent healing will bring Seventh-day Adventists to the test. Many who have had great light will fail to walk in the light, because they have not become one with Christ" (*Selected Messages,* bk. 2, 53).

Any rejection of truth, any acceptance of spiritualism, will make one susceptible to Satan's ultimate deception—the personation of Christ. In Isaiah 14:14 Satan made the claim, "I will be like the Most High." In the closing scenes of the contest between truth and error, Satan will deceive the world concerning the return of Jesus:

> "As the crowning act in the great drama of deception, Satan himself will personate Christ. The church has long professed to look to the Saviour's advent as the consummation of her hopes. Now the great deceiver will make it appear that Christ has come. In different parts of the earth, Satan will manifest himself among men as a majestic being of dazzling brightness, resembling the description of the Son of God given by John in the Revelation. [Revelation 1:13-15.] The glory that surrounds him is unsurpassed

> by anything that mortal eyes have yet beheld. The shout of triumph rings out upon the air, 'Christ has come! Christ has come!' The people prostrate themselves in adoration before him, while he lifts up his hands, and pronounces a blessing upon them, as Christ blessed his disciples when he was upon the earth. His voice is soft and subdued, yet full of melody. In gentle, compassionate tones he presents some of the same gracious, heavenly truths which the Saviour uttered; he heals the diseases of the people, and then, in his assumed character of Christ, he claims to have changed the Sabbath to Sunday, and commands all to hallow the day which he has blessed. He declares that those who persist in keeping holy the seventh day are blaspheming his name by refusing to listen to his angels sent to them with light and truth. This is the strong, almost overmastering delusion. Like the Samaritans who were deceived by Simon Magus, the multitudes, from the least to the greatest, give heed to these sorceries, saying, This is 'the great power of God'" (*The Great Controversy*, 624).

Without a clear understanding of the truth about death our only safety against the teachings of spiritualism is being firmly grounded on the Word of God in knowledge and practice.

> "None but those who have fortified the mind with the truths of the Bible will stand through the last great conflict. To every soul will come the searching test: Shall I obey God rather than men? The decisive hour is even now at hand. Are our feet planted on the rock of God's immutable word? Are we prepared to stand firm in defense of the commandments of God and the faith of Jesus?" (*The Great Controversy*, 554.)

Preparation to stand in the decisive hour before us must be made now. By God's grace and truth our stand on His Word will be firm.

SPIRITUALISM'S SUCCESS IS PREDICATED ON THE PROLIFERATION OF DARKNESS:

There was a time when exposure to any aspect of spiritualism meant you were sequestered behind a curtain, or in a dark room, speaking to a fortune teller or a palm reader. While those venues still exist, Satan has extended his tentacles through media portals. Movies, social media, On-demand, and portable digital devices have become the open door to the sinister world of spiritualism.

The forces of darkness have enlisted the occult industry to produce content that entangle young impressionable minds. Because the impact of media on the brain is closely studied, content creators produce the next sequence of a movie to be darker and more addicting than the previous. Movie watchers are demanding scarier and more satanic content as they find themselves helplessly incarcerated by the lure of spiritualism.

Satan also uses clean-cut mediums to present his demonic content in an apparently innocent fashion. Maybe you've seen the tear-filled audiences as a contemporary looking man or woman say that they have information, that they say, came from a dead relative that crossed over to life on the other side. On other occasions books are written that present the testimony of a young child that contradicts the Bible. Not only are audiences spell bound they embrace his apparently innocent experience as legitimate and reject the Scriptures. Therefore, we are warned, "Be sober, be vigilant; because your adversary the devil walks about like a roaring lion, seeking whom he may devour." 1 Peter 5:8 (NKJV).

Satan's ambition is clear, he is preparing the world for the overmastering delusion that will take the world by storm. We read in "And I saw three unclean spirits like frogs coming out of the mouth of the dragon, out of the mouth of the beast, and out of the mouth of the false prophet. (14) For they are spirits of demons, performing signs, which go out to the kings of the earth and of the whole world, to gather them to the battle of that great day of God Almighty." Revelation 16:13–14 (NKJV).

In these closing hours while spiritualism is bombarding the world, God calls us to be selective about the forms of media we expose ourselves to. There is no such thing as innocent darkness. When Jesus returns, spiritualism in all forms will be eradicated. Until then, we should adopt the declaration of David, "I will set nothing wicked before my eyes; I hate the work of those who fall away; It shall not cling to me." Psalm 101:3 (NKJV). In all forms of entertainment, guard your senses as one preparing for eternity.

THE RETURN OF JESUS ENDS SPIRITUALISM

The return of Jesus is the grandest event of human history. On that glorious day, the sorrows of life and the certainty of death will be forever erased. The lie of the archdeceiver will give way to the promise of the Lifegiver. Death is not an alternate route to heaven. It is simply the end of life— the sad fate of mortal man. That is why Paul summarized the two great contrasts of our reality, "For the wages of sin is death, but the gift of God is eternal life in Christ Jesus our Lord" Romans 6:23, NKJV.

God is calling us back to the truth of His Word so that those in darkness can have an opportunity to be rescued from the false teachings of spiritualism. This is the hour to return to the sure Word. Now is the time to abandon the teachings and practices that create confusion. Many are yet to come out of spiritual Babylon. God is calling His people out of spiritual Babylon. Faithfulness to God's Word will help lead them out.

The dead are sleeping, waiting the call of the Lifegiver. No conscious communication is taking place between the living and the dead. Every belief that we embrace must be established on the supreme authority of the Bible only. When we consult the Bible, the false teachings of spiritualism are refuted, and we can anchor our trust in God's Word.

AS YOU BEGIN THE NEXT CHAPTER...

In this book, we've been hearing a "prophetic call to faithfulness." And for we as Adventists, a part of that call is to take a look at what we call *church standards*. As a worldwide fellowship of currently around 22 million members, some areas of Adventist standards focus on: dress and adornment, health and diet, recreation and entertainment, sexuality and relationships, Sabbath-keeping, styles of worship, use of money, loyal citizenship, and speech (avoiding profane, vulgar, or blasphemous language).

For some—especially the young of the church—standards may seem negative: the "do's and don'ts"—the *rules*. One challenge as we close in on Christ's return and especially as church leaders issue that heartfelt "call to faithfulness," is to help the young and all members see that the love of Jesus is the most positive force in all the universe—and it is ***this*** that should saturate and be the foundation of every church standard we teach and believe.

The closer we draw to the end of time here on earth, the more divided our world's population becomes, and the greater the contrast between those who follow Jesus and those who don't. As the rest of the world sees the difference Christ makes in the lives of His followers, the more they are drawn to Him.

And that difference is best seen in how God's people choose to live by the highest possible standards in every area of their lives. Of course, those high standards are enabled as Jesus lives in His people through His Holy Spirit.

The writer of the next chapter offers a thought-provoking and fresh, new look at the topic of standards. May it challenge and bless you!

Lewis Walton is the author of 14 books, the latest of which is *The Lucifer Diary*, which is a portrayal of the Great Controversy theme as if seen through an angel's eyes. His other books include *Morning's Trumpet*, *Omega*, and *Omega II.* He is a tax attorney in Marina del Rey, a coastal community west of Los Angeles, and practices with his son. Prior to becoming a lawyer, he was a newscaster, and reported such stories as the Cuban Missile Crisis and the assassination of John Kennedy.

CHAPTER 12

STANDARDS: A SHINING LIGHT ON THE PATH HOME

STANDARDS: THAT'S JUST A QUAINT TERM OUT OF A FADING YESTERDAY, ISN'T IT?

- **A time when one might hear:** "Look, a lady with earrings just came into church. Must be a visitor. Be sure to welcome her."
- **Or see on a church potluck sign:** "This potluck is entirely vegetarian. Ask any of the hostesses for their recipe."
- **Or fail to see,** in an Adventist home, entertainment that looked more like Hollywood than Heaven.

Are standards just relics of a legalistic past? Or might they be rooted in Scripture?

Ask epidemiologists and secular filmmakers who come from around the world to Adventist enclaves like Loma Linda, seeking to learn how a surprising number of people can live to 100, free from diseases that claim others decades sooner.

Ask Bill Lee, a Chinese restaurateur who loved to wander around his establishment with a scotch in one hand and a cigar in the other—except when my father-in-law came in. Then, Bill's drink disappeared and his cigar was held behind his back. Why? Because he knew, without having to ask, that a table full of people with Dr. Marion Barnard *stood for something.*

Ask the thief on the Cross, whose first act after being promised salvation by the Redeemer, was to stop swearing and start acting like the Lord he had accepted.

So I ask again: are standards just a whimsical relic out of an era before we really understood that salvation is by faith? While reflecting on that, ask yourself this: why did Paul, who was the apostle of salvation by faith, use Hebrews 11 to recite what the giants of faith did?

"By faith Abel offered unto God a more excellent sacrifice..."

"By faith Enoch...pleased God..."

"By faith Noah...prepared an ark..."

Notably, Paul goes on to mention other biblical legends whom he deemed to be giants of faith: Barak, Samson, David. Or, if one remembers them by their failings: the weakling, the womanizer, and the murderous adulterer. If standards don't matter, why does so much of the Bible recount people's failure to live up to them, then learning from their mistakes and becoming heroes of faith? The giants of faithfulness described by Paul demonstrated the purity of their faith by the good works that followed.

So let's review some Adventist standards:

1. DIET AND WARDROBE

Basic health principles have made us a "peculiar" people since a June day in 1863 when Ellen White, while in a public meeting, moved to her husband's side, laid her hand on his shoulder, and prayed for him. James White had been ill from overwork but was instantly healed.

But the story didn't end there. The next thing the audience heard was "Glory to God!" uttered by Sister White as she was taken into vision. She later recounted that in this vision "the great subject of health reform was opened before me." (RH, Oct. 8, 1867). From that inspired view came ideas that were medical nonsense in 1863: tobacco, routinely prescribed by doctors for lung ailments, was declared by her to be a "most malignant poison." Meat, the favored dish on any dining table, was described as having "tuberculous and cancerous germs"—decades before doctors Rouse and Bittner demonstrated in the Twentieth Century that cancer was a virus and could be transmitted from one species to another by dietary ingestion.

We are not the only Christian denomination to claim a prophet. But when one measures the fruits of the insights received, self-serving "truths" like polygamy bear a stark contrast to Ellen White's counsel to give up meat—her favorite food at the time of the vision, and one she had previously felt was necessary to her own frail health: "Flesh meat... was ...my principal article of diet." (Ellen White, Letter 83, July 15, 1901). Nevertheless, against her own desires and wishes, she followed Divine counsel. "I at once cut meat out of all my bill of fare." (Ibid). These health standards created spectacular results—enough for the U.S. federal government to conduct major epidemiological studies showing that such dietary principles can reduce the risk of some cancers by up to 90 percent and give people eleven extra years of life. Cancer, heart disease, stroke—diseases that torment their victims for the last few years of the life after diagnosis—can be reduced by up to 90 percent simply by limiting one's intake of meat, dairy, and refined sugars. How? By following the principles one might have seen on that church potluck sign.

The same can be said of our wardrobe. There was a time, once, when you could spot a non-Adventist in church by the jewelry she wore. You knew to greet them and wish them well, inviting them back next week. Does jewelry, in the abstract, matter? It did to Jacob, when he faced an angry brother bent on killing him and his family. In a crisis so fundamental it threatened his very survival, Jacob built an altar and prepared to pray. But first he instructed his house to surrender their "strange gods" and "all their earrings" (Genesis 35:4). When facing an existential crisis, people typically lose the urge to draw attention to themselves. (There was a spectacular exception: Jezebel, who—prior to being devoured by wild dogs—painted her face).

Adventists believe that we are living during an ongoing judgment, which will soon transition to the living. When our lives are in review in the Highest Court, might we take a lesson from Jacob and put aside any adornment that would draw attention to self and highlight our imperfections? If our goal is to walk on streets paved with gold, why waste money on pavement?

2. ENTERTAINMENT

So long ago that some people conveniently dismiss her remarks as outmoded Victorian rhetoric, Ellen White specifically warned about amusements that could, with subtle power, change us into persons we never dreamed of becoming. At the head of the list was the theater. There was, she declared, "no influence in our land more powerful to poison the imagination" (4T 652).

Her words have the ring of old-fashioned Adventism, an absolute couched in terms that allow for no shades of grey, and in recent years people have had an increasingly hard time taking her seriously on the subject. A few generations back, most Adventists made at least some effort to stay away from the theater. But they soon encountered a new challenge: if they wouldn't go to Hollywood, then Hollywood obligingly came to them through the new medium of television. At first the device seemed reasonably harmless, delivering fuzzy black and white images of "Howdy Doody" and "Leave It to Beaver." But that was an era in which the worst you might expect to see was a plunging neckline, not full frontal nudity on a cable show, and a TV watcher did not hear street language fit for a waterfront bar. As television became an accepted part of Adventist family life, few people wondered what might happen if all this changed.

But change it did. Little by little the content of programming became more explicit, more profane, more overtly violent and sexual, until we learned to tolerate things we never dreamed we would accept in our living-rooms. The dangers foreseen by Ellen White had come into the heart of our homes through a window we ourselves had opened, and the effects showed in our spiritual lives. We read less in the Word, allowed popular culture to mold our priorities, and—without realizing what was happening—became more and more like the world we were put here to warn.

Worse, it was happening to our children. If we let Hollywood be their baby-sitter, it is not surprising when they sometimes prove inept at distinguishing between what is sacred and what is profane. Something was happening to us that Ellen White had described with dreadful clarity. There were two roads, she said, one leading to heaven and one to eternal night, and in the latter road she saw "many…who had the words written upon them: 'Dead to the world. The end of all things is at hand. Be ye also ready.'" This group of Adventists "looked just like all the vain ones around them, except a shade of sadness which I noticed upon their countenances. Their conversation was just like that of the gay, thoughtless ones around them; but they would occasionally point with great satisfaction to the letters on their garments, calling for the others to have the same upon theirs."

And the world's reaction? "Those around them would say: 'There is no distinction between us. We are alike; we dress, and talk, and act alike.'" (MYP 126, 127).

Which brings up the subject of how we speak. Do we reflect the high standard of speech expected of a Christian, or do we sound like the world? A painful personal example comes to mind.

Years ago I was invited to speak at a church in the Carolinas. I do not even recall which Carolina it was, but I was privileged to stay with a lovely family that owned two parrots. These birds were extremely smart and could hear, memorize, and repeat human conversations. One day I got a phone call about something terrible that had been done to a family member. It threatened his entire future career. Suddenly, I was no longer a Christian speaker—I was a military officer back on the quarterdeck of a warship, resuming a speaking style I thought I had left far behind. I exposed those poor parrots to words they probably had never heard, and which I can only hope they never repeated. Was I sorry? Deeply so—but the experience reminded me that the events we live through imprint our minds in ways we can scarcely imagine. So why should we expose ourselves to the profanity that now passes for entertainment?

By the time he or she graduates, the average high school student will have seen 15,000 hours of television, witnessed 18,000 murders, seen 800 suicides, and enough illicit sex to explain why marriage is no longer considered necessary by half the new couples in the country. "Every youth," Mrs. White warned, who is habitually exposed to such theatrical entertainment, "will be corrupted in principle" (4T 653). What might be the symptoms of such corruption? Inability to distinguish between right and wrong? Between the sacred and the profane? Between eternal life and eternal night? Inability to sense what it means to be an Adventist?

Worse, she said, there is something addictive about the entertainment process: "The love for these scenes increases with every indulgence, as the desire for intoxicating drink strengthens with its use ... The only safe course is to shun the theater. There is no influence in our land more powerful to poison the imagination, to destroy religious impressions, and to blunt the relish for the ... sober realities of life." (Ibid)

Speaking of intoxicating: Is it possible that we—or worse, our college-age youth—may have seen so much alcohol consumed in the movies that we (or they) now consider alcohol as harmless relaxation? If so, God help us. Airline pilots who show up for a flight can be grounded for violating the bottle-to-throttle prohibition. Why? Because alcohol distorts judgment. In the air, that can be fatal. But what about the Christian life?

Sure, it's easier to have entertainment that lauds easy living and the flouting of worldly standards provided by a large flat-screen TV. But in a crisis, when we have seconds to get the right answer, the punch line from last night's sitcom will be about as useful as a snow cone in a blizzard.

If we really are who we say we are, what we do in our spare time should reflect that.

3. SABBATH OBSERVANCE

Is there a risk that we could drift toward a post-modern view of the Sabbath, where it loses its awesome significance?

Revelation 14, which describes the angelic messages we are commissioned to proclaim, reminds us to "worship him that made heaven, and earth, the sea, and the fountains of waters"—words visibly taken from the fourth commandment. The Sabbath is an end-time message.

But why?

Think about it: In 1844, as Adventist pioneers were piecing together the scriptural truths that would become the Advent message, two other writers were also drafting documents that would change the world. One was Karl Marx, whose first draft of the Communist Manifesto was penned in 1844. The other was Charles Darwin, who wrote his first draft of Origin of Species that same year. However confused humans might become about the truths emerging in 1844, there was no confusion in the mind of Lucifer. As God raised up a people to proclaim the Advent, the Sabbath, and end-time warnings, the enemy would deluge the world with the intriguing idea that life, including human life, was the result of a cosmic accident.

What was heaven's remedy for that mistake? A weekly reminder that we are here because of intelligent design. Never in human history would the Sabbath be more important. *If people had been reminded every week, by Sabbath observance, of their divine origin, Darwin's theory would have died at birth.*

Without a clear view of the Sabbath and its memorial of God's *resting* from His Creation, it is all too easy for Pope Francis to allow that "evolution...is not inconsistent with the notion of creation"—as he did in 2014:

"When we read about Creation in Genesis, we run the risk of imagining God was a magician, with a magic wand able to do everything. But that is not so..."1 An end-time message that points people back to the Sabbath drives God's stake in the beginning of time and history: "In the beginning, God..." The Sabbath makes it impossible to think of the Lord, who could speak light itself into existence, as a "magician."

But is there a danger we might let that mighty truth drift out of our lives? Do we still observe the Sabbath as God intends? Do we still follow Heaven's instructions regarding Sabbath observance? Though Sabbath-keeping can be carried to legalistic extremes, we might learn something from our Jewish friends. As sunset approaches on Friday, a special service is held in the Jewish home to welcome the arrival of sacred time that memorializes Creation. The family is called together. Special food is prepared. The Sabbath candles are lighted, and prayers are said.

We need not adopt Jewish rituals, but in our own way do we as Adventists welcome the Sabbath with something special and memorable, something that children can carry with them throughout life? Or does sunset find us at the end of a mad scramble to get the groceries carried in before the sun's upper limb hits the horizon?

The Jewish Havdalah service at Sabbath's end is also quaintly beautiful. A box of spices is passed around the family to suggest that the Sabbath's spiritual fragrance will linger in the home. A candle is lighted and then extinguished under a gentle stream of wine. Think about the symbolic significance: the Light of the World is being extinguished in His own blood! One wonders how anyone can experience such symbolism and not recognize Jesus as Messiah—but in our own way do we also miss the deep symbolism of the Sabbath? Do we with mild impatience wait for it to end? I well remember hearing a youngster, as the Sabbath was about to end in a devout Adventist home, exclaim "Oh, boy! Only ten more minutes till sundown."

---

1. Gleddie, Cyril, Roman Catholic Beliefs: God's or Mans? FriesenPress 2016, p. 29.

Might we do better in honoring these holy hours?

What about worship style? Do we really act as if we are in the presence of a holy God? Has our worship shifted from a Bible-centered experience to an emotional encounter based on feeling? Worship based on the Word of God with clear, powerful Bible preaching is life-transformational. Worship centered on music that screams at our feelings rather than speaking to our minds has little lasting impact. Think about Ezekiel's description of heaven. Unfallen beings, who have never been stained by sin, bow in profound reverence when the name of God is spoken. Some cover their faces and feet with shining wings. Should worship be a hand-clapping, foot-stomping bedlam, or should we remember into Whose presence we have entered by faith?

"The Lord has shown me," Ellen White once wrote, that "just before the close of probation...there will be shouting, with drums, music, and dancing. The senses of rational beings will become so confused that they cannot be trusted to make right decisions. *And this is called the moving of the Holy Spirit....* The Holy Spirit never reveals itself ...in a bedlam of noise" (2SM 36).

Sister White, who was sometimes privileged to hear angels sing, described their music as melody, heavenly, divine. Do our worship services prepare us for that atmosphere?

4. STANDARDS ARE OBJECTIVE AND VERIFIABLE MEASURES OF OUR FAITH

I am an instrument-rated commercial pilot, and standards make perfect sense to me—as do the instruments on my airplane. Fly into a cloud, lose your view of the horizon, and you have no internal way of knowing which way is up. You will feel turns that aren't there, and think you are level when the airplane is turning. Ignore the instruments, rely on your feelings, and you will enter what pilots call a graveyard spiral. You will hit the ground while thinking you are still in control. Only by relying on your instruments can you bring yourself and your passengers safely home.

Like the instruments on my airplane, the law of God does not condemn me—gravity does. Standards exist to keep us on course for heaven.

Air Force Colonel Jack Broughton flew 102 combat missions over Hanoi, through the most formidable air defenses on earth at that time. He landed safely all 102 times, bringing his airplane back from every mission. On one mission alone, his flight augmentation system was shot out by flak, sending his F-105 into a violent climb and descent porpoising motion when he was only 800 feet above the ground.

Flying at near-supersonic speeds, he had only seconds to disable the malfunctioning system before the plane either yanked itself to pieces or hit the ground. The only way to do that was to ignore the ground as it kept getting closer, take off his glove, and reach behind his ejection seat to find one out of over 200 circuit breakers located there. He took a breath, reached back, felt the breakers, and carefully counted four down and three left until he found the right one and popped it out with a fingernail.

He brought his plane safely back. How? Because, before every mission, he would spend at least two hours in front of a huge map and fly the mission in his mind. He would imagine everything that could go wrong, and plan how he'd react to it. He also spent hours poring over his aircraft's emergency manual, memorizing everything. Because of that, on the day that enemy guns found his fighter aircraft, he was able to visualize the needed circuit breaker in a place he could not see and could barely reach—and find the right switch.

What are Adventists, if not frail creatures hurtling toward Home and facing hostile territory every moment until we get there? Does our use of time reflect what we claim to believe? If we really believe that there is a God and a devil, that the end is so near the only thing holding it off is four angels struggling against the inevitable, that our goal is to make it Home instead of crashing into the world around us, we should have our noses buried in Heaven's emergency manual every spare second.

If we really are who we say we are, what we do in our spare time should reflect that.

5. STANDARDS LEAD US BACK TO CREATION'S ORIGINAL DESIGN—AND LEAD US HOME

"[W]hen professed Christians do not live up to the light that God gives them, they can do more harm than open sinners" (Ellen White, Speech in Copenhagen, Denmark, October 12, 1885).

"I'd rather see a sermon than hear one any day." That old quote is a powerful commentary on the importance of living the Advent message. The three angels of Revelation 14 cry out with powerful messages designed to prepare a world for its final moments. Those messages have been entrusted to us. Nowhere else in the entire Christian community does one find that unique collection of end-time truths: gospel, judgment, Sabbath, an end-time collapse of liberty made on a global scale—and, as a capstone, a people who "keep the commandments of God." To know all this, to have access to such a treasure of truth, and not to live it—how can one imagine a sadder failure?

Perhaps the fairest criticism of Adventist standards is that they are "constricting." For people for whom this world is the final destination, that may be accurate. If there is nothing beyond this earth, then why worry about anything other than maximizing your pleasure while here? Secular ethicists wage endless debates over how to define right and wrong. But these debates are pointless where there is no goal, no home to reach. Many Christians get sucked into this debate by trying to marginalize standards through relativism and a grace that does not lead to obedience. And like a pilot taking his eyes off the instrument panel and trusting his feelings, they risk flying in circles that will eventually become a graveyard spiral.

One absolute has not varied since Eden. It is designed to bring us safely back to Creation's design. There is a principle built into Creation that I like to call the Principle of Return. In heaven's plan, every life form borrows from the biosphere everything it needs to survive—food, water, air, the stuff of life. It then returns what it borrowed, enriched by its own creativity. The canary, for example, breathes in oxygen, vital to its survival, enriches it with song and new life, and then gives it back as carbon dioxide—a gas poisonous to itself, but which is needed by the lily. The lily takes it in, processes it through the Krebs cycle, and then gives back oxygen—but not before making the world a happier and more beautiful place through the sheer fact of its existence. Life on such a plan, observed by all Creation, could go on into infinity.

But there was a danger: If one part of that system became *selfish* and decided to keep something rather than giving it back, there would no longer be enough for everyone. The result would be a terrible imposter called death. That was the frightful abnormality Lucifer introduced.

Standards reflect how we will interact with heaven. We visualize heaven as the perfect place to be, but that will be the case only for those who are happy with its underlying principles. Thou shalt not kill. Thou shalt not commit adultery. Honor they father and thy mother. *Take only to enrich and give again.* Those rules were no more done away with on the Cross than the law of gravity. And being stuck in a heaven that is premised around the Principle of Return would, for a selfish person, be the worst hell imaginable. A merciful Lord does not impose heaven on someone unprepared for its lifestyle. Standards matter because, until our choices reveal a character fit to live there, heaven is not a place we would enjoy. As always, Jesus said it best: "If ye know these things, happy are ye if ye do them" (John 13:17).

If this world is *not* your final destination, if heaven exists and is worth having, then there is only one instrument panel that can take you there. Trust it and not your instincts, and as you pass through Earth's last storm, you'll see the runway lights of Home.

AS YOU BEGIN THE NEXT CHAPTER...

Have you noticed how many of the Bible truths Adventist Christians cherish and share begin with the letter "S"?

- Salvation
- Sabbath
- Second Coming
- Sanctuary
- Spirit of Prophecy
- State of the Dead
- Signs of the End

Oh—and how about a couple more? Most recent chapter . . .

- Standards of Christian Living

And the chapter just ahead . . .

- Stewardship

Stewardship is based on the idea of being good *Stewards* (kind of an old-fashioned word meaning Managers). Even before Lucifer messed up God's beautiful new world and turned it into a war zone, God had already invited Adam and Eve to go into business with Him and become co-managers of His Creation.

Following God's principles of love-based management, the first couple on Earth could make the world into an ever-more-wondrous paradise. From their Creator, they learned how to manage their environment, their time, their resources, their very lives.

Satan, the fallen Lucifer, changed all that. He introduced force, fear, guilt, greed, theft, oppression, cheating, fraud, and a raft of other evil management principles. Today the world operates almost exclusively on the basis of his diabolical school of management.

But we are still free to choose the better, higher way. The next chapter is your invitation to once again go into business with your Creator.

G. Edward Reid is an ordained minister and licensed attorney. He served for many years as the Stewardship Director of the North American Division.

CHAPTER 13

BIBLICAL FOCUS ON FINANCIAL FAITHFULNESS

THE VERY FIRST THING THE BIBLE ESTABLISHES ABOUT GOD IS THAT HE IS THE Creator of heaven and earth (Genesis 1:1), and this forms the foundation for everything else the Bible says about Him, about who we are, and about how we should relate to Him.

The New Testament adds: "All things were made through Him, and without Him nothing was made that was made" (John 1:3). Since God is the only and exclusive Creator, He is at the same time the rightful and exclusive Owner. Within this world view, all creatures are expected to see themselves and their possessions as belonging to God, the Creator.

It is difficult for us to fully understand and grasp the relationship that our God, the great and awesome Creator, wants to have with us. "Behold what manner of love the Father has bestowed on us, that we should be called children of God!" (1 John 3:1, NKJV.)

> "Can any human dignity equal this? What higher position can we occupy than to be called the sons of the infinite God? Can any worldly honor equal this?" (Ellen G. White, *God's Amazing Grace,* 341.)

In the providence of God, He is the One who gives us guidance on how to earn money and utilize it wisely. In the more than 2,000 verses in the Scriptures that deal with money and possessions and our attitude toward them, God gives practical instruction on how to live above the stresses of life and manage in such a way as to understand what it means to be financially faithful.

God owns everything and has all power. When we work with Him, He allows us to handle His resources for Him.

> "It is the Saviour's purpose that human beings, purified and sanctified, shall be His helping hand. For this great privilege let us give thanks to Him who 'hath made us meet to be partakers of the inheritance of the saints in light: who hath delivered us from the power of darkness, and hath translated us into the kingdom of His dear Son'" (Ellen G. White, *Acts of the Apostles,* 478).

As Christians, one of the most unique features in our relationship with God, is that He trusts us to manage His affairs on earth. At the very outset of human history, God explicitly entrusted Adam and Eve with the personal care of a flawless Creation (see Genesis 2:7-9, 15). From naming the animals and caring for the garden, to filling the earth with children, God let it be known that we are to work on His behalf in the management of His affairs on this earth.

He blesses us with resources and opportunities, but we are the ones who manage those resources, collect the money, write the checks, do the electronic transfers, and make the budgets. God encourages us to spend the resources He entrusts to us for our own needs, the needs of others, and to advance the work of God in the world. Incredible as it may seem, we are the ones God entrusts with rearing His children, building His buildings, and educating each succeeding generation.

God's counsel to His children through the wise man, Solomon, is: "Honor the Lord with your possessions, and with the firstfruits of all your increase" (Proverbs 3:9, NJKV). This counsel is appropriate, because, "You are worthy, O Lord, to receive glory and honor and power; for You created all things, and by Your will they exist and were created" (Revelation 4:11, NKJV).

THE TITHE CONTRACT

God asks us to put Him first in the management of our possessions, as an acknowledgement of His ownership and as a demonstration of our faith in Him to provide for us. But even more than this, He says that if we will put Him first, then He will bless the rest.

> "Not only does the Lord claim the tithe as His own, but He tells us how it should be reserved for Him. He says, 'Honor the Lord with thy substance, and with the first fruits of all thine increase.' This does not teach that we are to spend our means on ourselves, and bring to the Lord the remnant, even though it should be otherwise an honest tithe. Let God's portion be first set apart" (Ellen G. White, *Counsels on Stewardship*, 81).

A close spiritual connection exists between the practice of tithing and our relationship to God. The children of Israel prospered when they obeyed God and were faithful with their tithing. And they fell on hard times when they didn't. They seemed to follow a cycle of obedience and prosperity followed by disobedience and troubles. During one of these periods of unfaithfulness God, through the prophet Malachi, proposed two bilateral contracts with His people (see Malachi 3:7-11, here and following).

God promised the people that if they would return to Him, He would return to them. When they asked what He meant by returning to Him,

He explicitly says, "Stop robbing Me of tithe and offerings." Their robbery was the reason they were being cursed. Here is God's solution to the problem of the curse: "Bring all the tithe [the whole tithe] into the storehouse." And if you do this, then "I will open the windows of heaven and pour out for you such blessing that there will not be room enough to receive it." If we don't have room enough to receive it, we have a surplus with which we can help others and help to advance the cause of God.

Tithing was and is God's idea. Tithing is not a plan devised by a committee of the church. Tithing is first mentioned in Scripture in Genesis 14. Abram had returned from a successful hostage rescue mission to save his nephew Lot and his family and the other people who were taken from Sodom.

This experience occurred more than 4,000 years ago, and more than 400 years before God gave His laws through Moses. The king of Sodom was so grateful for the rescue that he offered Abram "the goods"—all the spoils of the battle. Abram refused the offer and stated that he had made a covenant with God that he would take nothing from anyone (see Genesis 14:22). Then Abram did two notable things. He gave a tithe of the spoils to Melchizedek (Genesis 14:20; Hebrews 7:1, 2), the priest of the Most High God, and gave the remainder back to the people of Sodom.

Melchizedek did not request the tithe. Abram simply offered it. Apparently, early Old Testament characters knew about the sacrificial system as practiced by Abel, Noah, and Abraham. They also understood about the clean and unclean animals before the laws were given to Israel at Sinai. The faithful ones, like Jacob (see Genesis 28:22), practiced tithing. Ellen White notes:

> "The tithing system reaches back beyond the days of Moses. Men were required to offer to God gifts for religious purposes before the definite system was given to Moses, even as far back as the days of Adam" (*Testimonies for the Church*, vol. 3, 393).

Immediately after Abram's tithing experience, the Lord came to him in a vision and said, "Do not be afraid, Abram. I am your shield, your exceedingly great reward" (Genesis 15:1, NKJV). In effect, the Lord was telling Abram, "Don't worry, I have your back. I will be your protector and provider."

When Jacob left home, running from his angry brother Esau, the second night of his journey he had a dream of a staircase that ascended from earth to heaven. Angels were going up and down on it. And God stood at the top and promised to be with Jacob and someday bring him back home again. This man had a real conversion experience and said, "The Lord shall be my God. And of all You give to me I will surely give a tenth to You" (Genesis 28:21, 22).

Dictionaries define tithe as "a tenth part of something" or "10 percent." This definition is likely taken from the Bible narrative. Tithe is simply returning 10 percent of our income or increase to God. We understand that all we have belongs to Him in the first place. The tithing legislation given to Israel at Mt. Sinai points out that the tithe is holy and belongs to God.

"And all the tithe of the land, whether of the seed of the land or of the fruit of the tree, is the Lord's. It is holy to the Lord.... And concerning the tithe of the herd or the flock, of whatever passes under the rod, the tenth one shall be holy to the Lord" (Leviticus27:30, 32, NKJV). Here, tithe and tenth are given in the same setting.

God only asks for 10 percent in our contract with Him. Then He allows us to manage and distribute the remaining 90 percent. Our offerings of gratitude are separate from and in addition to the tithe. The tithe is the minimum testimony of our Christian commitment. Nowhere in the Bible do we find any indication that God's portion is less than a tenth.

Since God is the owner of everything (Psalm 24:1), obviously He doesn't need the money. But since the tithe is His, what could He do with it? Simple. Anything He wanted to do. He could take it to heaven.

He could burn it up like a sacrificial offering. Or...? But He has told us what to do with it—He has asked us to use His tithe for the support of the Gospel ministry (see Numbers 18:21). And therefore, the needs of the ministers and God's work are taken care of with God's tithe. As you remember, the tribe of Levi—the ministerial force in the Old Testament—were not given large properties like the rest of the tribes. Levi was given certain cities, including the cities of refuge, with enough land around them for personal gardens. They were supported by the tithes of the others, and they themselves also tithed their income.

The Bible gives reasons for and promises regarding tithing (see Proverbs3:9, 10; Malachi3:10, 11; Matthew 6:31-33). Several reasons or purposes of tithing are given in these verses. First, to establish a trust relationship with God. God says, in essence, "If you are faithful with Me, I will give you amazing blessings." We can be sure both that God exists and that He cares for us, because of His providences in our lives.

A second big reason for financial faithfulness is to access the promised tangible blessings of God. As part of the tithing contract, God has promised blessings that are so large that we won't have room enough to receive them. With our surplus we can help others and help to support the work of God with our offerings. "Remember the words of the Lord Jesus, how he said, It is more blessed to give than to receive" (Acts 20:35).

First Corinthians 4:2 states: "Moreover it is required in stewards that one be found faithful."

So what does it mean to be faithful with our tithe? Several constituent elements apply to the tithe. Four of them are:

1. The amount—which is a tenth, or 10 percent of our income or increase.

2. Tithe is to be taken to the storehouse—the place from which the Gospel ministers are paid.

3. We are to honor God with the first part of our income.

4. Tithe is to be used for the right purpose—support of ministry.

As individual members, it is our responsibility to uphold the first three items, and it is the responsibility of the storehouse managers to make sure that the tithe funds are used properly.

Unlike our offerings, the tithe is not discretionary on our part. The tenth and the storehouse are both part of our responsibility. We don't set the parameters—God does. If I am not returning a full 10 percent to the conference storehouse through my local church, then I am not tithing. With all of the blessings God offers in Malachi 3:10, 11, why would I not choose to be faithful?

> "'Bring ye all the tithes into the storehouse' (Malachi 3:10), is God's command. No appeal is made to gratitude or to generosity. This is a matter of simple honesty. The tithe is the Lord's; and He bids us return to Him that which is His own" (Ellen G. White, *Education*, 138).

Managing God's funds places us in a unique relationship with Him. He blesses and sustains us and asks for only a tenth; then He uses His tithe to provide for those in the ministry, as He did for the tribe of Levi.

When we are called upon to give an account of our management of God's funds, He says, "Well done" to those who have been faithful (see Matthew 25:19-21).

The question of the honest tithe is quite simple. It is the whole tithe taken to the right place taken. To read Ellen White's most comprehensive tithe document, go to vol 9 of *Testimonies for the Church,* 245-252.

> "If all the tithes of our people flowed into the treasury of the Lord as they should, such blessings would be received that gifts and offerings for sacred purposes would be multiplied tenfold, and thus the channel between God and man would be kept open" (Ellen G. White, *Testimonies for the Church*, vol. 4, 474).

This is an amazing statement. If we were all faithful tithers, God would bless us with funds to increase our offerings 1,000 percent.

> "In the third chapter of Malachi is found the contract God has made with man. Here the Lord specifies the part He will act in bestowing His great gifts on those who will make a faithful return to Him in tithes and offerings" (*Review and Herald*, December 17, 1901).

> "The Lord is under no obligation to grant us his favors, yet he has pledged his word that if we will comply with the conditions stated in the Scriptures, he will fulfill his part of the contract" (*Signs of the Times*, December 16, 1889).

What an amazing experience—to be in a contract with the Almighty God! He has promised to uphold His end of the bargain. Let us resolve that we will be faithful on our end.

> "He who gave His only-begotten Son to die for you, has made a covenant with you. He gives you His blessings, and in return He requires you to bring Him your tithes and offerings. No one will ever dare to say that there was no way in which he could understand in regard to this matter. God's plan regarding tithes and offerings is definitely stated in the third chapter of Malachi. God calls upon His human agents to be true to the contract He has made with them" (Ellen G. White, *Counsels on Stewardship*, 75).

Note in the first and last sentences of this statement that *covenant* and *contract* are used interchangeably.

OFFERINGS FOR JESUS

As part of God's family, we have a significant role to play in the management of the resources He has entrusted to us. In Jesus' last recorded conversation with His disciples, He repeated the "Great Commission." Just before ascending to heaven, He said, "But you shall receive power when the Holy Spirit has come upon you; and you shall be witnesses to Me in Jerusalem, and in all Judea and Samaria, and to the end of the earth" (Acts 1:8, NKJV). To us today that would mean our local church, the conference territory, and the world field. In an attempt to fulfill this challenge, our offerings can include our local church budget, our conference or mission work, and the World Budget. If we will systematically support these areas of God's work, the resources will be available to finish the work with God's blessing.

Our offerings come from the 90 percent that remains in our possession after our tithe is returned to God. This is where generosity begins. Several different types of offerings were given by God's people as recorded in the Bible. There were sin offerings—given in response to experienced grace, and thank offerings—given to recognize God's protection, blessings of health, prosperity, and sustaining power. There were also Offerings for the poor and offerings to build and maintain the house of worship are also ways we can express our gratitude to God for His great blessings to us.

When we consider the magnitude of God's gifts, we begin to see our giving as more than just paving the parking lot or buying choir robes. We bring our gifts in response to what God has done for us. The church, then, be it local, conference, or worldwide, uses our gifts to advance the cause of God—which adds to His happiness. There is joy in heaven, because the Church is being a light on a hill—reflecting the Light of the world.

We love God because He first loved us. Our giving is in response to His unspeakable gift to us. In fact, we are told,

> "The Lord does not need our offerings. We cannot enrich Him by our gifts. Says the psalmist: 'All things come of Thee, and of Thine own have we given Thee.' Yet God permits us to show our appreciation of His mercies by self-sacrificing efforts to extend the same to others. This is the only way in which it is possible for us to manifest our gratitude and love to God. He has provided no other" (Ellen G. White, *Counsels on Stewardship*, 18).

Our offerings are an expression of our offering of ourselves to God. They are a deeply religious experience, in that they are a token of our lives being wholly surrendered to God as our Lord. An offering comes from a heart that trusts in a personal God who constantly provides for our needs as He sees best. Our offerings rest on the conviction that we have found assurance of salvation in Christ. They are not an appeasement or a search for acceptance, but rather, our offerings flow from a heart that by faith has accepted Christ as the only and sufficient means of grace and redemption.

Offerings are not based on a percentage like the tithe but rather, "Every man shall give as he is able, according to the blessing of the Lord your God which He has given you" (Deuteronomy 16:17). Our offerings are an acknowledgment and expression of our gratitude to God for His abundant gifts of life, redemption, sustenance, and constant blessings of many kinds. As we noted in the passage above, the amount of our offerings is based on our ability to give and our thankfulness. "For everyone to whom much is given, from him much will be required" (Luke 12:48, NKJV).

The question is asked in Psalm 116:12: "What shall I render to the Lord for all His benefits toward me?" How could we ever repay God for all His blessings to us? The simple answer is that we never could. The best we can do is be generous with the cause of God and in helping those around us. When Jesus sent out His disciples on a missionary trip, He told them, "Freely you have received, freely give" (Matthew 10:8, NKJV). Our giving of offerings contributes to the development of a Christlike character. We are thereby changed from selfishness to love—to be concerned for others and the cause of God as Christ was and is. Let us always remember that "God so loved, that He gave" (John 3:16).

Our offerings are discretionary regarding the amount and to whom they are given. But bringing an offering to the Lord is a Christian duty with spiritual and moral implications. Failure to bring offerings to the Lord is considered by Him to be an act of robbery (Malachi 3:8).

As God's children who are tasked with the responsibility of managing His business on the earth, it is a privilege, an opportunity, and a responsibility to bring our offerings to God as part of our worship experience.

We believe that the end of all things is at hand, and we are expecting the Spirit of God in latter rain power. Why hasn't it come?

> "One reason why there is so great a dearth of the Spirit of God is that so many are robbing God" (Ellen G. White, *Testimonies for the Church*, vol. 5, 734).

MANAGING IN TOUGH TIMES

Our world seems to be spinning out of control, with wars, bloodshed, crime, violence, immorality, natural disasters, disease epidemics, an uncertain economy, political corruption, and every other kind of misery and evil. A strong urge prevails for individuals and families to think first of their own survival. Accordingly, much thought is given to seeking security in these uncertain times.

Life's common tasks consume our time. We have children to rear, property to maintain, and jobs to perform. And of course, we do need clothes to wear, food to eat, and a place to live. In His sermon on the mount Jesus addressed these very basic needs and then stated, "Your heavenly Father knows that you need all these things. But seek first the kingdom of God and His righteousness, and all these things shall be added to you" (Matthew 6:32, 33, NKJV).

Jesus has asked us to put Him first, not because He is selfish or needs anything that we possess, but rather, for our own good. He knows that if we don't learn to trust Him at the very basic levels of life, we can become distracted from our heavenly goal and eventually be lost. And when pointing out the need to prepare for His Second Coming, Jesus warned, "But take heed to yourselves, lest your hearts be weighed down with carousing, drunkenness, and cares of this life, and that Day come on you unexpectedly" (Luke 21:34, NKJV).

As the signs of the end continue to multiply, a change needs to take place in the hearts of God's true people. Instead of thinking only of ourselves, we will realize that we can't take it with us; so, before the time arrives when we can't buy or sell, we should liquidate assets and give all we can to advance the cause of God so that our possessions do not fall into the hands of those who are serving Satan.

TIME TO SIMPLIFY

What should Seventh-day Adventist Christians do in response to these difficult times? Should we hunker down in a survival mode? No, in fact, just the opposite is true. Since we know that the end of the world and the Second Coming of Christ is near, we want to use our assets to tell others the good news of the Gospel and of what God has prepared for those that love Him. We understand that someday soon, everything on this earth will be burned up.

We understand from the Word of God that He is not sending moving vans to take our stuff to heaven. Those belongings will all get burned up! (2 Peter 3:10.) What should we do with our possessions? Ellen White gives us counsel in this regard:

> "It is now that our brethren should be cutting down their possessions instead of increasing them. We are about to move to a better country, even a heavenly. Then let us not be dwellers upon the earth, but be getting things into as compact a compass as possible" (*Counsels on Stewardship,* 59).

The account of Lot's deliverance from Sodom by God Himself and two angels is recorded in Genesis 19:12-26. God's instruction was "Do not look back."

Lot entered Sodom a wealthy man. He came out with nothing. Why did Lot's wife look back? Apparently, there were three reasons: 1. Her heart was still in Sodom; 2) her possessions (wealth) were still in Sodom; 3) her children were still in Sodom (see *Patriarchs and Prophets,* 162). In one of the shortest verses in the Bible Jesus said, "Remember Lot's wife" (Luke 17:32). Every person who leaves this world alive will have to make the same decision that faced Lot's wife. Remember that no person or any "thing" is worth trading for eternal life.

If we don't want our stuff to get burned up, we should follow this counsel:

"The work of God is to become more extensive, and if His people follow His counsel, there will not be much means in their possession to be consumed in the final conflagration. All will have laid up their treasure where moth and rust cannot corrupt; and the heart will not have a cord to bind it to earth" (Ellen G. White, *Counsels on Stewardship*, 60).

WHEN NO ONE CAN BUY OR SELL

The Bible tells us that Satan's great end-time temptation is an economic embargo.

"And that no man might buy or sell, save he that had the mark, or the name of the beast, or the number of his name" (Revelation 13:17).

"In the last great conflict of the controversy with Satan, those who are loyal to God will see every earthly support cut off. Because they refuse to break His law in obedience to earthly powers, they will be forbidden to buy or sell" (Ellen G. White, *Maranatha*, 183).

The more money you have in your account at that time, the harder it will be to resist the temptation. This point can be made with a simple illustration. Suppose you have $300,000 in the bank. Then end-time events begin to unfold, and the authorities declare that no one can buy or sell unless they are willing to receive the mark of the beast.

In other words, your money—that you have worked so hard to save and now depend on to help take care of you—is worthless unless you accept the religious authority of the state. What would you do? Would you be willing to turn your back on your $300,000 and walk away? Unfortunately, many Christians with hoarded assets will go for the money and turn their backs on God, as did the rich young ruler, and lose eternal life. God made provision for this great temptation by establishing the tithing system.

God explained through Moses that one of the reasons He established the tithing system was "that you may learn to fear the Lord your God always" (see Deuteronomy14:23). We learn what fear means in this verse by letting the Bible interpret itself. In the poetic parallelism of Psalm 31:19 we see that fear is synonymous with trust.

"Oh! how great is Your goodness,
Which You have laid up for those who fear You.
Which You have prepared for those who trust in You."

These parallel lines show us that to fear the Lord is to trust Him. Therefore, we understand that God established the tithing system to protect us from selfishness and to encourage us to trust Him to provide for us. When Satan inspires evil men to issue a financial embargo against God's faithful children, those who have learned to trust Him in the tithing system will remain faithful then, too.

Have you learned to trust God through tithing? Are you faithful in your tithe? Do you set apart your tithe, a tenth, when you receive your paycheck from your employer?

From a merely secular perspective, we live in very challenging and stressful times. However, our Christian worldview gives us confidence and hope as we see the signs Jesus gave to let us know that the great climax of human history—the Second Coming of Christ—is very near, even at the door.

END-TIME STEWARDSHIP

> "In the last extremity, before this work shall close, thousands will be cheerfully laid upon the altar. Men and women will feel it a blessed privilege to share in the work of preparing souls to stand in the great day of God, and they will give hundreds as readily as dollars are given now. If the love of Christ were burning in the hearts of His professed people, we would see the same spirit manifested today. Did they but realize how near is the end of all work for the

salvation of souls, they would sacrifice their possessions as freely as did the members of the early church. They would work for the advancement of God's cause as earnestly as worldly men labor to acquire riches. Tact and skill would be exercised, and earnest and unselfish labor put forth to acquire means, not to hoard, but to pour into the treasury of the Lord" (Ellen G. White, *Maranatha,* 183).

"Faith sees Jesus standing as our Mediator at the right hand of God. Faith beholds the mansions He has gone to prepare for those who love Him. Faith sees the robe and crown all prepared for the overcomer. Faith hears the songs of the redeemed, and brings eternal glories near. We must come close to Jesus in loving obedience, if we would see the King in His beauty.... Food, clothing, station, and wealth may have their value; but to have a connection with God and to be a partaker of His divine nature is of priceless value.... The privilege of becoming sons of God is cheaply purchased, even at the sacrifice of everything we possess, be it life itself " (Ellen G. White, *God's Amazing Grace,* 34).

Let me tell you about Meropi Gjika. For decades after WWII, Albania was an atheistic country. It was illegal to practice any form of religion. Foreign visitors were lectured on the "wonders of atheism" and saw religious structures that had been turned into warehouses and cinemas. Enver Hoxa was the iron-fisted Albanian dictator who ruthlessly ruled the country.

Daniel Lewis, an Albanian from Boston, Massachusetts, responded to a call from the General Conference and became a missionary to Albania in the 1930s. He established a pharmacy, but his real mission was to present the most effective pill: the Gospel. Lewis reported five converts in 1939. His missionary activities landed him in prison, sentenced to twenty years, but four and a half years later, he died in brutal conditions. His Italian wife, Flora, was also imprisoned and later moved back to live with her daughter, Esther.

A small group of Adventist believers waited and prayed for over fifty years for someone to come from abroad, conduct Bible studies, and baptize them! Meropi Gjika was 87 when she met several Adventist leaders who were allowed to visit the country in 1991. "The Lord sent you to us," Meropi whispered, embracing our leaders.

One of Meropi's greatest desires, when the Adventist leaders visited with her, was to be relieved of the burden of keeping her tithe hidden. "What must I do with my tithe, which I have saved all these years?" she asked me. "Can you take it?" Meropi's two sons explained that their mother would not keep the money in a bank because she didn't trust the authorities.

Meropi was thrilled that at last she could support the cause of Christ and the church she loved. She brought out a plastic bag from under her bed. In it was a carton full of Albanian *leke* and a few American dollars. For more than twenty years she had been on a $4.00 per month pension, yet she put aside her tithe and offerings. All told, she had saved the equivalent of US$533.89. For over fifty years, Meropi trusted God and set aside her tithe, believing that one day she would be able to bless God's cause with it.

Returning our tithe to God is an act of faith. It is acknowledges God's goodness. It demonstrates our trust in God to meet our needs. It unites us with Adventists around the world in an act of sacrificial giving. It reveals our serious commitment to be part of God's mission of reaching the lost. It reveals that we are part of a worldwide body of believers committed at all costs to reaching the world for Christ.

AS YOU BEGIN THE NEXT CHAPTER...

- ***Of all*** the voices calling us to prophetic faithfulness . . .
- ***Of all*** the words pointing us to the True North . . .
- ***Of all*** the gifts most laser-focused on God's Everlasting Word . . .
- ***Of all*** the channels through which God speaks to us . . .

Is it not most unexpected and surprising ***of all*** that God called to be His messenger to the remnant a teenager with few evident abilities and little education?

But with the Bible as a guide, does the remnant really *need* a prophetic gift in its midst? Consider an illustration by early advent pioneer Uriah Smith:

Suppose we are about to start upon a voyage. The owner of the vessel gives us a Book of directions, telling us that it contains instructions sufficient for our whole journey and that if we will heed them, we shall reach in safety our port of destination. Setting sail, we open our Book to learn its contents. We find that its Author lays down general principles to govern us in our voyage . . . but He also tells us that the latter part of our journey will be especially perilous . . .

"But for this part of the journey," says he, "I have provided you a pilot, who will meet you, and give you such directions as the surrounding circumstances and dangers may require; and to him you must give heed." With these directions we reach the perilous time specified, and the pilot, according to promise, appears.

But some of the crew, as he offers his services, rise up against him. "We have the original Book of directions," say they, "and that is enough for us. We stand upon that, and that alone; we want nothing of you."

Who now heed that original Book of directions? Those who reject the pilot, or those who receive him, as that Book instructs them? Judge ye . . ." (Uriah Smith, *Review and Herald,* Jan. 13, 1863).

Blessed are we beyond all measure—as we approach our final port—to have a pilot sent to guide us through the dangers around us and bring us safely to our eternal harbor!

Dwain N. Esmond is an author, editor, and ordained minister. He currently serves as Associate Director/Editor for the Ellen G. White Estate, Inc., where he supervises the preparation and publication of all White Estate-related content. Elder Esmond also helps lead strategic planning and development for the White Estate. He is joined in ministry by his wife, Kemba, and their son, Dwain Jr.

DWAIN N. ESMOND

CHAPTER 14

A MESSENGER SENT FROM GOD: FAITHFULNESS TO THE SPIRIT OF PROPHECY

THE APOSTLE PAUL IS ONE OF THE MOST BELOVED FIGURES IN ALL OF SCRIPTURE. We see the misguided zeal that led him to persecute God's Church (1 Corinthians 15:9; Galatians 1:13) and the love of Jesus that intercepted him on the road to Damascus (Acts 9). We cringe as he recounts the pains he suffered for the Gospel (2 Corinthians 11:23-27), and we are awed by his desire to know the fellowship of Christ's sufferings (Philippians 3:10). He knew the personal pain of wanting to do right but doing wrong instead (Romans 7), and the victorious crown awaiting him for fighting the good fight, finishing the race, and keeping the faith (2 Timothy 4:7, 8). We find much in the life of Paul with which we can identify as fellow Christian athletes in running the "race" for eternal life.

Fired by a passion for Jesus and a near-manic compulsion to share the Gospel, Paul preached by day and wrote letters to fellow believers by night. In all that he endured, the beloved apostle remained faithful in the dispatch of his personal and professional calling as a servant of God. Indeed, it was Paul who encouraged the Corinthian believers not to lionize teachers of the Gospel instead of the God who had called them: "Let a man so consider us, as servants of Christ and stewards of the mysteries of God. Moreover, it is required in stewards that one be found faithful" (1 Corinthians 4:1, 2, NKJV).

People entrusted by God with divine revelations are required above all else to be faithful. They are not required to be successful, though success would attend their efforts for God. They are not required to be significant, though their names and messages would reverberate for centuries to come. They are not required to be found prosperous, though the favor of God would rest on them. The one non-negotiable for every follower of Jesus, wrote Paul, was faithfulness. Faithfulness was the test then for God's people, and faithfulness is the test now for His remnant Church.

GIFTS ONLY GOD CAN GIVE

The apostle Paul understood that gifts God gives are nurtured in the soil of faithfulness to His high and holy purposes. The One dispensing the gifts of the Holy Spirit is Jesus Himself (Ephesians 4:8). It is to the Corinthian Church that Paul first enumerates the gifts of the Spirit, in which the gift of prophecy figures prominently (1 Corinthians 12:8-10). In Ephesians 4:7-13, Paul offers another listing of spiritual gifts while making clear that the gifts are given,

> "for the equipping of the saints for the work of ministry, for the edifying of the body of Christ, till we all come to the unity of the faith and of the knowledge of the Son of God, to a perfect man, to the measure of the stature of the fullness of Christ" (vss.12, 13).

Additionally, God gives these gifts that His people may not be like children "tossed to and fro and carried about with every wind of doctrine but, speaking the truth in love, may grow up into Him who is the Head—Christ" (vs. 14). All the gifts of God are meant to edify and equip God's people for ministry, until we all grow into the fullness of Christ. For these reasons alone we should praise God!

The Holy Spirit has been equipping men and women for service since the dawn of time, and there is no sunset provision to His labor or the gifts He gives. God, through the prophet Joel, emphatically stated:

> "And it shall come to pass afterward [in the last days] that I will pour out My Spirit on all flesh; your sons and your daughters shall prophesy, your old men shall dream dreams, your young men shall see visions" (Joel 2:28).

Amos likewise declares, "Surely the Lord God does nothing, unless He reveals His secret to His servants the prophets" (Amos 3:7). God never leaves His people to grope in darkness without a word from Him. God promised that faithful messengers would come, and we must be able to recognize them, test their messages, and follow only that which bears the imprimatur of heaven.

A MESSENGER ARRIVES

Seventh-day Adventists believe that Ellen G. White received a modern-day manifestation of the gift of prophecy from the Holy Spirit. To say those words is to mask the reluctance with which this young (yet in her teens) former Methodist believer accepted her call. It was a blessing and a burden that often brought her to tears. The weight is evident in an 1874 letter she sent to Elder J. N. Loughborough, a minister whose preaching Ellen White enjoyed:

> "I have felt for years that if I could have my choice and please God as well, I would rather die than have a vision, for every vision places me

under great responsibility to bear testimonies of reproof and of warning, which has ever been against my feelings, causing me affliction of soul that is inexpressible. Never have I coveted my position, and yet I dare not resist the Spirit of God and seek an easier position."[1]

Ellen White received her first vision in December of 1844, during a morning prayer session at the home of a Mrs. Haines on Ocean Street in South Portland, Maine. As she would later tell it:

> "While praying, the power of God came upon me as I never had felt it before, and I was wrapped up in a vision of God's glory, and seemed to be rising higher and higher from the earth and was shown something of the travels of the Advent people to the Holy City"[2]

This vision of a small band of Jesus-focused believers on the narrow way to heaven provided confirmation of conclusions reached from deep Bible study after the "Great Disappointment" of October 1844, when tens of thousands of Millerites in the United States and around the world, as part of the Second Great Awakening, believed wholeheartedly that Jesus would come.

The disappointment led many believers in the Advent movement to give up their faith. But some felt the misunderstanding was their fault and not the Bible's. Through prayer and Bible study they discovered that the cleansing of the sanctuary spoken of in Daniel 8:14 was that of the heavenly sanctuary and not the earth, as they had mistakenly believed. Their reckoning that the 2,300 prophetic "days"/years would culminate in the fall of 1844 was right, but they had incorrectly concluded *what* was to happen then.

Through close study of the sanctuary doctrine in Scripture they found that, like the cleansing of the earthly sanctuary on the Day of Atonement, in 1844 Christ's ministry as our High Priest moved from the Holy Place of the heavenly sanctuary into the Most Holy Place, there to begin an investigative judgment of earth's inhabitants.

From this moment onward, Ellen White's more than 2,000 visions helped to guide and direct the group of believers God called to preach the Three Angels' Messages of Revelation 14. This remnant group would "keep the commandments of God and have the testimony of Jesus" (Revelation 12:17). What is the testimony of Jesus that they would possess at the end of time? Revelation 19:10 answers: "for the testimony of Jesus is the Spirit of Prophecy." In other words, God's end-time remnant will not only be obedient followers who love and proclaim His Word; they will also have a manifestation of the gift of prophecy in their midst. We believe that God gave Ellen White the gift of prophecy and manifested it during her lifetime.

INTERESTING TIMES

When God called Ellen White to be His messenger, He did so at one of the most momentous times in human history. In the year 1844 Charles Darwin published an essay that would later develop into *On the Origin of Species by Means of Natural Selection*, which developed into the evolutionary theory as we know it today. The year 1844 was also when Marxism was born. Karl Marx, the highly influential German philosopher and economist, published his early economic and philosophic manuscripts.

Is it a coincidence that God would call Ellen White and the Seventh-day Adventist Church into existence at the time when two seismic intellectual forces began shaking the world? Is it a coincidence that at a time when the godless theory of evolution and the godless economic theories of Marxism were born, God chose to raise up a people who would preach messages calling all to worship Him "who made heaven and earth, the sea and springs of waters" (Revelation 14:7)? Messages warning that Babylon, the pseudo-spiritual apostate with all its spiritual and economic confusion, "is fallen" (Revelation 14:8)? This is no coincidence. Ellen White was to be another in the long line of messengers sent by God when a crisis loomed on Earth.

But Ellen White was not without her critics, even back then. From the very onset of her ministry, some doubted whether Ellen White was receiving messages from God or simply experiencing latent mental issues due to her poor physical health. One skeptical believer who wrote James White captured the thoughts of some at the time:

> "I cannot endorse Sister Ellen's visions as being of divine inspiration, as you and she think them to be; yet I do not suspect the least shade of dishonesty in either of you in this matter. . . . I think that what she and you regard as visions from the Lord, are only religious reveries, in which her imagination runs without control upon themes in which she is most deeply interested."[3]

To make matters worse, there were others operating at the time who claimed to receive dreams and visions. Joseph Smith, the Mormon prophet, was killed in 1844. By that time, he was a known entity with a substantial following. Mary Baker Eddy, founder of the Christian Science movement, was considered a prophetess by her adherents. John Humphrey Noyes, founder of the Oneida Community in 1841, was just beginning to grow his Utopian socialist colony in Putney, Vermont. There was plenty of healthy skepticism to go around during America's Third Great Awakening.

ESTABLISHED AND BLESSED

Nevertheless, in the decades to follow, God would establish, bless, and distinguish Ellen White's life and ministry in ways that few could imagine at the time. For example, Ellen White's life and work right from the start focused on Jesus. The foundational orientation of her seventy-year ministry was Jesus. Merlin D. Burt, professor, church historian, and Ellen White scholar, comments:

> "Sometimes people do not realize that Ellen White's first three major prophetic visions during 1844 and 1845 had Jesus at the center. In her first vision—the Midnight Cry—it is Jesus that the

> Advent people were following on the path. When they were discouraged, Jesus raised His arm, and a light 'waved over the Advent band.' In her second major vision—the Bridegroom—it was Jesus who led His people from the Holy to Most Holy Place of the heavenly sanctuary. In her third major vision—the New Earth—it was Jesus who personally showed Ellen White the future glories of the new earth."[4]

In her writings, Ellen White used more than 840 names, titles, and appellations for Jesus. Her Christocentric life and ministry is perhaps the most powerful proof that she was a messenger sent by God. First John 4:2 reminds us that confessing Jesus and His incarnation is one of the tests of a prophet:

By this you know the Spirit of God: Every spirit that confesses that Jesus Christ has come in the flesh is of God." A true prophet will declare—not deny—both the deity and the humanity of Jesus. Ellen White passes this test in countless ways, but she also made it clear when she wrote that "in Christ is life, original, unborrowed, underived" (*The Desire of Ages*, 530).

EXALTING SCRIPTURE

Ellen White also exalted the Bible in her writings. "I recommend to you, dear reader, the Word of God as the rule of your faith and practice," she wrote. "By that Word we are to be judged. God has, in that Word, promised to give visions in the 'last days'; not for a new rule of faith, but for the comfort of His people, and to correct those who err from Bible truth."[5]

She further counseled, "Our position and faith is in the Bible. And never do we want any soul to bring in the *Testimonies* ahead of the Bible."[6] To underscore the point, in 1962 the Ellen G. White Estate—legal custodian of Mrs. White's writings—issued a Scripture index to the fifty-one books published under her name as of 1958.

Tim Poirier, vice-director of the White Estate, writes:

> "In abbreviated form, her citations or allusions to Scripture passages fill 156 pages in the index, and included nearly every chapter of the Bible. A conservative estimate of the number of unique references included in this index would give the total at over 40,000—amounting to an average of between one and two scriptural references per printed page."[7]

This is an astounding total for any writer, let alone a nineteenth-century spiritual leader. Ellen White is almost without equal on this point alone, and certainly so if one includes scriptural references in all of her writings. Critics who claim that Ellen White was simply a devotional writer fail to grapple with the depth of the biblical insights that underpin her writings.

Isaiah 8:20 tells us, "To the law and to the testimony! If they do not speak according to this word, it is because there is no light in them." Ellen White's bibliocentric writings pass the second biblical test of a prophet—complete harmony with Scripture.

The prophetic authority of her writings derives from the inspiration and guidance of the Holy Spirit in her life and work, though the function of her writings is somewhat different from the writings comprising the scriptural canon.

Scholar Gerhard Pfandl compares Ellen White to the non-canonical prophets mentioned in Scripture: people such as Nathan, Ahijah, and Iddo (2 Chronicles 9:29):

> "What the non-canonical prophets said or wrote was just as authoritative and binding for the people of their time as were the books of Moses and Isaiah (2 Samuel 12:7-15). The authority of a prophetic book lies in its inspiration—not in the book's place in the canon."[8]

AN EXEMPLARY LIFE

But what about Ellen White's life? Did her life bear witness that she was a servant of God? This third test, found in Matthew 7:15-20, has exposed the hypocrisy of many who claimed to be prophets of God. Consider this statement featured in a 1915 edition of *The New York Independent* newspaper upon the death Ellen White: "She was absolutely honest in her belief in her revelations. Her life was worthy of them. She showed no spiritual pride, and she sought no filthy lucre. She lived the life and did the work of a worthy prophetess." Even a secular paper clearly recognized the kind of spiritual leader Ellen White was.

Against the backdrop of this and many other glowing testimonies, some have tried to impugn her reputation with charges of plagiarism, pseudo-scientific statements, and even racism. None of these charges hold up under scrutiny. Take, for instance, the plagiarism charge. Ellen White faced this accusation during her lifetime and this misinformation persists today. Her introduction to *The Great Controversy* acknowledges the inclusion of other writers' words in her writings, but notice the reason given for not citing them:

In some cases where a historian has so grouped together events as to afford, in brief, a comprehensive view of the subject, or has summarized details in a convenient manner, his words have been quoted; but in some instances, no specific credit has been given, since the quotations are not given for the purpose of citing that writer as authority, but because his statement affords a ready and forcible presentation of the subject. In narrating the experience and views of those carrying forward the work of reform in our own time, similar use has been made of their published works.[9]

This statement has not mollified adamant critics of Ellen White; in fact, it has even emboldened some. In the early 1980s, the plagiarism charge rose again with great ferocity with the publication of *The White Lie* by Walter Rea, a former Adventist pastor. In response to Rea's accusations, Warren L. Johns, chief counsel of the General Conference of Seventh-day

Adventists, retained the services of Diller, Ramik, & Wright, a highly reputable law firm specializing in patent, trademark, and copyright law. Heretofore, the SDA Church had done no legal work with this law firm. They would be a wholly independent arbiter on the issue of whether Ellen White had plagiarized the writings of others or not. Vincent L. Ramik, a senior law partner of the firm, spent more than 300 hours examining 1,000 relevant legal cases. Ramik's entire report is available online, as well as excerpts from a revealing interview about his findings published in the September 17, 1981, issue of the *Adventist Review* magazine.

What did Ramik find? "Based on our review of the facts and legal precedents. . . . Ellen White was not a plagiarist, and her works did not constitute copyright infringement/piracy."[10] Ramik further stated, "Ellen G. White emphatically would not have been convicted of copyright infringement."[11] As if to leave no doubt about his findings, Ramik wrote, "Considering all factors necessary in reaching a just conclusion on this issue, it is submitted that the writings of Ellen G. White were conclusively unplagiaristic."[12] Ramik saw no legal case that could be mounted against Ellen White on the issue of plagiarism or any other type of copyright infringement: "If I had to be involved in such a legal case, I would much rather appear as defense counsel than for the prosecution. There simply is no case!"[13]

The allegations of plagiarism against God's inspired messenger are baseless and without merit, but Ellen White perceived, even back then, that the attacks leveled against her writings were not human in origin, writing in 1890:

> "Satan is. . .constantly pressing in the spurious—to lead away from the truth. The very last deception of Satan will be to make of none effect the testimony of the Spirit of God. 'Where there is no vision, the people perish' (Proverbs 29:18). Satan will work ingeniously, in different ways and through different agencies, to unsettle the confidence of God's remnant people in the true testimony."[14]

In addition to the plagiarism charge, some have vociferously questioned Ellen White's views on health matters, but these have stood the test of time, such as when she wrote in 1864 about the carcinogenic dangers of meat eating and tobacco.[15] In 1957, medical authorities in both the U.K. and the U.S. validated her claim that smoking tobacco was a causative factor in lung cancer, and more recent studies have confirmed the association between cancer and eating meat.[16] On the issue of racism, no Adventist pioneer worked harder to support ministry to former slaves and Blacks than Ellen White, so much so that her son Edson dedicated his life to that work. While she recognized the need to be pragmatic and careful in how the Church shared the Gospel in the post–Civil War Southern states where the bigotry and racism of many Whites was especially violent and rampant, Ellen White was unequivocal about the value of all human beings in the eyes of God:

> "Whoever of the human family give themselves to Christ, whoever hear the truth and obey it, become children of one family. The ignorant and the wise, the rich and the poor, the heathen and the slave, white or black—Jesus paid the purchase money for their souls. If they believe on Him, His cleansing blood is applied to them. The black man's name is written in the book of life beside the white man's. All are one in Christ. Birth, station, nationality, or color cannot elevate or degrade men. The character makes the man."[17]

Some ask, "But what about fulfilled prophecies? Did her predictions come true?" Jeremiah 28:9 makes clear that "When the word of the prophet shall come to pass, then shall the prophet know that the Lord has truly sent him."

One notable prediction from Ellen White comes from the early nineteenth century. Having received warnings of impending judgment upon the city of San Francisco, California, for many years, Ellen White had her final and most detailed vision regarding its destruction on April 16, 1906. She saw houses "shaken like a reed in the wind" and buildings falling to the ground.

"Pleasure resorts, theaters, hotels, and homes of the wealthy were shaken and shattered. Many lives were blotted out of existence, and the air was filled with the shrieks of the injured and the terrified. . . . It seemed that the forbearance of God was exhausted, and the judgment day had come."[18]

At 5:12 A.M. on April 18, 1906, the earthquake struck, destroying 80 percent of the city and taking more than 3,000 lives. Ellen White's prediction had come to pass, and the specter of this tragic event broke her heart.

FAITHFULNESS IS OUR TEST

Much more can be said about the prophetic gift of prophecy that God has entrusted to the Seventh-day Adventist Church. While traveling in one country of the world, a dear women's ministry leader approached me after I had given a seminar on Ellen White. She was frantic, and I wondered at the time if I had said something that upset her. After we spoke for a few minutes, the source of her concern became abundantly clear.

"Pastor," she began, "we have a huge problem in our area here. Many offshoot churches and leaders are using Ellen White's writings in ways that are harming the people." I listened to her recitation with great sorrow. How could such a precious blessing of God be so misused?

Perhaps the greatest modern challenge we have in remaining faithful to the Bible and Ellen White's inspired counsels is how to handle them with care. Here are some critical tips to help us rightly interpret the inspired word (2 Timothy 2:15):

Begin all study of Scripture and Ellen White's writings with a healthy outlook. We must pray for guidance from God, and we must come with an open mind, setting aside our preconceived ideas in order to learn what the Lord says.

Focus on central issues instead of tangential ones. We should focus on the important truths and the message for this time, rather than marginal issues which feed fanaticism.

Study all available information on a topic before coming to conclusions. Seek to base conclusions on the full context of Ellen White's thought on the issue(s) studied.

Take time and place into consideration. Remember that much of Ellen White's counsel is personal—to an individual or specific situation—and may not be fully applicable to everyone.[19]

Discover the underlying biblical principles for Christian living to make appropriate applications to life. Differentiate between universal principles and counsels which may be addressing a limited, localized concern.

Keep statements in their proper contexts. Ellen White warns strongly against bending her statements or removing them from their context to make them say what we want them to say.[20]

Recognize that Ellen White often makes statements that help put her strongest statements in perspective. Many of her statements on a subject present the ideal. But she also understood that real situations sometimes required practical solutions short of the ideal. Keep these balancing statements in mind.

IN CONCLUSION

God has given the Seventh-day Adventist Church a "more sure word of prophecy" (2 Peter 1:19, KJV). Now more than ever, the apostle Paul's call to faithfulness must be heeded by God's remnant Church! Before the return of Jesus, desperate times will descend upon the earth and its inhabitants. The world will be ripe for destruction (2 Peter 3:10); men and women will be captive to vices and sins (2 Timothy 3:1-5); apostasy will be global (1 Timothy 4:1); many of the righteous will be persecuted and exiled (2 Timothy 3:12); and a formal religion that denies God's power will substitute as a means of salvation (2 Timothy 3:5). Are not all these realities present in our world today? Given this dire situation, why would God not send someone to call His people to repentance and faithfulness to prepare them for end-time service?[21]

In Matthew 24:11, Jesus predicted that false prophets would arise, but we can be assured that Ellen White is not one of them. Now more than ever, we must embrace her inspired counsels and reclaim our status as "people of the book." Now more than ever, the call to acceptance of God's prophets found in 2 Chronicles 20:20 should characterize our view of this special messenger: "Believe in the Lord your God, and you shall be established; believe His prophets, and you shall prosper." God promised that the gift of prophecy would come in the last days, and we must be able to recognize it, test the prophetic messages, and follow only that which bears the imprimatur of heaven.

In the writings of Ellen G. White, the Seventh-day Adventist Church and the world has been gifted a treasure of immeasurable value. May this sacred counsel be deeply valued, richly lived, and faithfully shared as we near the Second Coming of Jesus!

ENDNOTES

1. White, E. G. (1874, August 24). Ellen White [Letter to J.N. Loughborough]. Battle Creek, Michigan.
2. White, A. L. (1985). *Ellen G. White: The Early Years* (vol. 1, 56) (Hagerstown, MD: Review and Herald Publishing Association).
3. White, J. S. (1847). *A Word to the Little Flock* (Brunswick, ME), 22.
4. Timm, A. R, Esmond, D. E., eds. (2015). Merlin Burt. *The Gift of Prophecy in Scripture and History*. Nampa, ID: Pacific Press Publishing Association, 274.
5. White, E. G. (2017). *Early Writings*. Silver Spring, MD: The Ellen G. White Estate, 78. https://egwwritings-a.akamaihd.net/pdf/en_EW.pdf
6. Ibid., 276.
7. Poirier, T. (1986). *Contemporary Prophecy and Scripture: The Relationship of Ellen G. White's Writings to the Bible in the Seventh-day Adventist Church, 1845-1915*. Wesley Theological Seminary 1986, Washington, D.C.
8. Pfandl, Gehard. (2004). *The Authority of the Ellen G. White Writings*. Biblical Research Institute. Retrieved from https://adventistbiblicalresearch.org/sites/default/files/pdf/AuthorityEGWwritings.pdf
9. White. E. G. (1950). Introduction *The Great Controversy* (Nampa, ID: Pacific Press) xii.
10. *Adventist Review*. September 17, 1981, 3.
11. Ibid.
12. Ibid.
13. *Adventist Review*. September 17, 1981, 6. For a link to the Ramik report and other information on the charge of plagiarism against Ellen White, visit: https://whiteestate.org/about/issues1/about-egw/writings/literary-productions/plagiarism-charge/
14. Letter 12, 1890.
15. White, E. G. *Counsels for the Church* (Nampa, ID: Pacific Press, 1991), 229; idem. (2018*Counsels on Health* (Silver Spring, MD: The Ellen G. White Estate), 84. https://egwwritings-a.akamaihd.net/pdf/en_CH.pdf
16. Medical Research Council, "Tobacco Smoking and Cancer of the Lung," *British Medical Journal*, June 29, 1957, https://www.ncbi.nlm.nih.gov/pmc/articles/PMC2121650/; Mark Parascandola, "The Other Surgeon General's Report: "History of the U.S. Public Health Response to Air Pollution, Cigarette Smoking, and Lung Cancer." *Annals of Cancer Epidemiology* 4 (March 2020), https://ace.amegroups.com/article/view/5500/html.
17. *Manuscript* 6, 1891.
18. White, E. G. (1906).*Manuscript* 47.

19 Ellen G. White, *Selected Messages,* bk 1 (Washington, D.C.: Review and Herald, 1958) 57, "Regarding the testimonies, nothing is ignored; nothing is cast aside; but time and place must be considered."

20. Ellen White was deeply troubled by the misuse of her writings, especially by those who took her writings out of context. (SM, bk. 3, 82; Letter 208, 1906; SM, bk. 1, 44, 58).

21. Simões Lima, Valdecir (March 2017). "The Sure Word of Prophecy," *Adventist World*, 26, 27. https://www.adventistworld.org/nad-march-2017/.

AS YOU BEGIN THE NEXT CHAPTER...

- Astronomers know about it.
- Many travelers also know about it.
- Any good compass shows it.
- Detailed topographic maps point it out.
- And both the title and content of this book focus on it.

True North.

If you follow Jesus, you have a True North within yourself. It's your life's orienting point—the fixed, steady point in your world as it spins and changes all around you. It includes your most deeply held values, beliefs, and principles.

Pastor, author, evangelist, and church leader Mark Finley, along with publisher Dan Houghton, referenced True North in their brief Preface to this book: "Before You Turn This Page." Pastor Finley also wrote chapters 10 and 15. This final chapter is just ahead, as, once again, you're invited to "turn the page."

The reason we can say that you have a True North within yourself is that the Truest North in all the universe is Jesus. So if you've invited Him to live in you, He is your True North—your constant, unchanging source of truth and life. Jesus is your internal compass, to guide your life in the ways He chooses for you.

This book is "a prophetic call to faithfulness." With Jesus as our True North, we will be faithful to Him, to His church, to the tasks He gives us to do, and to spending quality time getting to know Him.

Father God, please make us faithful to you. Thank you for living in us—our indwelling True North—until we see that eastern cloud about the size of a hand growing closer and brighter and know that it is You with countless angels, coming to take us home!

Mark Finley and his wife, Ernestine "Teenie," have teamed up in ministry throughout the years. Teenie is known worldwide for teaching natural lifestyle cooking. Together they have been involved in Christian ministry for over 40 years-preaching, teaching and offering spiritual growth workshops, and conducting over 100 evangelistic series that have spanned the globe with sermons translated into over 50 languages. Today, Pastor Finley and Teenie continue their ministry at the Living Hope School of Evangelism Training Center in Haymarket, Virginia.

MARK FINLEY

CHAPTER 15

A PROPHETIC CALL TO FAITHFULNESS

QUITE SOME YEARS AGO, THEN-SENATOR MARK HATFIELD OF OREGON VISITED Calcutta, India. He spent a life-changing day with Mother Teresa. He recounts touring the slums with her and visiting the so-called "House of Dying," where sick children were cared for in the final days of their lives. He viewed the long lines at the clinic where the poor waited by the hundreds to receive medical attention. As he watched Mother Teresa and her team minister to these impoverished, sick people, many of whom had been left by others to die, Senator Hatfield was overwhelmed by the sheer magnitude of the suffering she and her coworkers faced daily. "How can you bear the load without being crushed by it?" he asked. Mother Teresa replied, "My dear Senator, I am not called to be successful, I am called to be faithful."

The Word of God does not call us to a life of popularity, power, or prestige. It calls us to faithfulness: faithfulness to Christ, faithfulness to His teachings, faithfulness to His Church, and faithfulness to His mission. The Bible is filled with stories of men and women who were faithful to Christ at all costs. Think of Abraham, Moses, Joseph, Esther, John, and Paul, just to name a few. One of the stalwarts of faith was Daniel.

DANIEL'S FAITHFULNESS

In 605 BC Nebuchadnezzar, king of Babylon, attacked Jerusalem and overthrew it. Daniel and some of the brightest young Jewish minds were taken captive and brought as hostages to Babylon. Nebuchadnezzar's intent was to educate them in the philosophy, culture, and religious practices of Babylon, qualifying them to serve as puppet rulers for his regime. To abolish their Jewish identity, the Babylonian king changed their names. Hebrew names described the godly qualities an Israeli father and mother desired in their children. Babylonian names often reflected the names of the Babylonian gods. For example, the Hebrew name *Daniel* literally means *God is my judge* or *God is my vindicator,* while his Babylonian name, *Belteshazzar,* means *"keeper of the hid treasures of Bel."* Bel-Marduk was the chief god of Babylon.

God begins the book of Daniel with Daniel as a captive in Babylon's corrupt, godless society. His mind could easily have been shaped by that society. He was under almost incomprehensible pressure to conform to the practices and lifestyle of Babylon. But Daniel 1:8 says:

> "Daniel purposed in his heart that he would not defile himself with the portion of the king's delicacies, nor with the wine which he drank; therefore, he requested of the chief of the eunuchs that he might not defile himself."

"Daniel *purposed* in his heart." What does this signify? It means that Daniel *decided.* It means that he *determined.* It means that he *chose.* In the Bible, particularly in the Old Testament, the word *heart* is used in a special sense to refer to the seat of both the intellect and the emotions. *Heart* is the center of the thought processes. Proverbs 4:23 says, "Keep your heart with all diligence." Proverbs 23:7 adds, "As . . . [a person] thinks in his heart, so is he."

The book of Daniel begins with the story of a young man who makes a settled choice in the depths of his mind and emotions that he will not defile himself by conforming to the evil around him. The story begins this way and shows Daniel and his three God-fearing friends as they honor God and are in turn honored by Him. At the end, the story comes full circle. A battle fought and won in the hearts of His faithful servants leads to complete victory.

It's an appropriate story for our time, because the real battle at the time of the end, in the last days of earth's history, is not some battle in the Middle East. The real battle just before Jesus returns is the battle for your mind. The devil will do everything he can through this godless secular society to influence your thought processes, because the mind is the seat of our thoughts and emotions. Satan was there in Babylon, doing everything he possibly could to influence Daniel's mind and emotions through the enticements of the pagan culture around him. But Daniel "purposed in his heart that he would not defile himself." This young man clearly understood his identity. Even in captivity, in bondage to the Babylonians, God called him to be an ambassador for the King of kings.

In the book *Prophets and Kings*, Ellen White makes this insightful statement about Daniel's faithfulness to principle:

> "Among the children of Israel who were carried captive to Babylon at the beginning of the seventy years' captivity were Christian patriots, men who were as true as steel to principle, who would not be corrupted by selfishness, but who would honor God at the loss of all things. In the land of their captivity these men were to carry out God's purpose by giving to heathen nations the blessings that come through a knowledge of Jehovah. They were to be His rep-

> resentatives. Never were they to compromise with idolaters; their faith and their name as worshipers of the living God they were to bear as a high honor. And this they did. In prosperity and adversity, they honored God, and God honored them" (Ellen G. White, *Prophets and Kings*, 479).

The experience of Daniel and the Hebrew captives in Babylon powerfully reveals that it is possible to be faithful to God in the most challenging circumstances. God's call to faithfulness in this immoral and godless world in the last days of earth's history is a call to let the light of His love and truth shine brightly through our lives. As time comes screeching to a halt at the collapse of spiritual Babylon, God's call is once again never to lose a sense of our identity in Christ as part of a prophetic movement destined to lighten the world with His glory. His call is once again a call to faithfulness to our prophetic mission to proclaim the everlasting Gospel in the blazing light of the three angels to every nation, and kindred, and tongue, and people (Revelation 14:6). For this goal to be accomplished, our faithfulness to and relationship with Christ is paramount.

FAITHFULNESS IN A COMMITMENT TO OUR DEVOTIONAL LIFE

Not long ago a respected church administrator was discussing the challenges of ministry with one of his colleagues. The discussion turned to devotional life and its relationship to busyness. The administrator made this tragic admission: "With everything I am doing and all of my administrative responsibilities, I am just too busy to spend any significant time in prayer or Bible study. That's my wife's thing, not mine." Writing to the church at Ephesus from the rocky barren isle of Patmos, John informs us that although the Church was doctrinally pure and had labored for His (Jesus') namesake, "Nevertheless I have somewhat against thee, because thou hast left thy first love" (Revelation 2:4).

The leaders of the Ephesian church had labored to the point of exhaustion but neglected the one thing that would make their labors effective.

Knowing Christ personally and experiencing His presence individually is the only thing that will give real meaning to our spiritual life.

On another occasion, after an area pastors' meeting, one of the pastors in attendance approached the speaker and asked if they could have a private discussion. When they were alone in a quiet corner of the room, the pastor said, "No one knows this, but I am exhausted, burned out, fatigued, and feel I can no longer function in my ministry. I am out of gas and running on fumes. Is there any way you can help me?" Chuck Swindoll, in his book *Intimacy With God*, comments, "Noise and words and frenzied, hectic schedules dull our senses, closing our ears to His still, small voice and making us numb to His touch."

One of the major challenges facing western Christianity is superficiality. Many Christians long for an instant experience with God. In this era of fast moving images and quick solutions to complex problems, the tendency on the part of many, when we are bombarded with so much information, is to look for a Christian experience that costs them little. Our greatest need is for men and women of faith, who spend quality time with God.

I have thought about this a great deal. When you are incredibly busy and you perceive you have more to do than time to accomplish it, it is so easy to neglect the deep, reflective prayer and Bible study that is life transformational.

Ellen White puts it this way:

> "All who are under the training of God need the quiet hour for communion with their own hearts, with nature, and with God. In them is to be revealed a life that is not in harmony with the world, its customs, or its practices; and they need to have a personal experience in obtaining a knowledge of the will of God. We must individually hear Him speaking to the heart. When every other voice is hushed, and in quietness we wait before Him, the silence of the soul makes more distinct the voice of God. He bids us, 'Be still, and

know that I am God.' This is the effectual preparation for all labor for God. Amidst the hurrying throng, and the strain of life's intense activities, he who is thus refreshed, will be surrounded with an atmosphere of light and peace. He will receive a new endowment of both physical and mental strength. His life will breathe out a fragrance and will reveal a divine power that will reach men's hearts" (Ellen G. White, *The Ministry of Healing*, 58).

In the *quietness,* God longs to speak.
In our *challenges,* God longs to speak.
In our *difficulties,* God longs to speak.
In our *problems,* God longs to speak.
In our *perplexities,* God longs to speak.
In our *confusion,* God longs to speak.
In our *weakness,* God longs to speak.
In our *resounding successes in life* and also...
In our *flat-out failures,* God longs to speak.

Will you give God the time to speak to your heart? Will you fall on your knees and say "Jesus, all I want is to know your will in every given situation. Speak Lord. Give me the wisdom to know your will, the strength to do your will, and the courage to accomplish the purpose that I was born for." If we are not faithful in our devotional life, if we do not know Christ personally, if we do not experience His presence daily, if our lives are not transformed by His word, our religious experience will be shallow, superficial, and hollow. Faithfulness to Christ in our devotional life makes all the difference. This leads us to the second aspect of faithfulness.

FAITHFULNESS IN OUR COMMITMENT TO CHRIST'S CHURCH AND TEACHINGS

Throughout the Gospels, Jesus gives us the assurance that His Church will triumph at last. The New Testament writers echo this theme. No indication is to be found, either in the Bible or the writings of Ellen White, that the Church will fail in the mission it has been called into existence to accomplish. It gives us great confidence to know that this Church is in Christ's hands. He is its founder, its leader, its captain, its general, and its true head. He has continually guided this movement in the past, is daily sustaining it in the present, and will powerfully lead it into the future. Our Creator, Redeemer, and coming King is the Church's only hope for today, tomorrow, and forever. He has providentially raised this Church up for a unique mission, and it will not fail in rising to the destiny for which Christ created it. Seventh-day Adventists are a prophetic movement with an urgent prophetic calling. We are not merely another denomination on the landscape of religious movements. We are a divine end-time movement with an end-time purpose, an end-time message, and an end-time mission for the entire world.

"THE CHURCH IS GOD-MADE, NOT MAN-MADE"

This does not mean that the Church does not have its challenges. It does; but amid these challenges, the Holy Spirit is working powerfully, and the ultimate triumph of the Church is certain. In Matt 16:18, Jesus said, "I will build My Church, and the gates of hell shall not prevail against it." This Church is not some human, man-made, bureaucratic organization, as some would have us believe. According to the Savior's own words, He has built His Church, and the gates of hell will not prevail against it. First Corinthians 12 tells us that the Church is the body of Christ. Ephesians 5 states that the Church is the bride of Christ. In 1 Peter 2 we learn that the Church is the household of Christ. First Peter 2:9 proclaims that the people of God are a chosen generation, a royal priesthood, an holy nation, and a peculiar people. God's prophetic messenger to the remnant, Ellen White, puts it this way:

> "The church is God's fortress, His city of refuge, which He holds in a revolted world. Any betrayal of the church is treachery to Him who has bought mankind with the blood of His only begotten

> Son.... He has sent forth His angels to minister to His church, and the gates of hell have not been able to prevail against His people" (Ellen G. White, *Acts of the Apostles*, 11).

Christ holds His Church in His hands. It is His fortress, His city of refuge in a planet in rebellion. It is a light in the darkness, a beacon in the night, and a shining light on the dimly lit path ahead.

Ellen White continues in *Acts of the Apostles,* page 11, with these reassuring words:

> "Through centuries of persecution, conflict, and darkness, God has sustained His church. Not one cloud has fallen upon it that He has not prepared for; not one opposing force has risen to counterwork His work that He has not foreseen. All has taken place as He predicted. He has not left His church forsaken, but has traced in prophetic declarations what would occur, and that which His Spirit inspired the prophets to foretell has been brought about. All His purposes will be fulfilled. His law is linked with His throne, and no power of evil can destroy it. Truth is inspired and guarded by God; and it will triumph over all opposition" (Ellen G. White, *Acts of the Apostles*, 11).

Christ and His Church will triumph at last. Jesus has never yet lost a battle with Satan. On the Cross He triumphed over the principalities and powers of hell. You and I are on the winning side. As that old hymn, "Onward Christian Soldiers"—written in 1864 by Sabine Baring-Gould—so powerfully puts it:

Crowns and thrones have perished, kingdoms rise and wane,
But the church of Jesus constant will remain.
Gates of hell can never 'gainst that church prevail;
We have Christ's own promise that can never fail.

All the demons in hell cannot, will not defeat God's purposes for His Church. Christ's Church will triumph at last. His truth will shine brighter and grow stronger until Revelation's prediction in the 18th chapter that "the earth will be filled with the glory of God" will be gloriously fulfilled (Revelation 18:1). In these climactic hours of earth's history, we see evidence around the world that God's truth is triumphing over the powers of evil.

Today God is preparing a people to proclaim the marvels of His grace, the greatness of His love, the goodness of His character, the righteousness of His law, and the beauty of His truth. They are committed to Christ and faithful to His bride, His Church. You cannot please Jesus if you criticize His bride. How would you feel if you met somebody who was so negative that they spewed out their poisonous venom of criticism about your wife? What if they printed books about her faults? What if they had a flashy, well-designed website viewed by tens of thousands to expose her errors? How would you feel about that? Most likely you would be hurt and wounded. Jesus is likewise deeply hurt when people who should know better make it the passion of their lives to criticize His Church rather than focus their attention on winning lost people for the kingdom. I am reminded of Ellen White's statement in the devotional book *Maranatha* for May 1 on page 129:

> "God has a church upon the earth, who are His chosen people, who keep His commandments. He is leading, not stray offshoots, not one here and one there, but a people. There is no need to doubt, to be fearful that the work will not succeed. God is at the head of the work, and He will set everything in order. If matters need adjusting at the head of the work, God will attend to that, and work to right every wrong. Let us have faith that God is going to carry the noble ship which bears the people of God safely into port."

We can have the absolute assurance that the God who launched this movement will take this ship home.

We are living in a generation that questions all authority. There is a distrust of social, political, and even religious institutions. This mistrust runs deep and at times is justifiable. But keep this eternal reality in mind: God's remnant Church is not a human, bureaucratic institution. It is the body of Christ on earth, and Jesus knows how to take care of His body. Despite its imperfections and faults, He is still its leader and will work to right every wrong so that "He might present it to Himself a glorious church, not having spot or wrinkle or any such thing but that it should be holy without blemish" (Ephesians 5:26).

Faithfulness to Christ and His Church certainly includes faithfulness to Christ's teachings. Jesus said, "Sanctify them through your word. Your word is truth" (John 17:17). For some, doctrine has almost become something to be avoided. It is not only neglected but treated with skeptical contempt in some circles. The word *doctrine* simply meanings *teachings*. Where would the Church be without the teachings of Christ? His teachings on the role of scripture, salvation, the Second Coming of Christ, the state of the dead, and service—all give substance to our faith. The New Testament Church placed emphasis on both the person and teachings of Christ. Speaking of the Day of Pentecost, when 3,000 were baptized, Luke states: "Then they that gladly received his word were baptized: and the same day there were added unto them about three thousand souls" (Acts 2:41, 42). Notice carefully these two expressions. These new converts "received His Word" and "continued steadfastly in the apostles' doctrine." Jesus is the "way, the truth. and the life." You cannot separate Jesus from His Word, because He is the living Word, and you cannot separate Jesus from His truth, because He is the embodiment of truth, and you cannot separate Jesus from His teachings, because He is the author of all true doctrine.

His truth will triumph at last. The light of His Word will illuminate this world. His plans for this earth will be accomplished. His Church will be victorious over the powers of hell. His Church will not disappear into insignificance. It will not flicker like a candle in the wind and go out in darkness. Like the rising of the sun, God's truth will dispel the darkness. Jesus, the Light of the World, will shine more brightly through His people as the crisis at the close of this earth's history comes to a climax.

Ellen White states it this way:

> "The church is the repository of the riches of the grace of Christ: and through the church will eventually be made manifest, even to the principalities and powers in heavenly places, 'the final and full display of the love of God'" (*Acts of the Apostles*, 9).

You and I are on the winning side. No matter how challenging the days ahead, no matter how dark the future becomes, no matter what difficulties the Church goes through, Christ's people, Christ's Church, Christ's purposes, Christ's plan, will triumph at last. Many will leave the Church. Some will criticize the Church and its leadership. Some will cast doubt on the eventual triumph of the Church. These negative naysayers are wrong. Christ's Church will be victorious at last. We are destined for glory. The Bible is clear on this point. Christ's own words come echoing and reechoing down the centuries, "I will build my church and the gates of hell will not prevail against it"; therefore, I believe in the Church.

FAITHFULNESS IN OUR COMMITMENT TO CHRIST'S STANDARDS

Jesus stated it well when He prayed, "I do not pray that You should take them out of the world, but that You should keep them from the evil one" (John 17:15, NKJV). The apostle John added:

> "Do not love the world or the things in the world. If anyone loves the world, the love of the Father is not in Him. For all that is in the world—the lust of the flesh, the lust of the eyes, and the pride of life—is not of the Father but of the world. And the world is passing away and the lust of it; but he who does the will of God abides forever" (1 John 2:15-17).

The Church has always faced the danger of losing its perspective and compromising its loyalty to Christ through a growing tendency to allow the world to shape its thinking.

The closer we get to the end of time, the more the devil will redouble His efforts in this area. I am concerned about the almost overwhelming tide of worldliness that is sweeping into some of our churches.

Standards which were once cherished by Seventh-day Adventists in the areas of diet, dress, recreation, amusement, and Sabbath-keeping are fast becoming things of the past. When members are adorned like the world, dress like the world, love the world's entertainment, listen to this world's music, and are captivated by its Hollywood productions, genuine spirituality erodes, and the devil makes inroads into the soul.

When the Adventist health message, which so many honest-hearted people in the secular world are embracing, is made of "none-effect" by God's people and considered to be legalism or fanaticism rather than a glorious gift from a loving Creator, something is tragically wrong.

We are "ambassadors for Christ" (2 Corinthians 5:20). We are the "light of the world...the salt of the earth" (Matthew 5:13, 14). Jesus says, Let your light so shine before men, that they may see your good works and glorify your Father in heaven (Matthew 5:16). Millions all over the world are looking for something different from what they have.

Deep within, they are tired of the aching longing to satisfy their heart's desires through the things of this world. They long for genuine, authentic Christianity. We will never reach them by compromising our standards to come down to their level. We must "lift up the standard."

This is no time to flirt with the devil's dress, diet, amusement, and worldly influences. This is the time to hold the standard high for the world to see.

Christ living in our lives and dwelling in our hearts makes a dramatic difference in how we live. The call of the hour is a call to faithfulness in our lifestyle.

FAITHFULNESS IN OUR COMMITMENT TO WITNESS AND SERVICE

Biblical faithfulness always leads to action. The New Testament Church was passionate about witness. It was faithful to Christ's mission. Sharing Christ was the natural outgrowth of their relationship with Him. They were prepared to make supreme sacrifices for His cause. Many of these believers suffered persecution, imprisonment, and even death. No sacrifice was too great for the Jesus who gave so much for them.

Their commitment to Christ often led them to take a leap of faith. Christ called them out of their comfort zones. The task before them was far beyond their ability to complete. It was far too great for them to accomplish, but not too great for God to accomplish. They grasped the promises of God and in faith went out to change the world. The task before the Church today is far beyond our capacity to accomplish. Christ is calling us to take a leap of faith. The single-minded focus of Jesus' life was to redeem lost mankind (Luke 19:10). He now invites us to join Him in His mission by giving our lives in service.

David Livingstone once commented:

> "People talk of the sacrifice I have made in spending so much of my life in Africa. Can that be called a sacrifice which is simply acknowledging a great debt we owe to our God, which we can never repay? Is that a sacrifice which brings its own reward in healthful activity, the consciousness of doing good, peace of mind, and a bright hope of a glorious destiny? It is emphatically no sacrifice. Rather it is a privilege. Anxiety, sickness, suffering, danger, foregoing the common conveniences of this life—these may make us pause, and cause the spirit to waver, and the soul to sink; but let this only be for a moment. All these are nothing compared with the glory which shall later be revealed in and through us. I never made a sacrifice. Of this we ought not to talk, when we remember the great sacrifice which He made who left His Father's throne on high to give Himself for us."

David Livingstone clearly understood that whatever he sacrificed for the cause of Christ, Jesus' sacrifice was much greater for him. As the apostle Paul passionately stated, "The love of Christ constrains us" (2 Corinthians 5:14).

In the light of Christ's love and His soon return, the early Adventist believers were compelled to share the Christ-centered, grace-filled message of end-time truth found in the prophecies of Daniel and Revelation. They sensed they were part of a prophetic movement providentially raised up by God to proclaim the Three Angels' Messages to the world. As Ellen White so aptly put it...

> "In a special sense, Seventh-day Adventists have been set in the world as watchmen and light bearers. To them has been entrusted the last warning for a perishing world. On them is shining wonderful light from the Word of God. They have been given a work of the most solemn import—the proclamation of the first, second, and third angels' messages. There is no other work of so great importance. They are to allow nothing else to absorb their attention" (Ellen G. White, *Testimonies*, vol 9, 19).

They believed Christ's words, "And this gospel of the kingdom shall be preached in all the world as a witness to all the nations and then shall the end come" (Matthew 24:14). They accepted the challenge and were faithful to Christ's mission. Seventh-day Adventist missionaries have spanned the globe, bringing hope and healing to millions. Many of these early Adventist missionaries never returned home. They gave their lives in service, and their graves are scattered throughout the earth as they await the final call of the Life-giver at the glorious return of our Lord.

Considering the legacy of these faithful believers in the past and in the blazing light of eternity, Jesus invites us to take a step in faith and commit all our lives to His service. The task is not yet complete. The mission is not yet accomplished. The work of Christ on earth is not yet finished. His love compels us to give our all to His cause. Will you pause for a moment and once again commit your life to share His love and truth with the people in your sphere of influence? Will you just now dedicate your life to witness for Him in this crisis hour of earth's history? Will you ask Jesus to keep you faithful until He comes? Why not bow your head and ask Jesus to place a burning passion in your heart to be an ambassador for Him in this last-day generation?

This is a time to recommit ourselves to Christ and to His Church. For He is preparing a people who are *bathed in His righteousness, justified by His grace, and sanctified through His power. They love His truth, live His truth, and proclaim His truth. They count all things but loss for Christ. They care not for earthly fame or human accolades. Position, prestige, and earthly praise mean little to them. With the apostle Paul they say, "For me to live is Christ." Empowered by His Spirit, they proclaim His love and share His truth. The Holy Spirit is poured out in latter rain power. Hearts are touched. Lives are changed. The world is reached, and Jesus comes again.

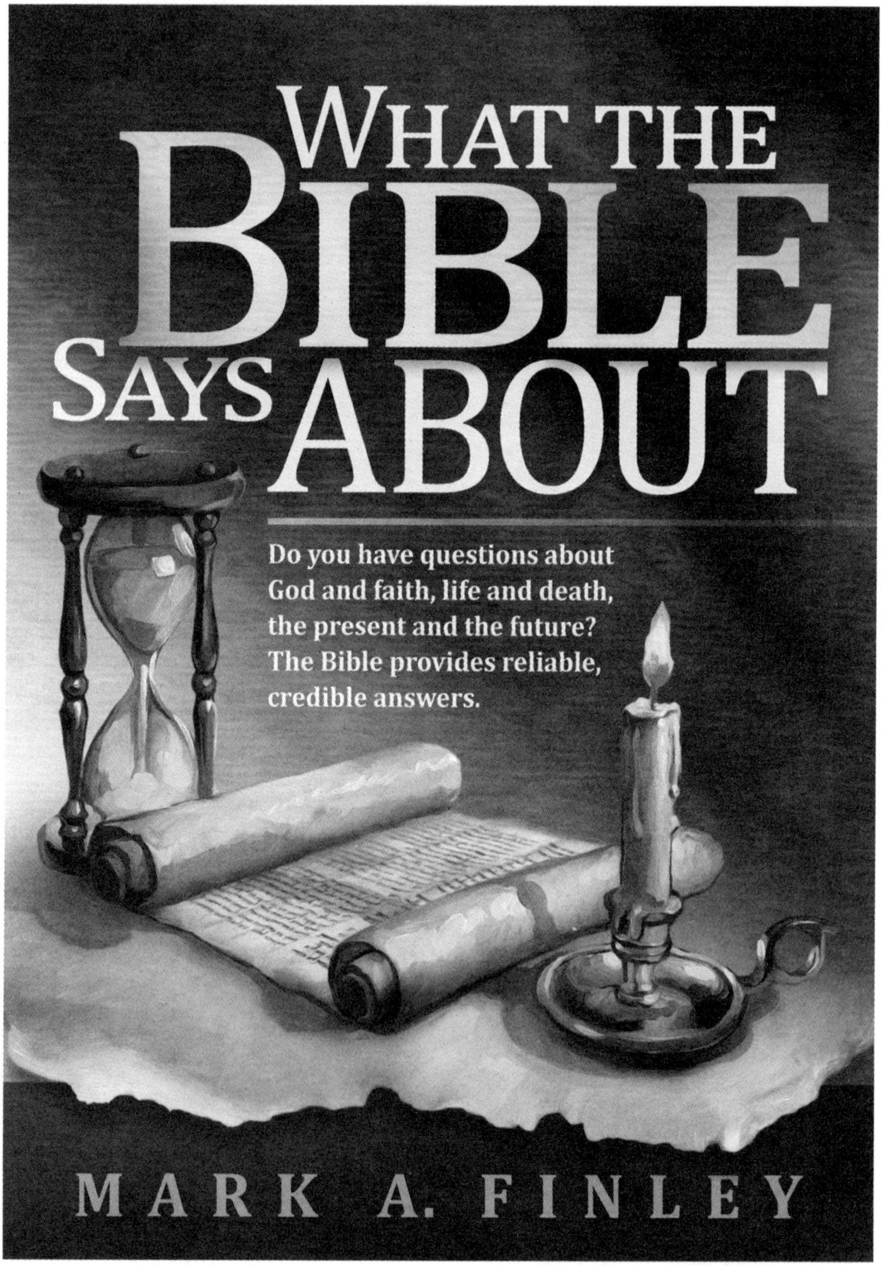

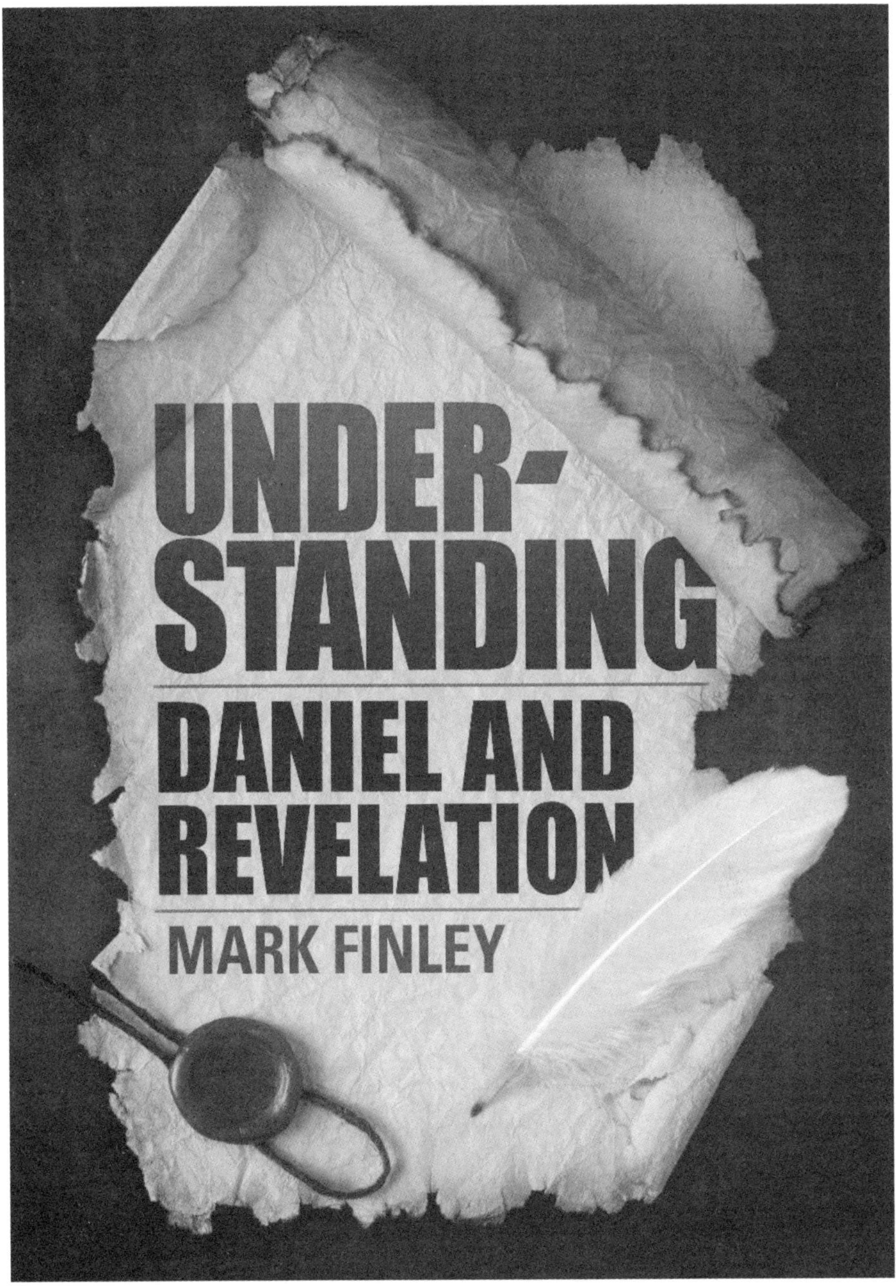
UNDER-
STANDING
DANIEL AND
REVELATION
MARK FINLEY

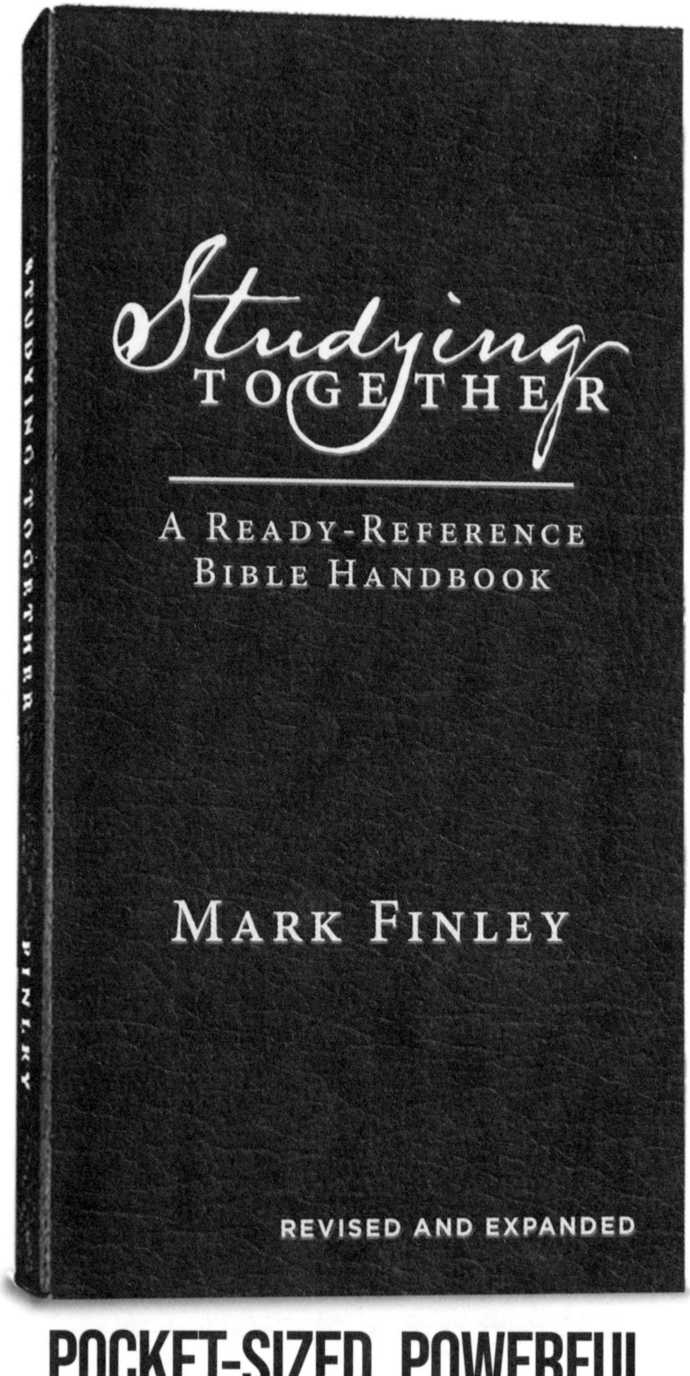